INTERNATIONAL BUSINESS AS RESPONSIBLE BUSINESS

Theory and Practice

John R. Bryson, Jennifer Johns, Laura Salciuviene
and James Blackmore-Wright

The companion website for this textbook is:
https://bristoluniversitypress.co.uk/
international-business-as-responsible-business/
companion-website

BRISTOL
UNIVERSITY
PRESS

First published in Great Britain in 2025 by

Bristol University Press
University of Bristol
1-9 Old Park Hill
Bristol
BS2 8BB
UK
t: +44 (0)117 374 6645
e: bup-info@bristol.ac.uk

Details of international sales and distribution partners are available at bristoluniversitypress.co.uk

© Bristol University Press 2025

British Library Cataloguing in Publication Data
A catalogue record for this book is available from the British Library

ISBN 978-1-5292-4114-3 hardcover
ISBN 978-1-5292-4115-0 paperback
ISBN 978-1-5292-4116-7 ePub
ISBN 978-1-5292-4117-4 ePdf

The right of John R. Bryson, Jennifer Johns, Laura Salciuviene and James Blackmore-Wright to be identified as authors of this work has been asserted by them in accordance with the Copyright, Designs and Patents Act 1988.

Cover design: Nicky Borowiec
Front cover image: Designed by Laura Johns, rendered by Nicky Borowiec

Contents

List of Figures, Tables and Boxes

Figures

Tables

Boxes

Acknowledgements

How do we know what we know? This is one of those metaphysical questions that is best avoided. Nevertheless, it is an important question to consider when completing a book. This is a co-authored book, and each author brought their own experiences and ways of seeing and interpretating the world to the project. The book's origins can be traced back over a decade and partly lie in our research experiences, and of teaching students at Birmingham, Bristol and elsewhere. In part, the book's origins were informed by numerous conversations with academics and those directly involved in international business and businesses of all kinds.

Students are important, and too often it is assumed that there is a one-way dialogue between teachers and their students. This should never be the case. Academics are also students and there are many opportunities for academics to learn from their students. We would like to thank all those individuals who have encouraged us to develop insights into the world of international business. This includes the wealth of businesses, organizations and entrepreneurs, policy makers and other practitioners whom we engage with through our research and education, some of whom have directly contributed to this book through case study examples.

A book is the outcome of a co-creation and co-development process. Given this, we would like to thank our current and former colleagues, PhD students and taught postgraduate students who have directly and indirectly supported this project. We must also thank our departments and universities.

Producing a book is a partnership between many different individuals. This includes Ellen Pearce, the Commissioning Editor at Bristol University Press, who has been extremely supportive and encouraging. It includes the reviewers of the book proposal and also of the first completed manuscript. The book was developed in sequence with the design of a new MSc International Business programme at Birmingham. It was the development of this programme that encouraged us to write this book which coincided with the delivery of a new MSc in International Business and Strategy: Global Challenges at Bristol. Individual chapters were used to inform our teaching at Birmingham and Bristol during 2024–5 and we thank our students for being receptive of this material and contributing to this book's co-creation process. At Bristol University Press we want to thank Isobel Green, assistant editor, Amber Lanfranchi, marketing executive and the production team including Koel Mukherjee and Polly Chester (Bourchier).

In some respects, this book seemed to write itself. One of the chapters was co-written online and in real-time. This was a very stimulating co-creation process.

However, the book cover was much more challenging. We started with five initial cover designs, but all were dismissed. Finally, we turned to an artist for some help, communicating to her our building-block framework and ideas around what we wanted the cover to say. That this artist so readily understood our approach and motivations galvanized our confidence in the project and she was able to produce the cover you see today. It should be noted that the cover was initially created using mineral paper, which is a more sustainable option. We would like to pass on our thanks to the artist, Laura Johns (Jennifer's mother), for her creativity and contribution to this shared project.

Preface

The world is facing uncertain times, but then all times are uncertain in their own way. Nevertheless, our current times come with enhanced uncertainty; governments, businesses and individuals must adapt to what has been defined as a 'polycrisis', or a complex situation where multiple interconnected crises converge and amplify one another.

One change that occurred on 2 April 2025, was President Donald Trump's so-called 'Liberation Day' for the US economy. New tariffs on all imports to the US were introduced. This could be the start of another trade war, but no one wins in a trade war. US residents will experience price increases and companies exporting to the US may experience a reduction in demand. Companies can adapt by shifting their market focus or US consumers may continue to purchase imported products. Some companies may shift production to within the US. One outcome could be a US wage-price spiral driven by workers demanding wage increases as prices rise combined with an increase in demand for labour that would lead to wage inflation. Another outcome is that the global terms of trade are changing. One development is that larger nation-states are trying to dictate how other countries engage in business and trade transactions. This includes selling raw materials, including rare earths and components, through a licensing system. These licenses restrict how nation-states can export products that contain material that has been obtained under license.

International business is operating in an era of increased geopolitical turmoil and faces profound challenges, such as disruptive innovation, including artificial intelligence, new forms of competition, alterations in consumption, ageing populations, the ecological crisis and a return to trade protectionism. Every individual experiences some aspects of these challenges, but context matters. Every individual, company and country must contend with the impacts of a different array of challenges.

In this book, we draw on existing work in international business and aligned disciplines to theorize this shifting contemporary geoeconomy. We seek to translate often abstract ideas into practice-oriented discussion framed around responsible business. This focus on practice is derived from our collective belief in the importance of inspiring and informing others to take their academic understandings into the 'outside' world and encouraging them to do so responsibly.

The chapters in this text are linked by a common focus on motivations – the motivations of entrepreneurs, managers, employees and organizations. We should not overlook our own motivations and those of our students, who join us for a time to share part of our journey as we seek to understand and reflect on business practices.

This book explores the ways in which the motivations of decision-makers shape, for example, business strategies, supply chains, operations, internationalization and approaches to marketing. This involves often complex trade-offs between different things and creates a high diversity of firm types and activities, even within the same sectors and geographies.

Acting responsibly is good business; it can enhance profitability and also attract highly talented employees. We have reflected on our own motivations for writing this book. Our intention is to produce an interesting and engaging textbook for our students who want to know more about how business can be more sustainable and create a more just and equitable future. Writing a text that focused on the practice of responsible business was an important step in helping to create business schools that do more to equip and embolden their students to create economic and social change for the better. This includes developing a dialogue between practice, responsible business and theory that would challenge existing approaches. Enhancing and challenging existing practices and encouraging the development of new business practices should be central to everything that goes on in business schools, but too often theory supplants a focus on practice.

Finally, we would like to reflect on the timing of the publishing of this book. During the writing of this book, several significant national economies have changed government. Some moved 'left', others 'right'. In general, the direction of travel for international business is towards enhanced responsibility. This is driven partly by consumers, generational change, efficiency savings, disruptive innovation, regulation and competition. However, this is never a unidirectional process as there are pushbacks. Pushbacks come from business leaders and governments as they respond to actual or perceived challenges or threats. What we know for certain is that nothing is constant, and we will continue to witness both drivers for change and counter-processes that seek to decelerate, stop or reverse change. The contemporary rise in pushbacks means that it is more important than ever that universities are educating the business leaders of the future to pursue responsible change. We thank those who engage with the ideas and responsible business practices explored in this book.

International Business as Responsible Business and the New Geoeconomy

Introduction

This textbook is the outcome of ongoing discussions between the authors regarding the practice implications of international business as responsible business. In this book, we seek to explore international business in all its dimensions. We begin this chapter by exploring the characteristics of international business and frame this within a discussion of responsibility. The chapter concludes by presenting an overarching framework for exploring the practice of responsible international business.

It is important to distinguish between those involved in researching and writing about business and those involved in the everyday practice of managing businesses. One could argue that there are too many books on international business, internationalization or globalization that present and review the current academic literature. Our book seeks to be different in that the emphasis is on understanding the challenges practitioners face in thinking globally and acting locally. The practice of managing an international business involves negotiating trade-offs, coping with tensions and frictions, responding to shocks, managing out uncertainty and prioritization of processes that include a focus on decisions regarding capital investment and revenue. An international business must manage out uncertainty or try to enhance certainty in multiple geographical (local, regional, national, supranational) contexts. This includes simultaneously enhancing certainty or security of supply and production processes, combined with commodity design, innovation and labour and in configuring routes to market, including different market entry modes.

In international business, uncertainty is everywhere, and this includes macro-economic turbulence and recessionary cycles, but also wars, epidemics and pandemics, technological and process innovations, information asymmetry and the impacts of extreme weather events linked to climate change. Uncertainty is a threat and an opportunity, but all businesses, like all individuals, must cope with living with uncertainty. Practice includes strategic decisions that may apply to the complete firm, a division, site or product line, as well as everyday decisions and many of these would be mundane or even repetitive decisions. Practice includes negotiating relationships with other organizations, including other companies and governments with the outcome being enshrined in a written or unwritten contract.

This distinction between the everyday practice of running or managing an international business versus more abstract theorizing is central to this book. Our ambition is to develop a critical and practice-informed account of international business. This is a pragmatic and practice-oriented approach to encourage students, or future business practitioners, and academics to develop an ongoing dialogue regarding the management of international businesses. The emphasis is on enhancing the benefits that come from international transactions and minimizing the negatives. The starting point for this dialogue requires an appreciation of responsible versus irresponsible business practice positioned within a discussion of the evolving international economy, or geoeconomy. This then requires an appreciation of the wider environment within which international business is enacted, with a focus on exploring the drivers and risks behind international business.

Characterizing international business

International business occupies a privileged and special place in corporate, political and media worlds. There is something distinctive about international businesses, given their size, complexity, diversity or heterogeneity and geographic reach. This diversity includes criminal multinational enterprises and illicit business activities (Buckley et al, 2024). International businesses matter. There is a paradox here. Most businesses are small and medium-sized enterprises (SMEs) and are only indirectly connected to the international economy; these are businesses that think and act locally. For example, in the UK in 2023, there were 5.51 million SMEs and these account for 99.9 per cent of this country's private sector businesses (Department for Business and Trade, 2023). The US is similar as SMEs account for 99.9 per cent of all US businesses.

International businesses are engaged in formal and informal transactions and commercial activities between companies, organizations, individuals and government entities that involve cross-border exchanges between different national jurisdictions. It is important to appreciate that whilst money and data makes the world go round, all types of international business play a central role in this whirlwind. This includes businesses involved in designing and fabricating the products and software, including cybersecurity tools, which underpin the activities of financial institutions and markets. The use of the term 'whirlwind' is deliberate as this highlights that it is often a turbulent and destructive process that is impossible to control. Conflating money with international business is intended to highlight that these two activities cannot be separated. International business is an exercise in financial investment and in the management and manipulation of money.

Like all businesses, the core purpose of an international business is configured around the creation of value. The key question is value for whom, where and what type of value? Too often, academics, politicians and managers overemphasize value defined very narrowly around profit. This is unfortunate as profit creation is the final stage in a much more complex process of value creation that begins with the identification of some type of consumer need and then shifts to designing a solution to this need that will create values-in-use for consumers. The creation of values-in-use supports monetarization processes based around realizing 'value-in-exchange' (Vargo et al, 2008). It is important to treat 'value-in-use' as a complex process that involves the creation of multiple values rather than a single value. There is additional complexity here for international businesses as the same commodity, a good, service or some combination, may create different values-in-use for consumers located in different countries. In any case, the act of consumption is both a universal and a particular process, with each consumer experiencing their own forms of values-in-use, based on the interactions between the acquisition of a commodity and their values, beliefs, lifestyles and biographies.

International business takes many different forms or market entry modes that include exporting, foreign direct investment including acquisitions, franchising, licensing agreements, joint ventures, partnerships and strategic alliances, setting up or acquiring subsidiaries, subcontracting and even piggybacking, in which a company negotiates a contract to assist another firm in exporting their products to other countries. Some companies will engage in all entry modes whilst others focus on one or more modes. Each mode comes with different drivers, risks and rewards. A firm's entry mode bundle reflects the company's history and approach to international business. An international business is in a continual state of becoming and change. A firm will add additional entry modes or might disinvest or decide to cease to engage in one type of mode. These market entry modes are applied in vastly different ways by companies and these differences matter. Thus, a firm which has experienced difficulties in one market related to one entry mode will have failed to read that market, with the outcome being failure to adjust an entry mode to local market conditions. Small firms, and even newly established ones, can operate as international businesses; scale is no longer a determinant of international business. Developments in telecommunications, combined with the growth in international travel, has enabled born global firms to be established, or firms that at the moment of their establishment think and act internationally (Hennart et al, 2021).

Most international businesses have a very restricted international footprint, with companies concentrating their activities on a few countries. There are 193 United Nation Member States and two recognized independent nations (Vatican City and Palestine) and yet no company has a presence in all these countries (Table 1.1). In 2023, Walmart, the US retailer, was the world's largest employer, with over 2.2 million employees and is widely cited as an example of a 'global' firm. Walmart is a typical international business that is connected to the international economy in two ways. On the one hand, it sources commodities for sale through configuring an international network of suppliers via Walmart Global Sourcing and, on the other hand, it provides retail services to customers located in the US and in just 24 other countries, but the majority of the company's stores are in the US. Walmart is developing its business through configuring a unique global perspective that reflects its history, existing infrastructure, relationship network and approach to business. This is a unique global perspective as every company configures its own engagement with the international economy. Every business has features that are shared with other

Table 1.1: The global reach of the top 10 international businesses

Rank	Company	Country	Sector	Revenue USD (billions)	Global spread reach (by number of countries)
1	Walmart	United States	Retail	$612.3	24
2	Saudi Aramco	Saudi Arabia	Energy	$603.7	Over 50 countries
3	State Grid	China	Energy	$530.0	51
4	Amazon	United States	Internet services and retailing	$514.0	Over 20 countries
5	China National Petroleum	China	Petroleum	$483.1	Over 30 countries
6	Sinopec Group	China	Petroleum	$471.2	Over 70 countries
7	ExxonMobil	United States	Petroleum	$413.7	118
8	Apple	United States	Technology	$394.3	Stores in 17 countries, Apple services are available in 175 countries
9	Shell	United Kingdom	Petroleum	$386.2 billion	Over 70 countries
10	UnitedHealth Group	United States	Healthcare	$324.2 billion	Over 70 countries

Source: Adapted from Fortune Global 500 (2023)

companies but also particular or specific firm characteristics that may be considered idiosyncratic or unique. These idiosyncratic characteristics may be unimportant for business performance or might be a critical aspect of a firm's competitiveness.

International business as responsible business

It is important to appreciate that establishing and managing a business is a complex multidimensional activity involving a set of business processes that must be managed in an integrated manner. Managing a business involves an intensive form of multitasking, with each task being critical for the firm's current and future performance. There is an important challenge here, in that effective business leadership is founded upon being able to recruit the right people and to delegate responsibility whilst also ensuring that a holistic approach is applied that is informed by a common set of principles.

Creating value and responsible business

All business activities come with risks, and all have negative environmental and social impacts. Even the best designed closed-loop circular economy production process has negative environmental and social impacts (Du et al, 2025). A core question to consider revolves around exploring the fundamental drivers that shape the decisions made by business practitioners. This is a complex issue. It is too often assumed that the primary driver is profit generation. For some firms, profit is the primary driver, but not for all firms. Amazon, for example, focused initially on borrowing to invest in infrastructure development, with the company being founded on 5 July 1994 but only becoming profitable in 2003. There are many tensions in the decision-making processes that set a firm's primary objective. A focus solely on extracting profit might initially be successful, but there is a real danger that corporate performance could collapse if sufficient revenue is not reinvested in the business. In addition, there are tensions between balancing profitability with defendable or justifiable societal and environmental impacts.

Establishing and running a business is an exercise in creating value. The question is how each business defines value. This definition is imposed on companies listed on the stock market by investors and analysts, but for private or cooperative firms, value might be defined rather differently, with the definition reflecting the motivations of owners or founders. International businesses may form around celebrities, but like all businesses, wider social and economic impacts will be created (Box 1.1).

Box 1.1: Taylor Swift as an international business phenomenon

Can an individual be an international business? The answer is 'yes'. Steve Jobs and Apple or Jack Ma and Alibaba come to mind. These individuals were critical for these firms, but ultimately each of these firms outgrew their dependence on one individual; leaders involved in running firms are often replaceable.

Much of the literature on international business focuses on multinational companies and more recently on born global firms, but there are many different forms of international business. One form is based around individuals. Taylor Swift, the famous singer-songwriter, is an excellent example of this type of international entrepreneurship that is configured around the reputation of one individual. This is an important point as there is only one Taylor Swift and any attempt at substitution or identifying someone to stand in for Swift would fail. In 2023, Swift earned around $2 billion, and this figure sets her apart from other celebrity-led international businesses. As an international business, Swift's primary concern is with creating, managing and controlling her music, but there is so much more to this. Swift's business includes negotiating contracts, marketing, image management and projection, international intellectual property protection and international logistics and this is all additional to the creative process that lies at the core of Swift's international business.

All businesses generate spillovers or multipliers that are the result of expenditure that is directly or indirectly related to the business. Swift is no exception. Swift's 2023 Eras tour made a measurable impact on the US economy as it catalyzed expenditure on hospitality and tourism in cities such as Minneapolis and Chicago. The lyrics of one of her songs included friendship bracelets and this stimulated sales in craft stores across the US. In 2023, Harvard University announced that a course on Swift would be taught under the title 'Taylor Swift and Her World'. Swift has entered a new 'supercharged pop-star mode' that included releasing several albums over the past three years.

Swift is very much a highly creative international entrepreneur. In 2019, she stated: 'I'm sick and tired of having to pretend like I don't mastermind my own business … it's a different part of my brain than I use to write' (Nicolaou, 2023). As an entrepreneur, Swift is concerned with creating social value and this includes significant charitable donations. For example, at the start of her Eras tour, Swift made a major donation to the Arizona Food Bank, and this was part of a strategy to donate to foodbanks in each US city that was included in the tour. One consequence is that she raised the profile of these charities and encouraged others to donate.

There are many dimensions of Swift as an international business to consider. This includes exploring the relationship between reputation and international business and the creation of wider societal impacts including her direct and indirect relationships with other businesses. It is worth reflecting on how Swift's business activities are simultaneously configured around values created through live performance, recordings and media engagement.

Houdini, a Swedish outdoor clothing company that ships products to 37 countries, is an excellent example of an international business that is configured around a set of core values: to 'do good, play hard, push boundaries, have fun' and moreover the approach is about working 'together with an odd band of scientists, artists, designers and athletes' to push 'the boundaries of how outdoor clothing is made' (Houdini, 2024). Managing Houdini, like many other international businesses, is a balancing act between being profitable and creating value for customers and for everyone involved in this firm's value chain. This is a company on a journey towards circularity that includes a focus on ecosystem restoration and an ambition to remove negative impacts and to focus on cultivating positive impacts. There are many ways of labelling this type of firm. This could be classified as a firm that is practicing a circular economy form of corporate social responsibility, or as a firm that is trying to balance a triple bottom line configured around profit, environmental and societal impacts. Alternatively, this is a company that is engaged in an ongoing dialogue regarding responsible versus irresponsible business practice.

There is an ongoing academic debate on responsible business that builds upon accounts of corporate social responsibility. There are different approaches to applying a responsible approach to business practice. The most important point for practitioners is to appreciate that every company is engaged in an ongoing dialogue regarding an applied and practice-orientated definition. While there are very academic definitions, for those involved in managing businesses, the key is to focus on a pragmatic approach that can be applied in practice. Configuring firms around responsible business practice is a relatively new approach. Every organization must develop its own applied definition, but isomorphic processes will eventually result in the creation of established conventions. Nevertheless, in practice, responsible business reflects the capabilities, capacities and ambitions of a firm to balance the creation of negative impacts against profitability. A good example of this balancing process is found in the Dora Larsen company. This is a small company, a lingerie brand, which was established in London in 2016 and which ships worldwide and has stockists in 13 countries. This is a responsible business, with the company's values based around being 'a small, family run business. As big believers in Karma, producing responsibly is our priority. Our focus is on making product that lasts, fits well enough to wear every day, and is manufactured using certified and sustainable materials. We're not perfect, but we're focused on becoming the most responsible version of ourselves' (Dora Larsen, 2024). Acting responsibly for this firm is an ongoing project with no real end point and an acceptance that the firm is not perfect. There is no such thing as the 'perfect' responsible business.

Defining responsible business and responsible business as practice

There are three approaches to defining responsible business. The first is based on accepting that there is no perfect definition but that a company is involved in a journey towards acting more responsibly. How this is defined depends on the company, but also on consumers and, in some sectors, rating agencies. Second, a responsible business is one that creates more value for society than it extracts as part of a monetarization or value capture process. This could be considered as a utilitarian approach based on the doctrine that actions are right or responsible when they benefit the majority within a society. This approach challenges firms to consider going beyond extracting value to making measurable societal and environmental contributions. The third approach is informed by Kant's deontological philosophy (Conaway and Laasch, 2014; Laasch and Conway, 2016; van Tulder and van Mil, 2022). This ethical theory proposes that an individual should act based on what they believe is morally right and, in doing so, ignore any negative consequences. One implication is that responsible business could lead to a reduction in profitability, but any such negative outcome should be ignored. Deontology is associated with a debate on duty based on respecting other's humanity. The outcome for Kant is the notion of a 'categorical imperative' or a universal ethical principle that an individual should always respect others and that actions should only be taken that align with the rules that are followed by all.

There is a developing debate in the international business literature on social value creation and responsible business. This includes a focus on the application of corporate social responsibility to overcome the 'liability of foreignness', and the transfer of social value creation processes from headquarters to subsidiary firms (Sinkovics and Archie-Acheampong, 2020). Part of this debate appreciates that an international business must acquire legitimacy in foreign markets and such legitimacy includes creating social values within the countries in which they transact business. There is a tension between the academic account of social value creation and a pragmatic approach to practice. Thus, Sinkovics et al (2015) suggest that a business can only create 'genuine social value' by alleviating some form of social constraint, or in the case of multidimensional wicked problems, addressing some significant symptom. This sets the responsible business bar at an extremely high level. One challenge is in defining and measuring what is a genuine social value. The primary problem is that a firm seeking to create such social values would have set themselves an impossible challenge. For business practitioners, the challenge is to develop a set of principles, including some stretch targets, but the core principles must come with SMART key performance indicators that are specific, measurable, achievable, relevant and time bound.

Responsibility applies to all individuals and organizations, and this includes journalists, media outlets, politicians and consumers. A company that claims to be acting responsibly ideally should be trying to encourage their consumers to act in a responsible manner. This includes ensuring that consumers acknowledge their social and environmental responsibilities, including those related to reducing negative environmental impacts and trying to avoid consuming products that are linked to exploitative labour practices and modern-day slavery. There is a debate on the politics of responsibility that is framed around concerns with space, place and politics. One version of this debate focuses on exploring 'What is, in a relational imagination and in light of the relational construction of identity, the geography of our social and political responsibility? What, in other words, of the question of the stranger without?' (Massey, 2004: 1). This concept of the stranger without and within comes from postcolonial feminist theory (Schutte, 2000), with the emphasis being placed on appreciating different perspectives and positions and being open to appreciating the 'other' and the 'international other'. It engages with ongoing debates on decolonizing academic debates, with the emphasis being on reimagining what, how and by whom knowledge is constructed, shared, taught, appreciated and applied to inform practice.

This is a very theoretical argument, but there are many practical applications for business. The primary issue is to consider the importance of trying to understand and embrace diversity in the context of engaging with consumers and producers located in many different national contexts. This is much more than being aware of cultural differences but involves establishing and applying responsible business principles that seek to ensure that environmental and social damage is limited. The production and sale of all products and services comes with some degree of environmental and societal negative impacts and all responsible businesses must be aware of these impacts and seek to minimize them. Minimization might be a zero-cost process and there might be costs associated with this activity, but the possibility also exists to apply this process to enhance market share and profitability. Acting in a responsible manner to strangers within and without should be seen as a pathway to profitability and sustainability. It is these businesses that will attract and retain talented employees. By understanding the other, these businesses will also be able to develop new commercially valuable products and services that embrace diversity by being challenged by the knowledge, beliefs, values and lifestyles of the other; the other in these terms is also a possible consumer.

Central to all international businesses should be this concern with understanding and appreciating consumer diversity. This process requires the identification of value propositions that provide solutions to societal challenges as experienced by consumers. The key issue is to focus on creating values-in-use for consumers. This concept has its origins in Karl Marx's discussion of exchange and use values, but the term 'value-in-use' comes from the more recent debate on service-dominant logic (S-D logic). Values-in-use are created through a consumer's use of a commodity, with the purchase reflecting the first stage in this process. Central to this process is the background or identity of the consumer and this includes their values, lifestyles and access to other resources. The S-D logic approach, like Marx's earlier analysis, recognizes that 'value is always co-created, jointly and reciprocally, in interactions among providers and beneficiaries through the integration of resources and application of competences'

(Vargo et al, 2008: 146). This approach then needs to be considered in relation to the ongoing debate on responsible business. The proposition made by Sinkovics et al (2015) that business should create 'genuine' social value needs to be reframed to acknowledge that multiple stakeholders, including consumers, governments, the media and academics, are responsible for this value creation process; genuine social values are better defined as 'values-in-use', and these are always co-created.

Isomorphism and irresponsibility/responsibility

There is a tendency for firms working in the same sector to become similar. Each firm will have its own set of principles, but isomorphism occurs, or the processes that encourage or force organizations to behave in a similar manner (DiMaggio and Powell, 1983). Isomorphism is an important societal process that encourages herd behaviour. This is a process that business practitioners must not take for granted as the danger is that companies become too similar. There are different types of isomorphic pressures: normative, coercive and mimetic. Normative occurs through the activities of professional practitioners, for example, lawyers or accountants, the movement of staff between firms and recruiting people from similar backgrounds. Coercive isomorphism comes from pressures imposed by other organizations and that might represent the emergence of conventions. These include pressures imposed by investors regarding expectations about profitability and the return on invested capital. Coercive isomorphism makes it difficult for public companies to develop alternative approaches or to break away from the behaviours expected by investors and financial analysts. Mimetic isomorphism results from a tendency for individuals and organizations to copy behaviours and structures developed by others. For example, Uber developed an innovative approach to providing taxi services that was rapidly copied by companies like Lyft. Isomorphism also includes the process by which new business models and/ or goods and services are transferred between countries.

Isomorphic processes ensure that too many firms adopt similar principles and approaches to balancing the relationship between risk versus reward with the outcome being too much of a focus on profitability with much more limited attention given to understanding and mitigating an organization's negative societal and environmental impacts. For practitioners, it is important to appreciate the ways in which isomorphic processes influence their behaviour. The key point is that an organization should have a clear understanding of its values and beliefs, and these should be developed from an internal debate rather than be imposed, or indirectly determined, by isomorphic processes.

Isomorphism is partly about the construction and transfer of conventions within a sector and between firms. Business or sector conventions are part of a debate on legitimacy building, with legitimacy defined in the context of organizational management as 'a generalized perception or assumption that the actions of an entity are desirable, proper, or appropriate within some socially constructed system of norms, values, beliefs, and definitions' (Suchman, 1995: 573). This includes an understanding of the ethics that guide business decision-making processes (Kline, 2010). Building legitimacy is a social process involving multiple stakeholders that includes investors, analysts, academics, regulators and competing firms. For any one international business there is a tension between accepting existing norms and conventions or challenging them. Challenge may come from competitors and new disruptor firms or from alterations in regulations or consumer behaviour. One such ongoing challenge has emerged with firms experimenting with shifting from production processes configured around linear flows of materials and energy to circular or 'closed-loop' systems that are designed to minimize resource use and waste residuals (Du et al, 2025). This approach can be traced back to the work of McDonough and Braungart (2002), who explored a cradle-to-cradle approach to production as an alternative to approaches that were defined as a cradle-to-grave approach, or in other words production processes configured to produce commodities that end up as waste and which are often sent to landfill or incinerated.

The evolving geoeconomy

All economic activities occur in place and are linked to a complex web of flows of money, ideas, expertise, raw materials, components, complete products, services and people. It is important to conceive place relationally; at any one time, each place is the outcome of practices, investment decisions made in the past and interrelations with other places. Space is shaped 'through interactions at all levels, from the (so-called) local to the (so-called) global, then those spatial identities such as places, regions, nations, and the local and the global, must be forged in this relational way too, as internally complex, essentially unboundable in any absolute sense, and inevitably historically changing' (Massey, 2004: 5). The same relational approach can be applied to all international businesses as these are shaped by similar influences that include interrelations with other organizations and places.

Space and place really matter. Place is the context within which all economic processes are enacted. But all places are connected to other places in different ways. There are exceptionally well-connected places, for example global cities, and places that are much less connected. All places are in an ongoing process of becoming. This includes alterations in their connectivity to other places combined with all types of infrastructure investments and enhancements. It is also important to remember that a place can experience disinvestment. Places can decline and even shrink, and this could be driven by an ageing population or some form of destructive or creative innovation that undermines some aspect of a place's economy or interactions with other places. Every place has some type of symbolic value based around difference to other places. Place is also 'the sphere of the everyday, or real and valued practices, the geographical source of meaning' (Massey, 2005: 5). Space is related to distance and this 'equates space with the land and sea' and this 'makes space seem like a surface; continuous and given' (Massey, 2005: 4). This is to highlight that space is imagined or conceived in different ways. There are major challenges here. Place can be imagined within the context of globalization, with each place playing multiple roles in global flows of people, ideas, money, raw materials and goods. Alternatively, place can be conceived as a retreat that must be protected or defended from external influences.

There are problems with equating space with geographic distance as innovation has resulted in time–space compression, or a set of processes that result in a contraction in the relative distance between places, and one consequence is a collapse in relative or perceptual distance between places. All this suggests that space and place are socially constructed and in a continual state of change. Massey identifies three propositions for considering space. First, that space is the outcome of interrelations and interactions and that these range from 'the immensity of the global to the intimately tiny' (Massey, 2005: 9). Second, that space is the 'sphere of the possibility of the existence of multiplicity in the sense of contemporaneous plurality' (Massey, 2005: 9). In other words, space is about accepting or recognizing the coexistence of heterogeneity. Space, or interactions between places, highlights difference and acknowledges the importance of all types of place-based differences. Third, space like place is also always under construction. This includes alterations in places that lead to new interactions or new flows forming between places. It also includes alterations in the processes and technologies that exist that facilitate interactions between places.

The history of economic activities is one based on a shift from transactions that were predominantly local to the development of economies that operated nationally, then internationally or even globally. One approach is to argue that a borderless world has developed in which nation-states have become irrelevant as economic processes are global rather than national or local. Part of this argument includes discussions of time–space compression. The outcome is a shrinking world that has been enabled by innovations in logistics and telecommunications.

It is important not to decentre or underemphasize the role played by nation-states in regulating economic transactions. International businesses are not all powerful; national governments still control their borders by determining and enforcing the conditions under which people, raw materials, components and commodities enter their territories. Borders between different nation-states still matter; for international business these borders matter as they influence decisions regarding market entry modes and product/service design. National governments set or approve the standards and regulations that are applied to products and services that are sold in their territories. The varied nature of these regulations adds additional complexity to transacting business internationally. A recent challenge concerns regulations regarding how data about individuals is collected and stored. What is occurring is segmentation of the international economy based on data regulations with at least four distinct national geodata geographic configurations forming: the US, EU, China and Russia. An excellent example is China's Great Firewall that is the product of a combination of legislative actions and technologies developed and enforced by the Chinese government to regulate and control the country's internet. This Great Firewall includes censorship and the blocking of selected foreign websites. Anyone living and working in China has partial access to the data that is available on the internet. As far as data is concerned, the concept of a borderless world is a mythical construct.

The debate on globalization or internationalization is one that can be too academic. There is no question that economic activity is increasingly international in its focus, but this does not mean that the dominant form of economic activity is international or even global. Much of the literature on international business is framed around internationalization or globalization. Both these terms are too laden with assumptions regarding the dominance of international processes over local processes. There is a tension here in that most people live their lives locally with very few people having multilocational lifestyles. Consumption is determined by highly localized drivers with some international influences. Every act of consumption links the consumer indirectly and sometimes directly with other locations (Box 1.2). The danger is that terms like internationalization or globalization are applied without due care to understanding the variegated nature of economic activity.

Box 1.2: Taylor Swift's indirect international impacts

Even when Taylor Swift is not working, she is working; every action made by Swift is carefully observed with every appearance creating what has been termed 'gossip art' (Petersen, 2023). On Wednesday 10 January 2024, Swift dined out with friends at a pizzeria located in Brooklyn, New York. This event created gossip art that impacted on Little Lies, a small and medium-sized indie family business located in Perth, Scotland. For Swift's stylist had sourced this firm's £58 'Sweet Jane Olive Crushed Mini Dress' and it was this dress that she wore to dine with friends. Little Lies had no idea that Swift had purchased this dress and were surprised when the gossip networks identified the dress. On 11 January 2024, the company checked the stock of this dress and discovered that it was sold out. Little Lies is an example of a born global firm in that it was established in 2015 as an online boutique based out of a bedroom in the founders' home, with a business model based on sourcing and stocking styles from wholesalers. This model changed in early 2023 as the firm developed its own in-house design team based at its headquarters in Scotland and began to produce own-label pieces. This is a company that does not follow fashion trends as the focus is on creating timeless pieces that are manufactured in small, limited production runs to minimize waste. It was one of this firm's own-label garments that had been purchased by Swift.

The example of Swift and Little Lies highlights the ways in which an individual act of consumption links a consumer with impacts that are created in other places. These impacts might be positive, as is the case with Little Lies and Swift; however, they might also be negative. These negative impacts include purchasing products whose production is based on labour exploitation or processes that pollute and are environmentally damaging.

This book applies the concept of a geoeconomy, with the term reflecting the combination of economic and geographic factors that are involved in all types of international flows. A geoeconomy emerges driven by place-based differences. One perspective on globalization is that all places are becoming similar. If this were to be the case, then one outcome would be a decline in international trade; trade is driven by place-based differentials. Nevertheless, change is a primary driver behind the geoeconomies' ongoing configuration. It is possible to argue that a new geoeconomy has emerged that is quantitatively and qualitatively different to earlier forms. The challenge is to identify critical inflection points, or those times during which radical alterations occurred, with the outcome being a radically new form of geoeconomy.

For business practitioners, this is more of an academic activity. The key point is that the fundamental drivers behind the ongoing deepening of a geoeconomy that is more oriented to international transactions are well known and are best described as processes that are fundamental to capitalist economic relationships and that reflect a form of timeless theory.

Theory, international business and the geoeconomy

The world of business and management scholarship is saturated with theory. Every publication is expected to make a major theoretical contribution. There are many perversities here with one being a reluctance by business and management scholars to refute established theory. Up front, it must be acknowledged that a disconnect exists between business and management theory and the needs of business practitioners. Such theory reflects the interests of scholars rather than practitioners. There are three points to reflect upon. First, the academic literature is typically peer reviewed by academics rather than a combination of academics and practitioners. There is thus no rigorous practitioner assessment of much of this theory. This raises the question: Does the academic work actually reflect what is happening 'on the ground' in business? Second, managing a business is a complex activity requiring an integrated or holistic approach to decision-making. An operational decision, or decision regarding market entry modes, will impact on other business processes and yet most business and management theory focuses on one precisely defined business process, with often no engagement with other processes. Third, much of the academic literature is based around exploring representative or average firms and such firms do not exist. Even with isomorphism at play, every company is unique in its own way. This is not to argue that business and management theory is irrelevant for practice, but it needs to be used with care. For the practitioner, theory should inform business decisions with the primary contribution being in identifying the questions, issues and processes that should be considered when developing a solution to a business challenge. Experiential learning, and learning by copying or shadowing more experienced practitioners, combined with intuition, underpins many business decisions; textbook learning is one starting point, but it must be acknowledged that other types of learning are more important in shaping business outcomes.

The role of theory in informing business practice

There are two ways of knowing the world. On the one hand, a detailed description can be made whilst, on the other hand, a theory can be applied. We relate to the world by applying simple theories that are learnt in childhood with the first such theories linked to understanding the relationship between a word and some characteristic of the world we inhabit. Ultimately, a theory is a simplification of a complex process or 'is a statement of relations among concepts within a set of boundary assumptions and constraints. It is no more than a linguistic device used to organize a complex empirical world' (Bacharach, 1989: 496). A theory is only ever a partial explanation as each theory illuminates some aspect of the world and throws into shadow other aspects. One must agree with Bacharach when he noted that 'the purpose of theoretical statements is twofold: to organize (parsimoniously) and to communicate clearly' but that 'many current theories in organizational behaviour fail to accomplish this purpose' as a 'collection of constructs and variables does not necessarily make a theory' (Bacharach, 1989: 496). There are different types of theory. Some theories are predictive with the aim being to provide answers to questions that focus on understanding why something happens, when it happens, how it happens and where it happens. All theories contain assumptions and these place limits on the theory's ability to enhance understanding of complex processes. Often these assumptions reflect the time and place of theory development, or in other words the time and place influences on those involved in the theory-building process.

A distinction must be made between theory and other ways of knowing the world; for example, via data, typologies or metaphors. The business and management literature, and the business world, is saturated with implicit and explicit metaphors – for example, clustering, ambidexterity, springboarding, networking; metaphors are valuable, but they simultaneously provide enlightenment and obscuration. Theory does and should inform practice but should be used with care. The key measure of the success of a theory is its ability to enhance understanding by highlighting some aspects of a complex process. For business practitioners, theory highlights the parameters of a business challenge and raises questions that should be considered by the management team. Nevertheless, localized solutions need to be developed that might challenge theory. Theory is one starting point to understanding organizational problems, but any solution must reflect the organizational context. Any attempt to apply a theory without contextualizing it could lead to isomorphism. There is a danger in applying what should be considered as fashionable theory, or time-limited theory, as this could lead to isomorphism; business practices and the geoeconomy are continually changing, and these changes require theory to be continually adapted or new theories to be developed.

Timeless theory and international business

There are a 'set of what can be termed "timeless" processes that emerged with the development of capitalism and continue to transform space and place' but 'these timeless processes produce different outcomes depending on context' (Andres and Bryson, 2018: 8). It is possible to identify timeless theories that are fundamental for understanding and managing international business. Two such timeless theories are critical for understanding international business and the evolving geoeconomy.

Comparative advantage

In 1817, David Ricardo developed the principle of comparative advantage that is the basis for understanding international trade (Ricardo, 1817). Comparative advantage is an economic model for understanding why one location has an advantage over other locations in producing a particular commodity. A location, given a combination of different factors that might be unique, will possess a lower relative opportunity cost to produce a commodity that provides that place with comparative advantage. The outcome will be trade with places that do not possess such an advantage. One of Ricardo's assumptions was that capital and labour would be localized, with no international movement; this is quite some assumption. Nevertheless, Ricardo's theory highlights that a place should specialize in those activities for which it holds the greatest comparative advantage. This theory does not explain why these place-based differences exist, but their existence is critical as they are the drivers behind flows between places.

Divisions of labour and the spatial division of labour

The 'division of labour' is an excellent example of a timeless process. This approach was subsequently developed by Massey (1984) into the concept of a 'spatial division of labour'. The concept of the division of labour is too often identified with Adam Smith ([1776] 1977) and his analysis of the ongoing transformation of the organization of work in a pin factory. David Harvey, for example, noted that the division of labour developed 'from simple beginnings in Adam Smith's example of the pin factory' and this has 'over time grown to encompass much of what is now covered in management and organisation theory' (Harvey, 2014: 98). This attribution of Smith to the identification of this concept is incorrect. In *The Wealth of Nations* (1776), Smith does identify, define and characterize the division of labour, but he was not the first scholar to identify this process. The concept can be traced back to Plato's *Republic*, a Socratic dialogue written around 380 BC. In this dialogue, Plato discusses with Adeimantus the benefits associated with a division of labour and the development of specialization within labour markets.

The division of labour explains the disaggregation of complex tasks into several simpler tasks that can be undertaken by different individuals or groups of individuals. This division of tasks can occur on the same site or at the same location, or tasks can be transferred to other places and a spatial division of labour (Massey, 1984) emerges that is the foundational process in understanding the ongoing fragmentation of global value chains (GVC). A GVC refers to all activities or tasks and their locations required to bring a product or service to market. There are three important points to make about the division of labour. First, a division of labour always precedes mechanization or automation; tasks are disaggregated, facilitating the identification of which tasks can be mechanized or replaced with artificial intelligence and robotics and which are more effectively undertaken by people. Second, the division of labour is the primary driver behind GVCs. At a city–region scale, tasks may be allocated to one place given the existence of concentrations of specialist labour or other forms of place-based processes or incentives that provides a specific place with a comparative advantage in the performance of a task. Third, the division of labour is ongoing. Day-by-day decisions are made to further subdivide tasks and to replace people with machines or robots and to alter the geographic distribution of tasks. In this process, jobs are restructured or reshaped, some jobs are destroyed and new jobs emerge.

For business practice, the application of a division of labour to the organization of tasks is part of an ongoing process to replace variable costs with fixed costs or to replace highly paid employees with either machines or less skilled or lower-paid labour. The division of labour is partly about deskilling, automation and productivity enhancement but it is also fundamental to understanding decisions made regarding where tasks or production facilities should be located. There is a major limitation with the division of labour as the focus of this approach tends to be on production processes and it overlooks the advantages of locating production and sales/servicing facilities close to major concentrations of demand. The approach also overlooks business decisions that may be focused on overcoming the liability of foreignness (Denk et al, 2012) or the additional costs that accrue to international businesses engaged in business activities undertaken in foreign markets compared to indigenous competitors. There are many solutions to this challenge, including celebrating the firm's differences, acquiring local competitors and setting up local facilities. For some firms, there may be no liability of foreignness as their very foreignness is a competitive advantage. This is especially the case with innovations in logistics, telecommunication and artificial intelligence (AI) that have partly overcome some of the difficulties of cross-border management and managing at a distance. But there are processes working against this. This includes governments who are concerned with economic sovereignty or with ensuring that their citizens can access the raw materials, goods and services required to support everyday living.

Drivers and risks and international business

International business and the ongoing transformation of the geoeconomy is dependent on 'so-called little things' that 'are the real material of globalization, the things that count, the things that guide or impose outcomes' (Thrift et al, 2014: 1). These little things include innovations linked to shipping, aviation, logistics, telecommunications, data analytics and cybersecurity. For international business, objects matter as 'there are very few practices which are not intermediated by objects and there are many practices where objects dictate the terms of trade' (Thrift et al, 2014: 7). This is rather academic, but innovations in international business emerge in response to alterations in the wider framework conditions that support economic activity. These might be tiny or major innovations, but such innovations are compounded, with the outcome sometimes being the emergence of a new way of engaging in international business.

Drivers behind international business

International business has many drivers and comes with risks and rewards. These drivers include the search for additional consumers, or market share in a new country context, and/or new ways of configuring a production-oriented spatial division of labour – a GVC. A central driver is to enhance profitability by growing a business combined with spreading risks related to sales and production across many different markets. There is a danger in assuming that a major international business is the outcome of rational decision-making processes in response to some vision or aim. The actuality is much more complex as all decision-makers experience bounded rationality and information asymmetry, with the outcome being that decision-making processes are semi-rational. All businesses are managed through a complex combination of informed decision-making with improvisation.

One of the most critical drivers behind international business is the existence of place-based differentials. Place matters for international business as each place has a different combination of assets and each is connected to other places in different ways. Each place reflects the outcome of the historic accumulation of many decisions made by governments, individuals and organizations and each place is experiencing ongoing processes of change. Place-based differentials include lifestyles reflecting different cultures and traditions, but also differences in factor inputs: land, labour and capital. These place-based differentials underpin most international business theories, and their origins can be explained by the emphasis Ricardo placed on place-based comparative advantage.

Place-based differentials must first be identified as business opportunities and there must be appropriate infrastructure in place to exploit these differentials. Disruptive change is always possible. For example, BA, the UK airline, suspended flights from London, UK, to Beijing, China, in October 2024 as a direct response to longer flight times and increased costs that come from the Russian airspace ban that was linked to Russia's ongoing war with Ukraine. The Russia–Ukraine War altered place-based differentials, but not for all airlines. Competing operators Air China and China Southern Airlines were still able to use Russian airspace, and this provided them with a competitive advantage over BA. For firms a competitive advantage comes from the combination of factors that enables one company to produce goods or services better or more cheaply than its competitors. This aviation example is one of a short-term impact, but there are examples of innovations that transformed the geoeconomy (Jeffrey, 2024). One such transformation occurred on 26 April 1956, when 'a crane lifted fifty-eight aluminium truck bodies aboard an ageing tanker ship moored in Newark' (Levinson, 2016: 1). This was the beginning of a major revolution, driven by disruptive innovation – the introduction of the container. Containerization revolutionized international business as

> in 1956 China was not the world's workshop. It was not routine for shoppers to find Brazilian shoes and Mexican vacuum cleaners in stores in the middle of Kansas … Before the container, transporting goods was expensive – so expensive that it did not pay to ship many things halfway across the country, much less halfway around the world. (Levinson, 2016: 1)

A more recent innovation that transformed international business was linked to the telecommunications revolution that includes the internet, intranets and smartphones. The ability to communicate and interact in real time, 24 hours per day and seven days per week transformed international business. This was then combined with logistics innovations that enabled firms to track components in real time through innovations in Radio-Frequency Identification tags (RFID).

International businesses are complex as they are embedded in complex GVCs and may be vertically integrated with a firm owning multiple stages of its supply chain – from mines to production facilities. There is a danger with oversimplifying international business. Much of the international business literature is guilty of this error as the focus is on one small aspect of firm performance or behaviour. International businesses like Amazon, Apple, Alibaba or Samsung are engaged in many different markets and configure many different business models. These firms coordinate production and sales processes and related supporting business processes, but there is another important aspect to these businesses. These firms are also financial institutions involved in managing and investing large amounts of capital. For some international businesses, a major profit-generating activity comes from returns on investment capital. This is to highlight the importance of financialization for international businesses (Hu et al, 2025), with this term highlighting 'the increasing role of financial motives, financial markets, financial actors and financial institutions in the operation of the domestic and international economies' (Epstein, 2005: 3). The outcome is that non-financial companies like Apple, Alphabet and Microsoft are involved in seeking investment returns from managing millions or even billions of dollars. Unlike a national business, for example, an international business can coordinate its exposure to taxation internationally rather than nationally. One approach involves not repatriating foreign-earned profits back to the home country as a tax management strategy.

International business, risk and Jenga capitalism

Focusing on the drivers behind international business distracts from appreciating that all business activities are saturated with risks; international business is exposed to a complex blend of home and foreign market risks, combined with logistical risks that can include a temporary blockage of the Suez Canal or the impacts of terrorism on shipping in the Red Sea. There are many risks, including disruptive innovations, war, alterations in trading relationships driven by the introduction of new regulations or trade barriers, alterations in demand, supply chain disruptions, epidemics/pandemics and climate change. There are known and unknown risks and sometimes known risks cannot be quantified. International business is a major contributor to climate change, with linear production processes creating waste and adding to carbon. Furthermore, the logistics that drive international business produce emissions from sea, air and road transport and from the data servers that underpin an increasingly data-inflected geoeconomy.

A new 'period of capitalism has emerged that is best described as Jenga Capitalism' (Bryson, 2022, 2025). Jenga capitalism combines the noun 'capitalism' with the proper noun 'Jenga'. Jenga is a game in which individual players take turns to remove 54 wooden blocks from a stack or tower, with the loser being the player whose actions cause the tower to collapse. Each block that is removed is placed on top of the structure, with the tower becoming increasingly precarious. Jenga capitalism highlights the increasing precarity of the geoeconomy that is associated with tight coupling or a situation where two or more elements or systems are closely connected and which might depend on one another to function properly. Tight coupling within national economies and GVCs is the outcome of an ongoing cumulative process of system or network convergence as the internet, for example, develops into an integrated Internet of Things (IoT) that includes IoT critical national and international infrastructure. Any IoT device is exposed to cybersecurity threats or internet disruptions. Added to this is that enhanced connectivity based on a complex network of flows has emerged with globalization and is central to the configuration of GVCs. The outcome is a tightly coupled international geoeconomy, in which any disruption to part of the network can lead to systemic disruption or even collapse. International business is also facilitated by the temporary relocation of people between countries and this process enables the rapid transfer of disease. The COVID-19 pandemic is one example of Jenga capitalism, with the 2023 terrorist disruption of sea freight in the Red Sea being another. The ongoing intensification of tight coupling as a core process driving the geoeconomy is one indication of the complexity of international business.

Reading international business: a framework for informing international business practice

A core challenge for students and analysts lies in understanding the complexity of international business. There are many different approaches. One approach is to focus on business processes and explore them in turn, whilst another approach is to review international business theory. In this book, we apply a very different approach by developing a practice-informed analysis of international business that is framed around three parameters:

1. A practice-orientated rather than an academic-critical appraisal of the literature on international business, internationalization and the geoeconomy.
2. A value-oriented approach that seeks to understand the multiple values that are created by all types of international businesses. This includes an appreciation of alternative values that are related to a practice-orientated understanding of responsibility or responsible business.
3. An integrated approach to managing international business that is practice orientated.

These three parameters come together through the application of an approach based on how to read a business. All business practitioners, investors and analysts are engaged in an ongoing process of reading businesses. This is about assessing current business performance and processes and identifying adjustments that need to be made focused on different time frames – from the decisions that need to be made immediately in response to some event to longer-term strategy. Unlike much of the business and management literature, the process of reading a business requires an evaluation of everything. The business and management literature subdivides business into neat silos, with each silo representing an ongoing academic debate about some business process. Practitioners also operate in silos, but they must attempt to develop a much more complex and integrated understanding of a business or businesses.

Managers and all business practitioners develop 'the knack of reading situations with various scenarios in mind and of forging actions that seem appropriate to the understandings thus obtained' (Morgan, 1997: 3). This capability of 'reading' situations 'usually develops as an intuitive process, learned through experience and natural ability' and this process includes 'reading and rereading' (Morgan, 1997: 3). This process of reading businesses blends learning with experience and represents a form of informed but applied practice that also comes with opportunities for creativity. To Morgan, this process of reading develops 'creative insights that open new action opportunities to give leverage on difficult problems' and the criteria for judging this process are not objective but pragmatic (Morgan, 1997: 372). With reading a business, practitioners draw upon their personal experiences and develop and apply interpretative frames. This is an active and not passive process as those involved with reading a business have the opportunity to shape the business and alter outcomes.

Reading a business is a process in which a reader tries to appraise the structures, systems, drivers, values, principles and processes that lie behind the creation of all forms of value by a business (Bryson, 2022). This process can focus on the now, the past or the future. There is a real danger in extrapolating a firm's future from its past without considering future disruptions, including alterations in consumer behaviour, regulatory change, innovation and new forms of competition. The first stage in reading a business is based on acquiring a vocabulary and this includes terms and concepts used in practice and theory. The outcome is a framework for understanding international business (Figure 1.1) that has been developed to support the analysis of international business as responsible business that is developed in this book. This framework includes four cross-cutting processes: value, practice and conventions, motivations and change. The term 'motivation' is used rather than responsibility. Motivation emphasizes the reason or reasons that lie behind practice or an individual or company behaving or acting in a particular way. Motivation, or motives, always precedes practice. There are then 11 building blocks that are subdivided into a group of six things, two processes and three facilitators. Things include money and people whilst facilitators involve the three 'i's of intersections, intermediaries and innovation. These are enabled by governance structures and decision-making processes. Each of these 11 building blocks is considered in different international business theories but no theory considers all of these. Each chapter in this book engages with these building blocks and cross-cutting themes in different ways.

The second stage involves understanding the grammar or rules of doing business. One could argue that there are no rules for doing business, but there should be principles that inform decision-making processes. Part of this grammar is understanding the relationship between societal, or consumer needs and the value propositions configured by businesses that are then monetarized. Reading a business requires understanding of a set of foundational questions that should inform business practice. These questions can be derived theoretically or from some combination of theory, theory-led empirical analysis and practice. Each subsequent chapter in this book explores the terms, concepts and processes required to read a business and then identifies the questions for which practitioners need to develop solutions and which relate to each chapter's theme. The outcome of this process will be a framework intended to inform business practice through identifying the core questions that every firm needs to solve. These may be partial solutions and, in any case, business is a process of continual change; today's solution to a problem may be tomorrow's obsolete solution. This is why it is important to focus on

Figure 1.1: International business as responsible business framework: building blocks

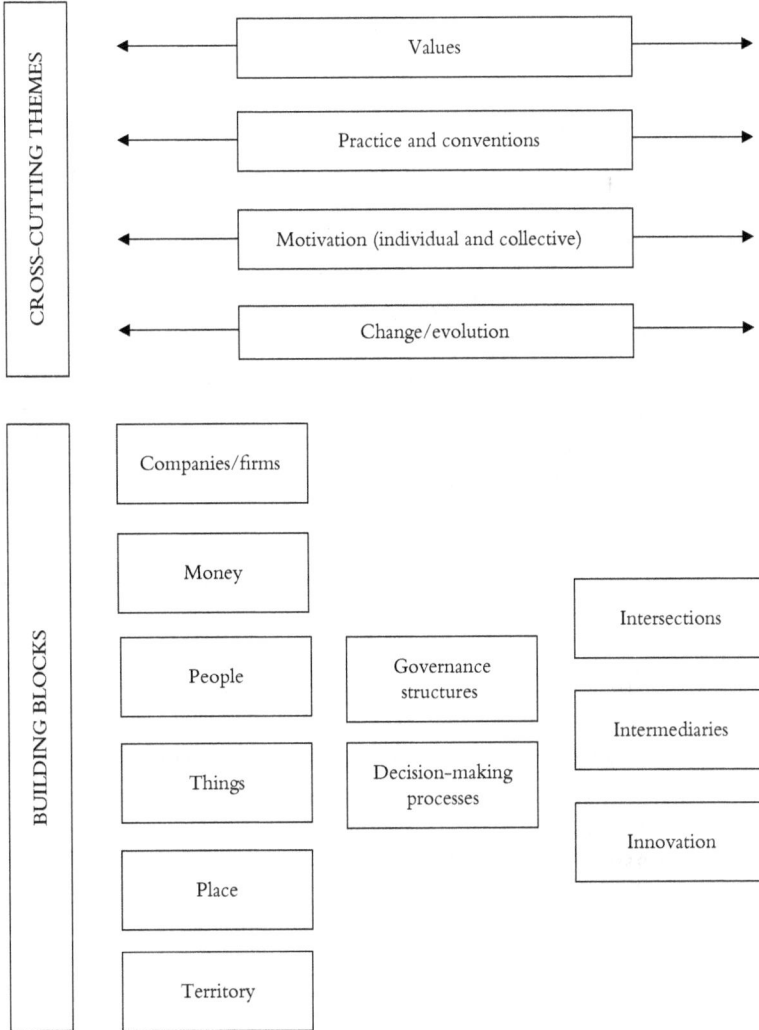

understanding the concepts, terms and processes rather than on solutions applied by existing businesses some time in the past; for business practice, the past should be considered as a very partial guide to the future.

This book has ten chapters, with this first chapter developing a building-block approach to understanding the practice of international business. Each chapter is designed to explore some dimensions of international business as responsible business, but each still engages with all the building blocks highlighted in our framework. In Chapter 2, the focus is on territory, or the institutional environment, whilst Chapter 3 explores the intersections between technological innovation and the emerging geoeconomy and this includes a focus on things and firms. This then leads to Chapter 4, which begins to unravel some of the dimensions of value and alternative values and this includes circularity. Chapter 5 builds on this debate by exploring business models, money and the monetarizing of value. Chapters 1–5 identify, explore and elaborate on a set of core processes that are critical for all international businesses. These come together in Chapter 6 that places these processes in the context of mainstream international business theory. Our intention is not to provide a detailed overview of these theories, but to highlight how they contribute to understanding responsible business practices. Our approach is designed around our building block framework, and this includes mapping this framework to international business theory in the context of a discussion of practice and responsibility. Place and territory are critical building blocks in international business, and these are explored in Chapter 7. There are many different types of business, including firms that create and sell services. Services have a very different set of characteristics compared to physical products, and these are explored in Chapter 8. It is important to understand intersections between people, place, territories and firms, and these are explored in Chapter 9 through a discussion centred on GVCs. Finally, Chapter 10 brings this analysis of international business and responsible practice together by identifying and exploring trade-offs and tensions.

Key terms

Geoeconomy – the outcome of the combination of economic and geographic factors that are involved in all types of international flows.

Liability of foreignness – the additional costs that accrue to international businesses engaged in business activities undertaken in foreign markets compared to indigenous competitors.

Responsible business – reflects the capabilities, capacities, motivations and ambitions of a firm to balance the creation of negative societal, environmental and economic impacts against profitability.

Recommended reading

Bryson, J.R. (2025) 'Jenga capitalism and the cyber-energy-production plexus: new forms of risk and uncertainty that are reshaping economic geography', in T. Neise, P. Verfürth and M. Franz (eds) *The Changing Economic Geography of Companies and Regions in Times of Risk, Uncertainty and Crisis*, London: Routledge, pp 47–65.

Buckley, P.J., Enderwick, P., Hsieh, L. and Shenkar, O. (2024) 'International business theory and the criminal multinational enterprise', *Journal of World Business*, 59(5): 101553. doi.org/10.1016/j.jwb.2024.101553.

Cook, G., Johns, J., McDonald, F., Beaverstock, J. and Pandit, N. (eds) (2018) *The Routledge Companion to the Geography of International Business*, Abingdon: Routledge.

Levinson, M. (2016) *The Box: How the Shipping Container Made the World Smaller and the World Economy Bigger*, Princeton: Princeton University Press.

Thrift, N., Tickell, A., Woolgar, S. and Rupp, W.H. (eds) (2014) *Globalization in Practice*, Oxford: Oxford University Press.

References

Andres, L. and Bryson, J.R. (2018) 'Dynamics and city–region regeneration economies', in J.R. Bryson, L. Andres and R. Mulhall (eds) *A Research Agenda for Regeneration Economies*, Cheltenham: Edward Elgar, pp 1–22.

Bacharach, S.B. (1989) 'Organizational theories: some criteria for evaluation', *Academy of Management Review*, 14(4): 496–515.

Bryson, J.R. (2022) 'Reading manufacturing firms and new research agendas: scalar-plasticity, value/risk and the emergence of Jenga capitalism', in J.R. Bryson, C. Billing, W. Graves and G. Yeung (eds) *A Research Agenda for Manufacturing Industries in the Global Economy*, Cheltenham: Edward Elgar, pp 211–43.

Bryson, J.R. (2025) 'Jenga capitalism and the cyber-energy-production plexus: new forms of risk and uncertainty that are reshaping economic geography', in T. Neise, P. Verfürth and M. Franz (eds) *The Changing Economic Geography of Companies and Regions in Times of Risk, Uncertainty and Crisis*, London: Routledge, pp 47–65.

Buckley, P.J., Enderwick, P., Hsieh, L. and Shenkar, O. (2024) 'International business theory and the criminal multinational enterprise', *Journal of World Business*, 59(5): 101553. doi.org/10.1016/j.jwb.2024.101553.

Conaway, R.N. and Laasch, O. (2014) *Principles of Responsible Management: Global Sustainability Responsibility and Ethics*, Nashville: South-Western.

Denk, N., Kaufmann, L. and Roesch, J.-F. (2012) 'Liabilities of foreignness revisited: a review of contemporary studies and recommendations for future research', *Journal of International Management*, 18(4): 322–34.

Department for Business and Trade (2023) *Business Population Estimates for the UK and Regions 2023*. [online]. Available from: www.gov.uk/government/statistics/busin ess-population-estimates-2023/business-population-estimates-for-the-uk-and-regi ons-2023-statistical-release [Accessed 8 August 2024].

DiMaggio, P.J. and Powell, W.W. (1983) 'The iron cage revisited: institutional isomorphism and collective rationality in organizational fields', *American Sociological Review*, 48(2): 147–60.

Dora Larsen (2024) 'Our values' [online]. Available from: https://doralarsen.com/pages/values [Accessed 14 June 24].

Du, B., Bryson J.R. and Qamar, A. (2025) 'Aspiring towards automotive circularity: a critical review and research agenda', *Journal of Environmental Management*, 380: 125–50.

Epstein, G.A. (2005) 'Financialization and the world economy', in G.A. Epstein (ed) *Financialization and the World Economy*, Cheltenham: Edward Elgar, pp 3–16

Harvey, D. (2014) *Seventeen Contradictions and the End of Capitalism*, London: Profile Books.

Hennart, J.F., Majocchi, A. and Hagen, B. (2021) 'What's so special about born globals, their entrepreneurs or their business model?', *Journal of International Business Studies*, 52(9): 1665–94.

Houdini (2024) Work at Houdini [online]. Available from: https://houdinisportsw ear.com/en-eu/about-houdini/work-at-houdini [Accessed 12 June 24].

Hu, H., Bryson, J.R., and Beaverstock, J.V. (2025) 'Triple-loop springboarding and simulacrum enterprises: financialization and new forms of emerging economy educational international businesses', *International Business Review*, 34(3): 102420. https://doi.org/10.1016/j.ibusrev.2025.102420.

Jeffrey, R. (2024) 'BA suspends costly Beijing route', *Air Cargo News* [online]. Available from: www.aircargonews.net/airlines/ba-suspends-costly-beijing-route/ [Accessed 18 September 2024].

Kline, J. (2010) *Ethics for International Business: Decision-Making in a Global Political Economy*, London: Routledge.

Laasch, O. and Conway, R. (2016) *Responsible Business: A Textbook for Theory, Practice, and Change*, Austin: Greenleaf.

Levinson, M. (2016) *The Box: How the Shipping Container Made the World Smaller and the World Economy Bigger*, Princeton: Princeton University Press.

Massey, D. (1984) *Spatial Divisions of Labour: Social Structure and the Geography of Production*, London: Macmillan.

Massey, D. (2004) 'Geographies of responsibility', *Geografiska Annaler: Series B, Human Geography*, 86: 5–18.

Massey, D. (2005) *For Space*, London: Sage.

McDonough, W. and Braungart, M. (2002) *Cradle to Cradle: Remaking the Way We Make Things*, New York: North Point Press.

Morgan, G. (1997) *Images of Organization*, Beverly Hills: Sage.

Nicolaou, A. (2023) 'Taylor Swift: a pop star at the peak of her powers', *Financial Times* [online] 23 December. Available from: www.ft.com/content/f37aaa87-043b-4d9c-98ad-d129f7ccc8db [Accessed 12 January 2024].

Petersen, A.H. (2023) 'Taylor Swift likes to work', *Culture Study* [online]. Available from: https://annehelen.substack.com/p/taylor-swift-likes-to-work [Accessed 12 January 2024].

Ricardo, D. (1817) *On the Principles of Political Economy and Taxation*, London: John Murray.

Schutte, O. (2000) 'Cultural alterity: cross-cultural communication and feminist theory in North–South contexts', in U. Narayan and S. Harding (eds) *Decentering the Center: A Philosophy for a Multicultural, Postcolonial, and Feminist World*, Bloomington and Indianapolis: Indiana University Press, pp 47–66.

Sinkovics, N. and Archie-Acheampong, J. (2020) 'The social value creation of MNEs – a literature review across multiple academic fields', *Critical Perspectives on International Business*, 16(1): 7–46.

Sinkovics, N., Sinkovics, R.R., Hoque, S.F. and Czaban, L. (2015) 'A reconceptualisation of social value creation as social constraint alleviation', *Critical Perspectives on International Business*, 11(3/4): 340–63.

Smith, A. ([1776] 1977) *The Wealth of Nations*, Harmondsworth: Penguin.

Suchman, M.C. (1995) 'Managing legitimacy: strategic and institutional approaches', *Academy of Management Review*, 20(3): 571–610.

Thrift, N., Tickell, A. and Woolgar, S. (2014) 'Respecifying globalization: an editorial essay for globalization in practice', in N. Thrift, A. Tickell, S. Woolgar and W.H. Rupp (eds) *Globalization in Practice*, Oxford: Oxford University Press, pp 1–15.

van Tulder, R. and van Mil, E. (2022) *Principles of Sustainable Business: Frameworks for Corporate Action on the SDGs*, Abingdon: Taylor & Francis.

Vargo, S.L., Maglio, P.P. and Akaka, M.A. (2008) 'On value and value co-creation: a service systems and service logic perspective', *European Management Journal*, 26(3): 145–52.

2

The Geoeconomy, Responsible International Business and the State

Introduction

One of the primary agents in the geoeconomy is the state. Business activities do not occur in a vacuum and politics and economics are highly interdependent. Each national government has an explicit or implicit agenda regarding business activities within its boundaries and often concerns itself with how it is connected to other economies through trade agreements (multi- or bilateral), imports and exports, inward and outward foreign direct investment and integration into global value chains. Contrary to some of the pervasive media narratives around the strength of international companies, national governments still exert considerable power, as demonstrated by national responses to the global financial crisis and the COVID-19 pandemic. This chapter examines the growing significance of geoeconomics and the role of the state in the global economy. The chapter's starting point is the cross-cutting theme of practices and conventions and the building block of governance structures. Discussion in the chapter includes the building blocks of territory, place, intersections and intermediaries.

The chapter understands the state as having multiple roles. We begin by defining the state, before then addressing each of these roles in turn. First, states as regulators, providing the rules of the game for international firms. We outline the different forms of regulation and how they impact on international firms. Second, states as collaborators. The chapter discusses the ways in which countries can work together, highlighting regional integration and its importance in shaping the geography and organizational form of international firms. Third, states as competitors. Here we examine national competitiveness and the emergence of state-owned enterprises (SOEs); see Chapter 6. Fourth, states as containers, with a particular focus on the cultural dimensions of states and the implications for international business.

Defining the state

Even predating the advent of globalization, there has been intense debate around the power, scope and role of the state in economies. Dicken (2011) reminds us that as early as 1969, economic historian Charles P. Kindleberger claimed that 'the national state is just about through as an economic unit' (Kindleberger, 1969: 207). Hyperglobalists assure us that the state is a weakening actor in the global economy (hence narratives around the end of the nation-state and the unrivalled power of international businesses). This is countered by Hirst and Thompson (1995), who argue that national-level economic processes remain central and that the international economy is far from ungovernable. For them, major nation-states have a pivotal role to play in creating and sustaining such governance but their role is less as autonomous national macroeconomic managers than as agencies that are representative of their populations and sources of legitimacy for new forms of governance. In this chapter, we suggest that the state is not merely a backdrop to business activities, but rather an active force that *shapes*, *regulates* and *directs* the economic environment in which businesses operate. Recognizing the state's influence is critical for those engaged in global markets, as it sets the parameters within which businesses must operate.

'Geoeconomics', a relatively new term in international business discourse, extends the concept of geopolitics by focusing on the strategic use of economic resources to achieve national goals, often through trade and investment rather than military means. The growing importance of geoeconomics highlights the need for global managers to understand the geographical and political factors shaping national economic strategies, which, in turn, influence corporate decision-making. Historically, the state's role has been rooted in its authority to create and enforce laws. While this text does not delve into a deep historical analysis of state formation, a basic understanding of the state's evolution is necessary to appreciate its current role in international business. Today, the state is defined not only by its government but also by its interactions with other nations and businesses on the global stage. This dynamic requires global managers to stay alert to changes that could impact the business environment. Including the state's role in strategic planning is important, as businesses must adapt their strategies to align with the specific characteristics of each country in which they operate.

Key thinkers such as Hobbes (1651/2008), Locke (1690) and Marx have shaped our understanding of the state. Hobbes (1651) and Locke (1690) challenged the divine right of kings, arguing instead for a state whose authority comes from the consent of the governed – a principle foundational to modern democracy. Marx and Engels (1848) viewed the state as a tool of class control, a perspective that still influences debates on economic and social policies today. Max Weber's (1919) concept of the state's monopoly on legitimate violence highlights its unique role in maintaining order and authority. His insights into bureaucracy are essential to understanding the organizational structures that underpin modern states. The advocation by John Maynard Keynes (1936) for government intervention during economic downturns has had a lasting impact, particularly during crises like the 2008 financial collapse. Later scholars such as Anthony Giddens (1985) and Joel Migdal (2001) further explored the state's roles in legal and international contexts. Giddens characterized the state as a legal entity exercising power within a territory, while Migdal emphasized its sovereignty and leadership in global affairs.

These perspectives illustrate the multifaceted role of the state as a regulator, protector and key actor in international business. However, while we can debate the role of the state in general terms, there exists multiple forms of national governance and overlap in the terms used. The *state* is a geographical space that has externally recognized sovereignty over its territory. There are currently 205 states recognized by the United Nations. The *nation* is a larger group of people with a common culture and sharing cultural traits. It may not be externally recognized. There are currently 574 federally recognized Indian nations in the United States of America. As well as being contained within states, nations can cross the geographical boundaries of states. A *nation-state* is a nation with a state wrapped around it; for example, Singapore. Globally we see wide variations in the motivations of national governments and the tools they use to regulate and control their economies. In this chapter we adopt Dicken's (2011) conceptualization of the state as a regulator, competitor, collaborator and container, though we recognize that since Peter Dicken published *Global Shift* in 2011, the geoeconomic landscape has undergone significant transformations, marked by intensified and more nuanced competition. The intervening years have seen a shift from the dominance of traditional economic powers to a more multipolar world, where emerging economies play increasingly significant roles. This change is driven by the rapid advancement of technology and innovation in countries like China and India, challenging the established hegemony of Western economies.

The nature of competition has also evolved, moving beyond sheer economic and military might to encompass technological leadership, control over data and influence in global governance structures. Digital technology, in particular, has become a critical battleground, with nations vying to lead in sectors such as artificial intelligence, cybersecurity and biotechnology. These changes have led to a more complex and interconnected geoeconomic environment, where strategic alliances and partnerships are critical, and where economic interdependence coexists with rising protectionism and strategic rivalry. This nuanced landscape demands a re-evaluation of traditional geoeconomic theories and strategies, urging states and corporations alike to adapt to a swiftly changing global context.

States as regulators

The contemporary geoeconomy is a complex mosaic of interconnected but highly differentiated spaces. One of the reasons for this is that states regulate how their economies operate to try to control what happens within and across their boundaries (Dicken, 2011). Table 2.1 outlines the four main ways in which states regulate their economies.

Table 2.1: State methods of regulation

---

1. Managing national economy
- *Fiscal policies* – raising or lowering taxes on companies or individual citizens and public expenditure
- *Monetary policies* – influencing the size of the money supply within the country to speed up, or slow down, its rate of circulation; manipulation of the interest rate on borrowing

---

2. Trade strategies

Policies towards imports:
- Tariffs
- Non-tariffs (includes import quotas, import licences and surcharges, rules of origin, anti-dumping measures, special labelling and packaging regulations, customs requirements and procedures, subsidies to domestic producers, local content requirements, exchange rate manipulation)

Policies towards exports:
- Financial and fiscal incentives to export producers
- Export credits and guarantees
- Setting of export targets
- Operation of overseas export promotion agencies
- Establishment of export processing zones and/or free trade zones
- Embargo on strategic exports
- Exchange rate manipulation

---

3. Foreign direct investment strategies

Policies relating to inward investment by foreign firms:
- Entry – government screening of investment proposals, exclusion of foreign firms from certain sectors or restriction on the extent of foreign involvement permitted, restriction on the degree of foreign ownership of domestic enterprises and compliance with national codes of business conduct (including information disclosure)
- Operations – instance on involvement of local personnel in managerial positions, insistence on a certain level of local content in the firm's activities, insistence on a minimum level of exports, requirements relating to the transfer of technology, locational restrictions on foreign investment
- Finance – restrictions on the remittance of profits and/or capital abroad, level and methods of taxing profits of foreign firms
- Incentives – direct encouragement of foreign investment: competitive bidding via overseas promotional agencies and investment initiatives

Policies relating to outward investment by domestic firms:
- Restrictions on the export of capital (eg exchange control regulations)
- Necessity for government approval of overseas investment projects

---

4. Industry strategies

The range of potential industry policies:
- Investment incentives (capital related, tax related)
- Labour market policies (subsidies, training)
- State procurement policies
- Technology policies
- Small firms policies
- Policies to encourage industrial restructuring
- Policies to encourage digital transformation
- Policies to promote investment
- Merger and competition policies
- Company legislation
- Taxation policies
- Labour market regulation (labour union legislation, immigration policies)
- National technical and product standards
- State ownership of production assets
- Environmental regulations
- Health and safety regulations

Application of these policies may be selective based on several criteria:
- Particular sectors of industry (bolster declining industries; stimulate existing industries; preserve key strategic industries
- Particular types of firm (encourage entrepreneurship and new firm formation; attract foreign firms; help domestic firms against foreign competition; encourage firms in import-substituting or export activities)
- Particular geographical areas (economically depressed areas; areas of 'growth potential')

Source: Adapted from Dicken (2011: 178–85)

No two states will have the same set of regulatory conditions (Box 2.1). This has profound managerial implications as firms need to consider the multitude of regulations in a new market and be vigilant regarding regulatory change in existing markets. Companies need to consider both the regulations that shape the state in terms of domestic market conditions, and also pay particular attention to the regulations and policies around foreign direct investment. Some states may prohibit some or all forms of foreign direct investment (although total prohibition is unusual), others may be actively seeking foreign direct investment by offering inducements. For responsible businesses, some consideration may have to be made to the impact that state regulations have on foreign investors, domestic firms and workers. Some policies – for example, the prohibition of trade unions – may not be considered in line with a company's values.

Box 2.1: State regulation: when the illegal becomes legal

Each state decides what activities are legal within its boundaries and regulates these to different degrees. Many illegal or illicit practices take place within countries, some of which are tolerated and some of which are actively prevented/prosecuted. As well as endemic illegal activities within legal mainstream economies, there are extensive illegal economies (which can involve theft, bribery and extortion, drugs, people trafficking and illegal arms dealing) organized by a variety of criminal organizations (such as the Italian Mafias, Chinese Triads, Japanese Yakuza and Russian Mafia) (Hudson, 2018). Despite the extensive geographical scope and size of these illegal operations, they have received limited academic attention—particularly in relation to how they intersect with legal economies (notable exceptions include contributions by geographers Hall, 2013; and Hudson, 2018).

States have within their power the ability to legalize particular activities and will do so for a variety of reasons. In 1986, the Japanese government partially legalized temporary staffing, extending it to full legalization in 1999. This was part of their strategy to make the Japanese labour market more flexible. It resulted in a booming market, serviced by large domestic firms and the market entry of global temporary staffing firms. Thus, a new industry was created to support the Japanese government's attempt to 'modernize' its labour market. By 2007, temporary staff in Japan numbered 1.6 million, representing 2.8 per cent of the total working population (Coe et al, 2012).

A second example is the legalization of cannabis in Canada in 2018. It is now legal for companies in Canada to cultivate, grow and distribute cannabis and related products for both recreational and medical use. A plethora of firms have now entered this new market. Deloitte (2023) estimated that between 2018 and 2021, the industry accounted for $11 billion in sales, contributed $43.5 billion to Canadian GDP and created 98,000 jobs. The largest firms in Canada include Tilray Brands (US-owned). It works with Novartis subsidiary Sandoz to sell, distribute and co-brand its medical products in legal markets worldwide. Tilray are motivated to 'shape the market but also inviting consumers to be part of the journey in this vibrant, health-conscious lifestyle'. They aim to 'empower the worldwide community to live their very best life, enhanced by moments of connection and wellbeing' through their mission to be the 'most responsible, trusted and market leading cannabis consumer products company in the world' (Tilray, 2024). Another large company in Canada is Canopy Growth, which is 'channelling the power of this extraordinary plant to build an organization made with intention and defined by purpose, serving as a new model for a transformational industry'. It believes that cannabis can be 'a catalyst for positive change in the world' and takes pride in its 'robust and stringent product safety control, responsible consumption education programs and environmental initiatives' (Canopy Growth, 2024).

We can therefore observe an industry that has been transformed by state legalization. The newly opened and highly regulated cannabis industry in Canada has attracted domestic start-ups and investment by international firms (particularly from the US). Canadian firms now supply the larger US market. The scale of cannabis production is new (much expanded), but the origins were once illegal. On the professional websites and in promotional materials of the firms, nothing is said about how the sector draws upon knowledge, expertise and labour from previously illegal activities (which inevitably it must in some ways). The previous quotes illustrate a sector that strives to convince us of its responsible practices, without mention of the darker sides of global cannabis production and trade. This highlights two points. First, state legalization does not remove the tracks of illegal activities and second, international business theories are currently limited in their capacity to understand the intersection and interaction of legal and illegal economic activities (see Buckley et al, 2024).

All nation–states outline the wider framework conditions that support economic activity. There are variations here. In countries like the US, Australia and the Netherlands, for example, businesses are encouraged to apply corporate social responsibility (CSR) practices, but CSR adoption is not highly regulated by government. However, a country like India has introduced regulations that mandate companies to adopt CSR practices. This regulation is intended to assist India in meeting the UN's Sustainable Development Goals (SDGs). In 2013, India's government passed the Companies Act of 2013. Under this Act, CSR provisions are mandatory for large firms. This Act was amended in 2014 to enhance CSR engagement across India. Companies with a net worth of over INR5,000 million or with a turnover of INR10,000 million or a net profit of INR50 million during any fiscal year must spend 2 per cent of their average net earnings generated over the last three years on CSR activities (Dharmapala and Khanna, 2018). Later in this chapter we explore the state as a container and discuss cultural differences and varieties of capitalism.

States as collaborators

Where a state shares a mutual interest with another, they may collaborate to achieve specific economic goals. A particular manifestation of this collaboration is the regional trade agreement, in which states group together, typically based on geographical proximity, to create supranational agreements. These regional trade agreements began after 1945 (eg the European Economic Community (EEC) and the Council for Mutual Economic Assistance). They then proliferated after 1990: for example, the European Union (EU) in 1992 and the North Atlantic Free Trade Agreement (NAFTA) in 1994. Each regional trade agreement utilizes a combination of different mechanisms to achieve its common ambitions. Integration can be achieved through establishing a free trade area, removing restrictions to trade for member states. This is the most common form of regional trade agreement integration as it does not prohibit member states from having their own trade policies towards non–member states. The next stage of integration is to develop a customs union in which member states also agree a common external trade policy towards non-members. Further integration comes with a common market or economic union (the latter is the highest form of regional economic integration). In common markets, the free movement of capital, labour and other factors of production between member states is permitted. The EU is the only true example of an economic union, with higher degrees of supranational control over economic policy.

The presence of regional trade agreements can significantly impact on the internationalization decision-making of firms. As there may be varying degrees of integration, managers need to consider how a presence in one state could afford them access to others. For example, by locating in Mexico, a firm has greater access to the US and Canada through NAFTA. If a firm locates in an EU member state, they have free movement across the whole of the EU, with very few barriers to trade, movement of people and common regulations. Such considerations can shape internationalization strategies, particularly for service and/or digital firms, where a central command hub within a regional trade area could allow coverage of the whole territory. For many firms, a driving factor of internationalization may be to establish a presence within a free trade area to avoid tariffs and restrictions imposed on imports from non-member states. Such regionalization of trade is common in many sectors, including automotive and agriculture. Box 2.2 discusses foreign direct investment in the UK since Brexit, illustrating a case of regional disintegration.

Box 2.2: Shifting foreign direct investment: the UK post-Brexit

For many years, the prevailing narrative within international business both in academia and practice, has focused on the trend towards increased global economic integration. This was illustrated by the rise of regional trade agreements and technology facilitating integration (communications technologies, digitalization, etc). However, since the global financial crisis in 2008, there have been a series of disruptions to this trend that include war, geopolitical conflict and pandemic. With greater economic integration comes greater political collaboration. This can cause discontent, dissatisfaction or disagreement about shared goals and outcomes. International business tends to focus on the impact of integration on multinational firms but finds itself needing to draw on understandings from international relations and industrial policy studies.

A famous example of economic disintegration is the exit of the UK from the EU ('Brexit') in January 2020. The consequences of this exit are varied. In terms of foreign direct investment, Brexit has witnessed a shift in investment patterns. There has been a substantial uplift in UK companies investing in Europe, particularly in Germany. Large UK companies sought a foothold in the EU to ease the red-tape burdens. These included Frasers Group (owner of Sports Direct), which is spending €300 million on a new distribution centre that will become its European headquarters; Mura Technology, which is building a chemical recycling plant; and THEMPC, a promotional and branding company, which set up an operations hub in Munich to produce and distribute printed goods and bespoke packaging inside the EU without customers needing to pay extra duties and taxes (Chazan and Giles, 2023).

The ability of the UK to attract FDI has declined from a peak of 1,205 projects in 2017 to 985, but this mirrors general trends across Europe. It still ranks second in Europe (to Germany) in terms of investment. The UK's largest sector for FDI is in digital technology, making it the leading country for tech FDI. The top source of FDI for the UK is the US, followed by India and Germany. The UK attracted 55 per cent of all FDI projects from India in 2023. However, there are some areas of decline, particularly in some high-value areas (EY, 2024). Investment in research and development projects has been falling (a drop of 44% between 2022 and 2023), as have manufacturing projects and projects to establish corporate headquarters (the lowest level since 2018) (EY, 2024).

The UK is still an attractive investment location for international firms. It is a large economy. The longer-term consequences of Brexit are yet to be revealed and some sectors, like agriculture, are suffering, particularly due to the availability of seasonal labour as a result of the absence of the free movement of labour by EU citizens to the UK. The sustained decline of projects in higher-value activities is a concern and the shift in headquarters (both in relocation away from the UK and slowdown in new headquarters being located in the UK) suggests that the UK is losing some of its prominence in Europe as a command centre.

For managers, the primary lesson in relation to states acting as collaborators is that while we have witnessed a general trend towards economic integration, nothing is certain. Individual states still have the power to decrease either integration or to leave agreements. This is easier for larger economies that may be better able to weather the turbulence of comparative isolation in the global economy, but much harder for smaller states. These factors should be considered when firms think about their internationalization strategies. Moreover, much greater attention is now being paid to local, regional and global forces that are causing commentators to discuss, and reflect upon, increases in the competition between states.

States as competitors

While there are numerous instances where states collaborate, the contemporary geoeconomy is increasingly shaped by geopolitical conflict and competition for resources. States act as powerful agents in areas of competition. International business has characterized the state as strategist, viewing the state as deliberately oriented to make strategic choices and implementing policies that can affect the international strategies of firms (Murtha and Lenway, 1994). Cerny (1997) characterized the 'competition state', highlighting that most Western industrialized states pursue marketization, the liberalization of cross-border movement and privatization of public services. Recently, Mariotti (2024) noted that the weakening of cooperative international governance is exacerbating the competition between rival states. Thus, 'Strong contradictions and imbalances have accompanied globalization, opening to the deterioration of international economic relations and a season of geopolitical conflicts and wars' (Mariotti, 2024: 642). This is intensifying firm–firm and state–state competition and states are acting as strategists, implementing policies to weaponize economic interdependence. To examine how states compete with each other, we will consider semiconductors and geopolitics, then discuss state-owned enterprises (when the state itself directly competes with international businesses).

Semiconductors

Semiconductors, the tiny chips powering much modern technology, have become central to global economic power, influencing industries from automobiles to defence. Their strategic importance now rivals that of traditional resources like oil, shaping international relations, driving economic growth and ensuring national security (Shih, 2020). While oil was once the cornerstone of geopolitical strategies, semiconductors are increasingly assuming this role.

The semiconductor industry is concentrated in the Indo-Pacific region, with firms located in countries such as Taiwan, Japan, China and South Korea as key players. Taiwan produces over 60 per cent of the world's semiconductors and over 90 per cent of the most advanced ones (*The Economist*, 2023). This concentration of production has significant implications for global power dynamics (Kim and Kim, 2021). While the US was once a leader in both the design and manufacturing of semiconductors, it now focuses primarily on design, with much of the production having shifted to Asia. This shift has left global supply chains vulnerable to geopolitical tensions, particularly between the US and China. In response, the US has enacted policies such as the CHIPS and Science Act to bolster domestic production and strengthen national security (White House, 2022). The CHIPS and Science Act, passed in 2022, reflects a broader US strategy to re-establish semiconductor manufacturing within its borders. Through subsidies supporting research, development, production and workforce training, the US aims to vertically integrate its chip production capabilities, a move that contrasts with previous global network strategies. A key aspect of this initiative was attracting investment from TSMC, Taiwan's leading semiconductor producer, to establish operations in Arizona. With a $40 billion budget, this investment is one of the largest foreign direct investments (FDIs) in US history. However, the implementation of this strategy is influenced by various geopolitical factors, reshaping both old and new political landscapes (Hsu, 2024), as firms and states seek access to this critical resource. Recent global shortages have underscored the fragility of the semiconductor supply chain. To mitigate these risks, geographic diversification and factors like climate change and water resources must be considered (Miller, 2020). With the semiconductor market projected to reach US$1 trillion by 2030, technological self-sufficiency and geopolitical concerns will increasingly intertwine.

The interest of national governments in the production and supply of semiconductors is motivated by a variety of factors, including national security and competitiveness. Semiconductor chips made by companies such as Taiwan's TSMC and South Korea's Samsung Electronics are critical for civilian and military applications. The criticality of these semiconductors raised concerns around availability (nations competing for access to supply), currency (nations competing for access to the most advanced chips) and national security (nations concerned about chips creating security vulnerabilities). This has instigated some protectionist policies, with national governments using diplomatic routes to try to ensure supplies and leading to discussions about domestic supply. China in particular, given its large presence in manufacturing, is developing strategies towards semiconductor self-sufficiency. Some concerns have been raised by US allies about potential Chinese dominance over semiconductor production. The US has implemented stringent export controls on semiconductor technologies to China, citing national security. These restrictions impact not only Chinese companies but also global firms like TSMC and ASML, which depend on US technologies. Simultaneously, the EU has recognized the strategic importance of semiconductors, launching the 'Digital Compass' initiative to double its output by 2030, aiming to ensure resilient supply chains in the face of global turbulence. In September 2024, the UK government acquired a semiconductor factory in County Durham. The factory was owned by Coherent and was threatened with closure. It manufactures gallium arsenite semiconductors that are needed for military applications, including fighter jets. UK Defence Secretary John Healey stated that:

> Semiconductors are at the forefront of the technology we rely upon today, and will be crucial in securing our military's capabilities for tomorrow. This acquisition is a clear signal that our government will back British defence production. We'll protect and grow our UK Defence supply chain, supporting North East jobs, safeguarding crucial tech for our Armed Forces and boosting our national security. (UKDJ, 2024)

The semiconductor industry illustrates the causes and consequences of high geographical concentration of the production of a commodity in high demand, and that innovates quickly. It is situated within evolving geopolitical contexts, but also itself shapes some dynamics. This demonstrates how industry and politics co-evolve, interacting to shape the sector in variable ways in different geographical contexts. Box 2.3 reviews the national competitiveness of Taiwan, the leading producer of semiconductors.

Box 2.3: National competitiveness and the global semiconductor industry

While originating from economics, Porter's diamond model (1990) is often applied in international business to understand national competitiveness. It uses four key factors: 1) factor conditions; 2) demand conditions; 3) related and supported industries; and 4) firm strategy, structure and rivalry. These can be applied to nations like Taiwan to understand the sources of their competitive advantage in semiconductors. First, Taiwan leads in the manufacturing of semiconductors due to the country's advanced technical education systems, labour force skill and productivity, significant R&D investments and advanced production facilities. Second, demand conditions are high. There is strong domestic demand for semiconductors, fuelled by consumer electronics markets and advanced industrial sectors, which drives domestic innovation. Third, Taiwan benefits from a robust network of related industries, including raw material suppliers, specialized equipment manufacturers and complementary sectors like consumer electronics and computing. This interconnected network strengthens Taiwan's semiconductor manufacturing capabilities. Fourth, intense competition among firms has driven remarkable advancements and efficiencies in semiconductor production. This competitive environment pushes firms to continually innovate.

Analysing the factors contributing to the competitive advantage of Taiwan has its limitations. The model has been critiqued for focusing mainly on domestic factors and may not fully capture the complexities of global supply chains and the international collaborations essential to the semiconductor industry (Moon et al, 1998). Semiconductor production spans multiple countries, and as such the national focus of the model can miss some important dynamics. ASML is a Dutch supplier of the most advanced photolithographic equipment for chip production. They have proprietary ownership of the extreme ultraviolet lithography (EUV) technology that is needed for the most advanced wafer fabrication. The firm has co-invested in technology development with all three lead firms (Intel, Samsung and TSMC). In 2024, ASML's market share was 83 per cent (Fox, 2024). EUV systems are oversubscribed – just one of TSMC's Fab 18 site required more than 50 EUV sets but the most ASML has been able to make in total (for the whole market) since 2020 is 63 sets (Wong et al, 2024). We can therefore observe that national competitiveness can be predicated on access to other suppliers and their capabilities, and these may well be outside the domestic market.

Finally, the model's static nature may fail to capture the dynamic evolution of the semiconductor industry, where technological advancements and market conditions change rapidly. It does not fully account for how countries can alter their competitive positions over time through strategic policies and targeted investments (Grant, 1991). Although the model recognizes the role of government, it does not sufficiently emphasize the critical impact of government policies – such as subsidies, tariffs and research funding – on the semiconductor industry. Government interventions in Taiwan have been pivotal in developing their semiconductor capabilities (Breznitz and Murphree, 2013).

The application of Porter's diamond model to the Taiwanese production of semiconductors highlights the insights gained from the model and some of its weaknesses. The model also assumes that competitiveness is uniform across nations (see Chapter 7 on place-based differentials). Having explored how firms operate across competing national economies, we now turn to examine a more direct form of competition by nations, that of SOEs.

State-owned enterprises

The state sector is an important element of many economies and there are legitimate reasons for state ownership. State-owned enterprises (SOEs), also called 'Businesses of the State', can act on the basis of commercial considerations or may have non-commercial priorities. They play important roles in many economies, often providing public goods and services (energy, resources, infrastructure, finance). These enterprises are fully or partially owned by the government and are established to pursue broader economic or policy objectives while operating under commercial, legal and institutional frameworks similar to those of private sector businesses. Unlike private enterprises, SOEs often benefit from certain privileges granted by the state, such as financial backing or regulatory advantages, which can influence their competitive position within the market. Their primary mandate frequently extends beyond profit maximization to include economic or social goals, such as job creation, infrastructure development and the provision of public services. The World Bank has identified 76,000 enterprises with more than 10 per cent state ownership in 91 countries (World Bank, 2023a). Examples include the Industrial and Commercial Bank of China, Federal Home Loan Mortgage Corporation (United States), Saudi Aramco, and Electricite de France. Kowalski et al (2013) state that SOEs are increasingly expanding to foreign markets. Some countries may use SOEs as a vehicle for pursuing non-commercial or strategic objectives and this may involve anti-competitive effects for their trading partners. This can have impacts on markets as these SOEs may be benefiting from domestic support that gives them a competitive edge over foreign (and domestic) private competitors in home or international markets.

The state can also take an indirect stake in firms through sovereign wealth funds (SWFs). These are state-owned investment funds or entities that are created and managed by national governments to invest in various financial assets. Funds are typically derived from a country's surplus revenues, which may come from sources such as commodity exports (like oil or gas), foreign exchange reserves or other financial assets owned by the state. Among the top 100 SWFs, there are several established by low- and middle-income countries, including Egypt, Ethiopia, Mongolia, Rwanda and Vietnam, although 80 per cent of these top 100 SWFs are found in high-income and upper-middle-income countries; for example, Australia, China, the United Arab Emirates (UAE) and the US (World Bank, 2023a). SWFs have grown from less than US$1 trillion in assets under management in 2000 to more than US$11 trillion in June 2022. Collectively, these state-owned investors have become the largest holders of financial assets globally, after banks and insurance companies (World Bank, 2023a).

The opaque operations of SWFs can raise concerns about their motivations. Global managers need to understand SWF dynamics, as these entities act as strategic players aligning investments with national interests. The regulatory landscape governing SWFs varies, adding complexity for businesses operating across different jurisdictions. SWFs like China Investment Corporation (CIC), established in 2007 with US$200 billion, exemplify the scale and complexity of these funds. CIC, managing over US$1 trillion, targets sectors like energy and resources, reflecting China's strategic goals (Lardy, 2012; Zhang and He, 2013; Rozanov, 2009). CIC's political motivations are monitored internationally, underscoring the need for managers to grasp SWF influence on global markets (Schwartz, 2010).

SOEs and oil

The oil and energy sectors serve as microcosms for international business dynamics, dominated by SOEs. Saudi Aramco, the world's largest oil producer, raised US$29.4 billion in its 2019 Initial Public Offering (IPO), showcasing its financial power (FI, 2023). China's Sinopec, a major oil-refining and petrochemical company has significant contracts with Saudi Aramco, and reflects China's strategy of using state-controlled companies to secure natural resources. Russia's Rosneft, while not directly state-controlled, remains closely tied to the political leadership of Russia. Other examples include Brazil's Petrobras and India's Indian Oil Corporation.

Nations controlling energy resources leverage this advantage for diplomacy, trade negotiations and global power projection. Conversely, countries dependent on energy imports must navigate complex geopolitical tensions to secure resources, highlighting the interconnectedness of state ownership in global trade. The fossil fuel sector's role in climate change adds to this complexity, as the 2023 International Energy Agency (IEA) report noted a resurgence in fossil fuel investment alongside increased funding for renewables. This reflects diverse national approaches (Hajer and Versteeg, 2018) to balancing energy dependency with environmental stewardship.

Russia's military actions in Ukraine in 2022 reshaped the global geoeconomic landscape. The EU led a response, condemning the invasion and imposing sanctions aimed at crippling Russia's economy, including excluding Russian banks from the SWIFT system and freezing central bank assets. Despite Europe's reliance on Russian energy, sanctions targeted this sector, though China's increased imports of Russian oil highlighted the limitations of these measures. By 2023, Russia's oil revenues returned to pre-2022 levels, aided by a shadow oil fleet and logistical networks (Kaufmann and Weber, 2023). The effectiveness of sanctions was limited by state behaviour, as Russia redirected its exports to China and India, illustrating the complex interplay between state actions and global markets. This situation underscores the critical role of SOEs in global markets, especially in oil, where nearly 70 per cent of the world's companies are state-owned (O'Sullivan, 2017).

The use of SOEs by nation-states to further their political ambitions is not always successful in economic terms. Venezuela's PDVSA is based on vast reserves, but the company's global presence has been weakened by mismanagement and political interference (Corrales and Penfold, 2015). There is widespread fraud and corruption in SOEs, particularly in oil and energy, which distorts markets, reduces competition and increases geopolitical tensions (Victor et al, 2012). Addressing these challenges requires transparency, compliance with regulations and collaboration among governments, industry players and civil society. It provides a particularly tricky environment for international businesses and their managers, especially for responsible businesses. The existence and growth of sovereign wealth funds is a reminder of the dynamism of the geoeconomy, where economic and political forces can create shifts in the activities of competitor firms which may have both significant opportunities and vulnerabilities due to high state involvement.

States as containers and models of capitalism

The geoeconomy is not homogenous as states act as 'containers' of distinctive cultures, practices and institutions, which are interconnected yet retain local variations (Dicken, 2011). Understanding these differences is important for global managers in assessing the international business environment. A key question for managers is whether a market is viable. This involves evaluating the economic system and how the prevailing model of capitalism influences organizational dynamics, risks and objectives. In 'free' market capitalism, minimal government intervention promotes competition and innovation but can lead to market failures, inequality and short-termism (Stiglitz, 2019). In contrast, 'coordinated market economies' (CMEs) rely on non-market relationships for competitive advantages, while 'liberal market economies' (LMEs) favour competition through market mechanisms (Hall and Soskice, 2001). These distinctions, or varieties of capitalism, impact global strategy, market entry, alliances and regulatory navigation.

Free-market capitalism highlights the need for balanced regulatory measures to prevent excesses. The relationship between economic models and GDP varies; while the US laissez-faire model shows strong growth, China's state-capitalist system also achieves high economic output despite differing social and market freedoms. Nordic countries' 'social capitalism' blends free-market principles with social welfare (Andersen et al, 2007), achieving high GDP and human development (World Bank, 2023b). The debate between state-managed and free-market capitalism underscores the need for balance. While state control ensures fairness, it can lead to inefficiencies; conversely, underregulated markets risk instability, as shown by the 2008 financial crisis (Roubini and Mihm, 2010). Sustainable or 'green' capitalism offers a potential path forward, linking long-term business success with environmental stewardship. However, challenges like 'greenwashing' and financial barriers, particularly for SMEs, remain (Busch and Lewandowski, 2018; Criscuolo and Menon, 2015).

In today's interconnected global economy, state influence, cultural traits and economic systems play vital roles in shaping business strategy. Recognizing these complexities, global managers must adopt a holistic approach, aligning business decisions with both local conditions and broader geoeconomic dynamics. Beyond profitability, businesses face a growing responsibility to adopt sustainable practices, recognizing that long-term success depends on the health of society and the planet. The move towards sustainable capitalism reflects the urgent need for companies to integrate responsible practices into their strategies as global challenges like climate change intensify.

The location of a company's global headquarters really matters. Governments are becoming increasingly concerned with national sovereignty and economic sovereignty. This includes a focus on security. This is becoming an increasingly important dimension of the intersections between international business and the state. TikTok, the social media app, for example, has experienced major problems with the American government. This app is owned by ByteDance, a Chinese company. The US government is concerned that TikTok represents a national security risk as an entity affiliated with the Chinese government owns 1 per cent of a ByteDance subsidiary. One concern is that the Chinese government could use TikTok to influence users, control their devices and to collect data. This is a complex case as TikTok has argued that it is incorporated in California and Delaware and thus subject to US laws and regulations. This raises the question of what constitutes the relationship between a company and a state. Lenovo, the Chinese multinational technology company, for example, has two global headquarters, with one being located in Beijing, China, and the other in Morrisville, North Carolina, US. The company's registered office is in Hong Kong. Shein, the Chinese global e-commerce platform, was founded in Nanjing, China, but the company's headquarters are based in Singapore. Similarly, Temu, the online marketplace owned by PDD Holdings, the Chinese e-commerce company, has a complex legal geography. PDD Holdings, for example, is registered in the Cayman Islands and Dublin is also listed as its principal office address. Temu, in the US, is owned by a subsidiary of PDD Holdings, Whaleco Inc., with this subsidiary being registered in the states of Delaware and Massachusetts. These locational decisions matter as they reflect strategies that involve decisions regarding tax, trade tariffs and regulations.

Companies like Shein and TikTok shifted their headquarters from China to reduce their exposure to American regulatory and reputational risk and also to distance these firms from Chinese government oversight. Nevertheless, both these firms have not broken away from China and are still considered as Chinese companies. This suggests that an international business can have multiple territorial identities. Dyson, the multinational technology company, was founded in 1991 in Malmesbury, UK, but in 2019 this firm relocated its headquarters to Singapore. This shift reduced the distance between the firm's Asian customer base and supply chains. Dyson, however, is still considered to be a British firm, but in legal terms it is Singaporean.

Cultural dimensions

Culture presents a significant challenge for international businesses due to its inherent complexity and, in part, the absence of a universally accepted definition. How can a manager improve their understanding of culture when faced with ambiguity? It profoundly influences how nations, businesses and individuals respond to geoeconomic developments. For global managers, the challenge goes beyond merely navigating cultural complexities; it involves understanding how culture fundamentally shapes behaviour. By expanding their understanding of diverse cultural contexts, managers can gain deeper insights into a nation's economic and business landscape, which is directly relevant to responsible business practices.

Culture, encompassing collective customs, norms, values, beliefs and practices, influences every aspect of social interaction and economic decisions. Geertz (1973: 196) defines culture as 'a system of inherited conceptions expressed in symbolic forms by means of which men [sic] communicate, perpetuate, and develop their knowledge about and attitudes toward life'. Similarly, Hall (1959) describes culture as 'the silent language' that underpins human behaviour and interaction, emphasizing its often subtle yet pervasive impact. These perspectives are profoundly relevant in contemporary business, especially as the success of international enterprises often hinges on their ability to operate effectively and responsibly across diverse cultural contexts. Despite its undeniable significance, culture is frequently misunderstood and undervalued in the analysis of international trade and geoeconomic events. Understanding the cultural context allows for a more nuanced interpretation of a company's motivations, decision-making processes and overall strategies. This focus on location or place ensures that analysts consider how cultural factors shape business practices, fostering a deeper and more comprehensive understanding of international business dynamics.

The influence of culture in international business goes far beyond surface-level customs and communication styles. It fundamentally shapes the economic policies and strategies of nations, affecting how they respond to global economic events. Understanding the cultural context of a market is not just advantageous but essential for those involved in international business. One significant cultural dimension is the divide between collectivism and individualism. In collectivist nations like Japan, social welfare and communal stability are paramount, shaping economic responses. For instance, during the 2008 global downturn, Japan's strategy prioritized collaboration between government, businesses and financial institutions to stabilize the economy and protect employment – reflecting a collective approach over aggressive market competition (Fackler, 2008). In contrast, individualistic nations such as the US tend to favour market-driven policies with minimal state intervention. During the 2008 financial crisis, the US government promoted entrepreneurial activity and innovation, reinforcing the cultural values of individualism and competitiveness. The focus was on empowering individuals and businesses to drive recovery, which is emblematic of this approach.

Cultural attitudes towards authority and hierarchy also shape economic strategies. In societies like China, where respect for authority is deeply ingrained, strong centralized decision-making dominates economic policy. China's swift, large-scale stimulus actions during economic downturns align with cultural norms favouring collective action for the greater good. This top-down approach contrasts with Scandinavian countries' more egalitarian governance, where policies are shaped through inclusive processes, reflecting their cultural emphasis on equality, consensus and social welfare.

Risk tolerance is another critical cultural factor. Countries comfortable with uncertainty, such as Israel, often adopt innovative and flexible approaches to economic challenges. Israel's focus on high-tech industries and entrepreneurship demonstrates resilience and agility in navigating global economic shifts. Conversely, risk-averse nations like Germany prefer cautious, well-planned policies, focusing on stability and precision (Dohmen et al, 2018), particularly in uncertain times. Cultural views on time also influence economic responses. Long-term planning and sustainability are prioritized in countries like the Netherlands, where policies promote enduring resilience and environmental protection. In contrast, countries like the UK often opt for quick, pragmatic solutions in times of economic stress, reflecting a cultural preference for immediacy and practicality. Social equity and justice further impact economic policies. In Brazil, for example, the focus on social justice drives efforts to reduce inequality, with policies supporting vulnerable populations during economic downturns (Barrientos, 2013). Conversely, countries like Singapore emphasize meritocracy and economic efficiency, prioritizing growth and competitiveness, while maintaining limited social safety nets.

Understanding these cultural characteristics is important for interpreting a nation's economic policies and strategies. For global managers, it means asking critical questions about cultural influences in current or potential markets to anticipate how these factors might shape business practices, enabling more effective navigation of international markets. Examples from Africa and the Middle East further illustrate the impact of culture on economic strategies. In Kenya, a focus on community and social networks influences crisis responses, with informal support systems reflecting the cultural value placed on collective effort. In Saudi Arabia, tribal affiliations significantly shape business practices, with strong family and clan ties influencing centralized decision-making.

Cultural traits profoundly affect national responses to geoeconomic events, shaping policy decisions, business strategies and resilience. The examples of Japan, the US, China, Scandinavia, Israel, Germany, the Netherlands, the UK, Brazil, Singapore, Kenya and Saudi Arabia highlight the complex interplay between culture and economics in a globalized world.

Conclusion

This chapter has discussed the different ways in which the state can impact on the geoeconomy and the activities of international businesses. Just as there are multiple forms of state intervention, there are also a variety of forms of state organization. Each has its own motivations, ambitions and views on its place within the global economy and the activities of international firms. The debates in this chapter highlight the intersection of politics and the economy. For responsible businesses, there is an additional layer to consider beyond the standard understanding of the different regulatory landscapes in which it is present or expecting to be present in. They also need to consider more deeply the political dimensions of the role of the state, especially where states hold views that may conflict with the values of the responsible business. The challenge for responsible businesses lies in capitalizing on the support offered by states while negotiating the fragile and often dangerous spaces of conflict between states. This is easier in some sectors than others, being particularly fraught in the cases of natural resources and critical components such as semiconductors.

Looking ahead to Chapter 3, the rapidly evolving technological landscape is reshaping the geoeconomy. In the next chapter, we will explore how disruptive innovation transforms international business practices and creates new opportunities and challenges. We will examine how the platform economy, digitalization and emerging technologies such as artificial intelligence (AI) and machine learning are accelerating internationalization. States are often key actors in technological development. Additionally, we will consider the rise of born global firms and the trade-offs between technological advancements and entrepreneurial behaviour. These insights will provide a deeper understanding of how technology is both a catalyst and a challenge in the new geoeconomy, offering further opportunities to align business with responsible and sustainable practice.

Key terms

Geoeconomics – refers to the study and application of economic tools, policies and resources to achieve geopolitical objectives. It encompasses the strategic use of economic power, including trade policies, investment strategies, energy resources and financial instruments, by states or other actors to influence global political and economic outcomes.

Sovereign wealth funds – state-owned investment funds or entities that are created and managed by national governments to invest in various financial assets.

State-owned enterprises – legal entities created by a government to partake directly in commercial activities on the state's behalf. The World Bank adopts the term 'Businesses of the State'.

Recommended reading

Hirst, P. and Thompson, G. (1995) 'Globalization and the future of the nation state', *Economy and Society*, 24(3): 408–42. doi.org/10.1080/03085149500000017.

Holton, R.J. (2011) *Globalisation and the Nation State* (2nd edn), Basingstoke: Palgrave Macmillan.

Mariotti, S. (2024) ' "Win-lose" globalization and the weaponization of economic policies by the nation-state', *Critical Perspectives on International Business*, 20(5): 638–59. https://doi.org/10.1108/cpoib-09-2023-0089.

References

Andersen, T.M., Holmström, B., Honkapohja, S., Korkman, S., Söderström, H.T. and Vartiainen, J. (2007) 'The Nordic model: embracing globalization and sharing risks', Research Institute of the Finnish Economy (ETLA). Available at: http://www.etla.fi/wp-content/uploads/2012/09/B232.pdf [Accessed 2 June 2024].

Barrientos, A. (2013) 'Social protection in Brazil: triumphs, challenges, and the path ahead', *Development and Change*, 44(5): 889–910.

Breznitz, D. and Murphree, M. (2013) *Run of the Red Queen: Government, Innovation, Globalization, and Economic Growth in China*, New Haven: Yale University Press.

Buckley, P.J., Enderwick, P., Hsieh, L. and Shenkar, O. (2024) 'International business theory and the criminal multinational enterprise', *Journal of World Business*, 59(5): 101553. https://doi.org/ 10.1016/ j.jwb.2024.101553.

Busch, T. and Lewandowski, S. (2018) 'Corporate sustainability governance: insights from the semiconductor industry', *Journal of Business Ethics*, 147(3): 723–40.

Canopy Growth (2024) 'Canopy Growth reports fourth quarter and fiscal year 2024 financial results: Q4 FY2024 net revenue increased 7% year-over-year, or 16% excluding divested businesses', Canopy Growth Corporation. Available from: https://www.canopygrowth.com/investors/news-releases/canopy-growth-reports-fourth-quarter-and-fiscal-year-2024-financial-results-q4-fy2024-net-reve nue-increased-7-year-over-year-or-16-excluding-divested-businesses/ [Accessed 22 May 2025].

Cerny, P.G. (1997) 'Paradoxes of the competition state: the dynamics of political globalization', *Government and Opposition*, 32(2): 251–74.

Chazan, G. and Giles, C. (2023) 'Post-Brexit UK investments drive FDI in Germany to record level', *Financial Times* [online]. Available from: www.ft.com/content/d88ad 354-9c4e-41a4-a439-06513ece665f [Accessed 4 September 2024].

Coe, N., Johns, J. and Ward, K. (2012) 'Limits to expansion: transnational corporations and territorial embeddedness in the Japanese temporary staffing market', *Global Networks: A Journal of Transnational Affairs*, 12(1): 22–47. https://doi.org/10.1111/ j.1471-0374.2011.00333.x.

Corrales, J. and Penfold, M. (2015) *Dragon in the Tropics: Hugo Chávez and the Political Economy of Revolution in Venezuela* (2nd edn), Washington: Brookings Institution Press.

Criscuolo, C. and Menon, C. (2015) 'Environmental policies and risk finance in the green sector: cross-country evidence', *OECD Science, Technology and Industry Working Papers*, 2015/01.

Deloitte (2023) 'Canada's cannabis report: a look at 2023 and beyond'. Deloitte Canada. Available from: https://www2.deloitte.com/content/dam/Deloitte/ca/Documents/consumer-business/ca_cannabis_annual_report-en-aoda.pdf [Accessed 12 April 2024].

Dharmapala, D. and Khanna, V. (2018) 'The impact of mandated corporate social responsibility: evidence from India's Companies Act of 2013', *International Review of Law and Economics*, 56: 92–104.

Dicken, P. (2011) *Global Shift: Mapping the Changing Contours of the World Economy*, London: Sage.

Dohmen, T., Falk, A., Huffman, D., Sunde, U., Schupp, J. and Wagner, G.G. (2018) 'Stability of risk attitudes and media coverage of economic news', *Journal of Economic Behavior & Organization*, 150, 93–117. Available from: https://www.sciencedirect.com/science/article/abs/pii/S0167268118300131 [Accessed 28 March 2025].

EY (2024) *EY UK Attractiveness Survey July 2024* [online]. Available from: www.ey.com/en_uk/newsroom/2024/07/foreign-direct-investment-in-uk-grows-as-eur ope-declines [Accessed 4 September 2024].

Fackler, M. (2008) 'Japan falls into recession, joining a club of countries that could soon grow', *The New York Times* [online] 18 November. Available from: www.nytimes.com/2008/11/18/business/worldbusiness/18yen.html [Accessed 18 August 2024].

FI (2023) 'Saudi Aramco: world's largest oil producer and most profitable company', *Financial Intelligence* [online]. Available from: www.financialintelligence.com/saudi-aramco/ [Accessed 19 August 2024].

Fox, J. (2024) 'Is ASML stock poised to outperform the market?' [online]. Available from: www.nasdaq.com/articles/asml-stock-poised-outperform-market [Accessed 25 September 2024].

Geertz, C. (1973) *The Interpretation of Cultures: Selected Essays*, New York: Basic Books.

Giddens, A. (1985) *The Nation-State and Violence*, Cambridge: Polity Press.

Grant, R.M. (1991) 'The resource-based theory of competitive advantage: implications for strategy formulation', *California Management Review*, 33(3): 114–35.

Hajer, M. and Versteeg, W. (2018) 'Imagining the post-fossil city: why is it so difficult to think of new possible worlds?' *Territory, Politics, Governance*, 7(2): 122–34.

Hall, E.T. (1959) *The Silent Language*, Garden City: Doubleday.

Hall, P.A. and Soskice, D. (eds) (2001) *Varieties of Capitalism: The Institutional Foundations of Comparative Advantage*, Oxford: Oxford University Press.

Hall, T. (2013) 'Geographies of the illicit: globalization and organized crime', *Progress in Human Geography*, 37(3): 366–85. https://doi.org/10.1177/0309132512460906.

Hirst, P. and Thompson, G. (1995) 'Globalization and the future of the nation state', *Economy and Society*, 24(3): 408–42. doi.org/10.1080/03085149500000017.

Hobbes, T. (1651/2008) *Leviathan*, J.C.A. Gaskin (ed.), Oxford: Oxford University Press.

Hsu, S.-Y. (2024) 'Critical approaches to geoeconomics: Taiwan's positioning in the global chip war', *Environment and Planning A: Economy and Space*. doi.org/10.1177/0308518X241269362.

Hudson, R. (2018) 'The illegal, the illicit and new geographies of uneven development', *Territory, Politics, Governance*, 8(2): 161–76. https://doi.org/10.1080/21622671.2018.1535998

Kaufmann, D. and Weber, T. (2023) 'The shadow oil fleet: how Russia maintains its energy revenue', *Energy Policy Journal*, 78(2): 121–35.

Keynes, J.M. (1936) *The General Theory of Employment, Interest and Money*, London: Macmillan.

Kim, H. and Kim, S.Y. (2021) 'The Indo-Pacific and the global semiconductor supply chain', *Asia Policy*, 28(1): 7–28.

Kindleberger, C.P. (1969) *American Business Abroad*, New Haven: Yale University Press.

Kowalski, P., Büge, M., Sztajerowska, M. and Egeland, M. (2013) 'State-owned enterprises: trade effects and policy implications', *OECD Trade Policy Papers*, No. 147, Paris: OECD Publishing. dx.doi.org/10.1787/5k4869ckqk7l-en.

Lardy, N.R. (2012) *Sustaining China's Economic Growth after the Global Financial Crisis*, Washington: Peterson Institute for International Economics.

Locke, J. (1690) *Two Treatises of Government*, London: Awnsham Churchill.

Mariotti, S. (2024) '"Win-lose" globalization and the weaponization of economic policies by the nation-state', *Critical Perspectives on International Business*, 20(5): 638–59. https://doi.org/10.1108/cpoib-09-2023-0089.

Marx, K. and Engels, F. (1848) *The Communist Manifesto*, London: Pluto Press.

Migdal, J.S. (2001) *State in Society: Studying How States and Societies Transform and Constitute One Another*, Cambridge: Cambridge University Press.

Miller, R. (2020) 'The semiconductor shortage: understanding the crisis and its impact on global supply chains', *Supply Chain Management Review*, 24(3): 30–7.

Moon, H.C., Rugman, A.M. and Verbeke, A. (1998) 'A generalised double diamond approach to the global competitiveness of Korea and Singapore', *International Business Review*, 7(2): 135–50.

Murtha, T.P. and Lenway, S.A. (1994) 'Country capabilities and the strategic state: how national political institutions affect multinational corporations' strategies, *Strategic Management Journal*, 15(2): 113–29.

O'Sullivan, M.L. (2017) *Windfall: How the New Energy Abundance Upends Global Politics and Strengthens America's Power*, New York: Simon & Schuster.

Porter, M.E. (1990) *The Competitive Advantage of Nations*, New York: Free Press.

Roubini, N. and Mihm, S. (2010) *Crisis Economics: A Crash Course in the Future of Finance*, New York: Penguin Press.

Rozanov, A. (2009) 'Sovereign wealth funds: defining liability profiles', *Financial Analysts Journal*, 65(4): 79–86.

Schwartz, H.M. (2010) *States Versus Markets: The Emergence of a Global Economy*, 3rd ed. New York: Palgrave Macmillan.

Shih, W.C. (2020) *Global supply chains in a post-pandemic world*, Harvard Business Review. [online]. Available from: https://hbr.org/2020/09/global-supply-chains-in-a-post-pandemic-world [Accessed 19 August 2024].

Stiglitz, J.E. (2019) *People, Power, and Profits: Progressive Capitalism for an Age of Discontent*, New York: W.W. Norton & Company.

The Economist (2023) 'Special Report: Taiwan's dominance of the chip industry makes it more important', 11 March [online]. Available from: https://www.economist.com/special-report/2023/03/06/taiwans-dominance-of-the-chip-industry-makes-it-more-important [Accessed 25 September 2024].

Tilray (2024) 'Tilray receives first new cannabis cultivation license in Germany under new regulations'. Tilray Brands. Available from: https://ir.tilray.com/news-releases/news-release-details/tilray-receives-first-new-cannabis-cultivation-license-germany [Accessed 20 March 2025].

UKDJ (2024) Britain buys semiconductor factory for defence purposes. Available from: https://ukdefencejournal.org.uk/britain-buys-semiconductor-factory-for-defence-purposes/ [Accessed 30 September 2024].

Victor, D.G., Hults, D.R. and Thurber, M.C. (2012) *Oil and Governance: State-owned Enterprises and the World Energy Supply*. Cambridge: Cambridge University Press.

Weber, M. (1919) *Politics as a Vocation*. Philadelphia: Fortress Press.

White House (2022) The CHIPS and Science Act. *White House Briefing Room* [online]. Available at: https://www.whitehouse.gov/briefing-room/statements-releases/2022/08/09/fact-sheet-chips-and-science-act/ [Accessed 19 August 2024].

Wong, C-Y., Yeung, H.W-C., Huang, S., Song, J. and Lee, K. (2024) Geopolitics and the changing landscape of global value chains and competition in the global semiconductor industry: Rivalry and catch-up in chip manufacturing in East Asia. *Technological Forecasting and Social Change* 209 https://doi.org/10.1016/j.techfore.2024.123749

World Bank (2023a) *The Business of the State*, Washington: World Bank [online]. Available from: https://www.worldbank.org/en/publication/business-of-the-state [Accessed 1 September 2024].

World Bank (2023b) *World Development Indicators*, Washington: World Bank [online]. Available from: https://databank.worldbank.org/source/world-development-indicators [Accessed 13 August 2024].

Zhang, Y. and He, L. (2013) 'Sovereign wealth funds: governance, risk, and returns', *Global Finance Journal*, 24(1): 1–12.

3

Technology, Responsibility and the New Geoeconomy

Introduction

Internationalization is underpinned by technological innovation. It has been enabled by innovations such as marine navigation, logistics (including containerization) and communications (particularly the internet). In the context of social and environmental pressures, particularly around climate change, the intersections of technological progress and economic growth, stability and productivity are often the focus of policy makers and international business practitioners. Technological solutions are often assumed to be the primary mechanism for economies to grow and to solve 'big problems'. For example, economies struggling with fluctuations in both the supply and cost of energy are seeking renewable forms – predicated on advancements in renewable technologies – to generate, transfer and store energy rather than to tackle the underlying cause of these fluctuations or to drastically reduce energy use or change processes. This 'technological determinism' views technological revolution as the primary cause of major social and historical changes in economies and societies. Technological determinists (both optimistic and pessimistic) view technology as autonomous and an inevitable force with wide-reaching consequences. Nation-states often try to compete with each other on technology. A contemporary example of this is the ongoing semiconductor chip war between China and the US, which commenced in 2017. This chapter places technological change in the context of international business, resisting technological determinism to understand the ways in which international businesses utilize technology to create value in new, often responsible, ways. It enters our framework with the cross-cutting theme of change/evolution and discusses the building blocks of things, innovation, intermediaries and decision-making.

While technological change is one of the primary drivers of change in the contemporary global economy, it is neither a new phenomenon nor a neutral process. Technological change does not occur in a vacuum. It is not apolitical and there has been a recent resurgence in national government interest in how technology can solve grand challenges and how it can reduce the dependency of national economies on global markets (eg political strategies around domestic manufacturing, like America Makes or China's strategy which seeks to reduce its dependency on other countries, whilst making global value chains (GVCs) more dependent on China). This creates an interesting dialogue, and sometimes conflict, between initiatives to develop technologies to solve ecological, political and social problems at the international scale, and national policy-making that draws on rhetoric around national 'self-sufficiency', economic sovereignty and competitive 'races' to develop and lead technological revolutions. International firms are operating in this geoeconomy, responding to numerous sets of expectations about the focus of technological change, its purpose and speed, and interacting with other stakeholders outside industry such as politicians, academics and national agencies, including those focused on defence. This chapter first discusses disruptive and responsible innovation, digitalization and platform economies and then companies that internationalize early ('born global firms').

Disruptive and responsible innovation

Innovation can be understood as something that is invented for the first time and successfully taken to market. It is new to the world or new to a company and/or sector. Within international business, innovation is understood to be central to business success but is not always considered alongside the broader strategies of international firms, their motivations and geographical footprints. We can observe that international businesses tend to keep high-cost innovation (R&D) facilities at, or close to, headquarters and other centralized nodes/command points in their international networks. However, when international business scholars wish to understand the role of innovation in multinational firms more deeply, they draw on approaches from business and management (disruptive innovation) or from science and technology studies (responsible innovation). We examine each approach in turn, addressing process innovation and linking this to internationalization debates.

Disruptive innovation

Disruptive innovations are innovations that involve significant new technologies, significant changes in consumption patterns and are considered to offer substantially enhanced benefits (Sandberg and Hansén, 2004). In 1995, Bower and Christensen published an article on 'disruptive innovation' in the *Harvard Business Review.* They identify failures by leading companies to stay at the top of their industries when technologies or markets change, drawing on analysis of the hard disk drive industry in the 1970s and 1980s. In *The Innovator's Dilemma* (1997), Christensen argues that managers face a dilemma, because by doing the things they need to do to succeed (listening to customers, investing in the business, building distinctive capabilities), they also run the risk of ignoring rivals with 'disruptive' innovations. 'Managers must be aware of ignoring new technologies that don't initially meet the needs of their mainstream customers' (Bower and Christensen, 1995: 44). When a company evaluates proposed technological innovations, its revenue and cost structures play a critical role. Disruptive technologies may appear to be financially unattractive to established companies as potential revenues are small and with unpredictable future revenues, it is difficult to balance the unknown rewards against the effort of pursing disruptive technologies. There is also the challenge of writing off all the sunk costs related to a company's existing technological footprint. If a company does seek to apply disruptive innovation, they can either accept initial lower profits as a new market develops or focus on developing a high-profit niche configured around a new technological solution.

Christensen extended the concept of disruptive innovation (Christensen and Raynor, 2003), arguing that technology itself is not inherently disruptive. Instead, it is how and to whom value is delivered in the marketplace – the business model – that makes an innovation disruptive (see Chapter 5). They suggest that 'disruptive innovations usually do not entail technological breakthroughs. Rather, they package available technologies in a disruptive business model' (Christensen and Raynor, 2003: 143). Thus, they deliver value to previously unserved markets or new value to previously overserved consumers. Here we also need to consider how to innovate responsibly. There is a danger that innovations can be adopted without proper consideration of the impacts (particularly societal). Examples include 3D printing (polymer printing can increase demand for plastic), recycled polyester in fabrics for garments (again, increasing demand for plastic bottles to recycle) or the consequences for individuals employed on insecure contracts for large platforms like Uber.

What do we mean when we label something, be it a technology, a service, a process or a business model, as 'disruptive'? This lies at the centre of debates around disruptive innovation, with Christensen et al (2015: 46) stating that: 'Many researchers, writers and consultants use "disruptive innovation" to describe *any* situation in which an industry is shaken up and previously successful incumbents stumble.' To disrupt something is to cause disorder and turmoil, often to the point of destruction. But can you do this without any disruptive innovation? Zipcar founder Robin Chase (2016) points to new businesses that have upended the hotel industry (Airbnb), taxi services (Uber) and navigation (Waze), labelling them as 'completely disruptive'. We could also point to classified advertising (Craigslist) and file sharing (Kazaa). However, Christensen would not consider this disruptive innovation, rather these are business models that create value by tapping excess capacity (Gobble, 2016). Disruptive innovation is limited to instances where the innovation is lower cost, lower forming and appeals to a subset of the existing market or a new market (see Table 3.1). This has managerial implications as individuals running companies need to think carefully, and strategically, about the practice of disruptive innovation. Commercializing these innovations could have implications, including producing sunk costs that need to be written off.

Academic literature has tended to focus on how geography is important during the development of innovation – situated in debates around the requirement for spatial proximity in idea generation and development – but rather less attention has been paid to disruptive innovation in the context of international business. In the examples noted in Table 3.1 we can observe three main types of disruptive innovation:

- *Export-oriented trade in physical goods* – the Toyota and Japanese steel manufacturer examples demonstrate downmarket disruptive innovation where cheaper and

Table 3.1: Examples of disruptive strategies and companies

Company or product	Country of origin	Description
eBay	US	Most of the internet start-ups of the late 1990s attempted to use the internet as a sustaining innovation relative to the business models of established companies. eBay was a notable exception because it pursued a new-market disruptive strategy by enabling owners of collectables to sell items they no longer needed but that would not be sold by auction houses.
Email	US	Email is disrupting postal services. The volume of personal communication that is conducted by letter is dropping precipitously.
Japanese steelmakers	Japan	Firms such as Nippon Steel, Nippon Kokkan and Kobe and Kawasaki Steel began their growth in the late 1950s by exporting low quality steel to Western markets. As their customers (including disruptive Japanese car manufacturers like Toyota) grew, the Japanese steel industry had to increase capacity dramatically, enabling it to incorporate the latest steelmaking technology such as continuous casting and basic oxygen furnaces in the new mills.
Kodak	US	Until the late 1800s, photography was extremely complicated. Only professionals could own and operate the expensive equipment. Kodak developed a simple 'point and shoot' Brownie camera that allowed consumers to take their own pictures. They could then post the roll of film to Kodak who would develop it and return the photographs by post.
Online travel agencies	Various, examples cited are from the US	Enabled by electronic ticketing, online travel agencies such as Expedia and Travelocity have so badly disrupted full-service, bricks-and-mortar agencies such as American Express that many airlines have dramatically cut the substantial commissions that they historically paid to travel agencies.
Sony	Japan	Sony pioneered the use of transistors in consumer electronics. It developed portable radios and televisions that disrupted companies making large TVs and radios using vacuum tube technology. Sony launched several new-market disruptions in the 1960s, 1970s and 1980s, such as videotape players, handheld consumer video recorders, the Walkman and the 3.5-inch floppy disk drive.
Toyota	Japan	Toyota entered many markets, including the US, with cheap subcompact cars. The cars were so inexpensive that people who could not previously afford a new car now could. Similar firms include Nissan and Honda. All three have now progressed to higher-value cars (Toyota now makes Lexus cars).
Ultrasound	Various, examples of soft tissue imaging companies are from the US	Ultrasound technology is disruptive relative to X-ray imaging. HP, Accuson and ATL created a multibillion-dollar industry by imaging soft tissues. Firms like GE, Siemens and Philips were the leading X-ray equipment makers, leading with CT scanning and MRI. Ultrasound was a new-market disruption. None of the X-ray companies participated in ultrasound for several years, only entering the market later by acquiring major ultrasound companies.

Source: Adapted from Christensen et al (2015: Table 2.2)

lower-quality products are sold across international markets, followed over time by the introduction of new production techniques (just-in-time manufacturing in the case of Toyota) and movement into higher-value products. While we associate this type of disruptive innovation with Japan, there are other examples including South Korean shipbuilding and South Korean car manufacturers like Hyundai and Kia. This export-oriented trade tends to be conducted by large firms in (what where then) emerging economies who compete on price to enable entry to large consumer markets.

- *Digital online services* – the development of email, online travel agencies (like Expedia) and online platforms (like eBay) that facilitate the exchange/trade in physical goods. At the start of the digital revolution, much online technological development came out of the US. US companies then rapidly expanded their digital networks to reach consumers globally. Over time, this US dominance has decreased. Other examples include Bolt (Estonia) and Skype (Sweden). These firms often internationalize rapidly and some are 'born global' firms (discussed further on). These disruptive innovations have developed digital networks to access consumers, delivering services in new ways.

- *New physical technologies* – companies develop technological innovations that radically change the market, creating new ways of consuming and often at the global scale. In the cases of Kodak (US) and Sony (Japan), the firms developed cheaper, and more portable, products that lead to a global explosion in the consumption of consumer electronics and cameras. This category also includes the development of new technologies that radically change manufacturing processes (eg 3D printing), medical procedures and testing (eg ultrasound, key-hole surgery) and medical treatments for humans and animals (eg new drug development). Here, new markets are created, or existing markets radically changed. International business can disrupt local markets and local players.

Here it is important to reflect on the disruptive innovations that have been behind the ongoing development of the geoeconomy, and these include those that have transformed logistics and communication. While the concept of disruptive innovation has been widely and enthusiastically adopted within business and management studies, it is not without critique. These include questions regarding the case study methodology used by Christensen and his co-authors, with suggestions made that cases were handpicked to suit the concept (Lepore, 2014). It has also been widely covered that Christensen predicted that Apple's iPhone would fail. Weeks (2015) explores the intriguing assertion by Christensen that managers are behaving rationally when they respond to disruptive innovations by retreating to higher-margin markets to avoid the disruptive technology. Christensen and Raynor (2003) make some proposals for managerial action. They suggest that founders are better equipped to deal with disruption than later 'professional' managers, but their supporting data is anecdotal rather than empirical (Weeks, 2015). Contemporary work on managerial decisions and disruptive innovation suggests that in order to provide stronger managerial guidance, the assumption that innovating firms are controlled by their environment also needs to recognize that the environment can also be influenced by the firms (see also Chapter 7 on firms in territories). A firm can take the role of market maker by introducing a disruptive innovation that transforms consumer behaviour.

Responsible innovation

The relationship between innovation and the environments in which it occurs is the focus of other fields of study within and beyond international business. One of these areas is that of responsible innovation. If you have seen the film *Oppenheimer*, you will be aware of the ethical agonizing by the scientists working on the Manhattan nuclear fission project. This highlights how innovation can involve profound tensions. Some innovation results in impacts that are later found to be unacceptable or harmful to society or the environment and it is increasingly recognized that governance of innovation by market choice is limited (Stilgoe et al, 2013). Controlling innovation is difficult, particularly emerging technologies where there are few agreed structures or rules to govern them. Science and technology are not only technically but also socially and politically constituted. This links back to Chapter 2, in which we explored the role of the state in internationalization. State regulation (or lack of) can be critical in technological innovation, as is the development of international standards (or lack of).

For Stilgoe et al (2013: 1570), 'responsible innovation means taking care of the future through collective stewardship of science and innovation in the present'. This concept is seen as a way of embedding deliberation around societal concerns within innovation processes. Stilgoe et al (2013) suggest four dimensions to this – anticipation, reflectivity, inclusion and responsiveness. In their review of existing academic work on the application of responsible innovation in multiple contexts, including business environments, Lubberink et al (2017) outline some of the strategies firms use when conducting responsible innovation (see Table 3.2). We can observe that the existing literature that focuses on understanding responsible innovation within business does so without any specific consideration of the specific demands of international business. Many of the strategies utilized by companies are exponentially more difficult when operating across multiple territories, particularly where firms are seeking to sell goods and/or services across numerous markets (with each containing different stakeholders, regulators, standards, end-user requirements, etc).

International firms question how, and in what ways, technological innovation is central to their business models and their values. Technological 'progress' is not necessarily progress in all its possible manifestations and change can add to uncertainty and ignorance. There are counterpoints to the dominant view of technological progress. Bihouix (2014: xiii) presents the idea that, 'instead of seeking top-down solutions to current environmental and societal challenges, instead of seeking ever more innovation, high technology, digitalization, competition, networking, growth ... we must instead direct ourselves ... to a society based primarily on simpler technologies, undeniably cruder and more basic, maybe a little less powerful, but much more resource efficient and locally controllable'. Thus, responsible international businesses may decide that they can meet business and societal needs through less reliance on technology or considering how advanced the technologies they use need to be. This is challenging while the prevailing narrative in the global economy is

Table 3.2: Firm strategies using a responsible innovation framework

---

Anticipation:
- Organizations engage in multiple activities to enhance their understanding of the innovation context (ie societal trends, market trends, technological developments, legislation and regulations), monitoring the external environment to identify changes in the innovation context. International firms do this across multiple territories.
- Firms need to be aware of possible unforeseen consequences that come with innovation and develop coping mechanisms implemented to reduce uncertainty.
- Firms can develop road maps consisting of alternative ways in which the desired impact can be achieved. These road maps may vary across geographical markets.

Reflexiveness:
- Reflexive innovators engage in several elements that need to be managed when innovating. They evaluate whether current and previous actions support the governance of the innovation process and help to achieve the desired outcomes of the innovation.
- Firms can use formal evaluations (is performance meeting the objectives set?) but can also encourage self-reflective methods in the firm.
- Innovators think about the effect of their own values and motivations on innovation governance and outcomes. Values and motivations are used as heuristics when decisions must be made under uncertainty or when faced with conflicting options. Personal ethics appear to be critical for achieving truly sustainable or social innovations when they are compatible with business sensibilities. This is particularly true of the personal ethics of the owner/manager as their values and motivations affect leadership, organizational culture and ultimately the management of the innovation project across multiple territories.

Inclusion:
- Firms conduct stakeholder engagement, where innovators determine who to involve, how and during which stages of the innovation process. Most of these engage with customers and end-users in order to be responsive to their needs. Other stakeholders could include partners in the supply chain, experts, government agencies, and external knowledge institutes (eg universities or research centres). Dialogue with stakeholders can include crowdsourcing, focus group discussion, workshop settings and community visits.
- Achieving and maintaining high levels of commitment and involvement by stakeholders is more likely when information is shared between the firm and its stakeholders. There may be tension between advantages of more open innovation processes (higher stakeholder engagement) and the costs (can have negative effects on the competitiveness of the firm).

Responsiveness:
- Firms need to be aware of new information about external environments that would require adjustment of the innovation. Companies aim to monitor the circumstances in which the innovation is implemented, including after the innovation is launched onto the market/markets.
- Some companies argue that since one cannot fully anticipate all risks and uncertainties, it is better to develop and launch the innovation and to then make subsequent effective adjustments afterwards (learning-whilst-doing).
- Exchange with stakeholders (through application and inclusion) can help firm responsiveness.

Source: Adapted from Lubberink et al (2017: 10–18)

around digitalization and advanced technologies. We will turn to address the role of technological change over time, examining the technologies that are enabling and accelerating internationalization and opening new sources of value for businesses (and creating new types of business).

Digitalization and platform economies

The geoeconomy is always evolving. Technological innovation has accelerated the ability of people, objects and ideas to circulate, creating the highly interconnected international economy of today. These changes are often characterized as industrial revolutions:

- *First Industrial Revolution – Mechanization* (1780). The introduction of industrial production equipment was driven by water and steam power. 'Time–space compression' (the shrinking of communication and transportation times across the globe) increased as transportation shifted from sailing ships to steam ships.
- *Second Industrial Revolution – Mass Production* (1870). Electrical power was used to create mass-produced goods. A significant decrease in transportation times through the adoption of rail travel and propeller airplanes. Telecommunication technologies made international business easier. In the 1950s, containerization greatly increased the efficiency of logistics.
- *Third Industrial Revolution – Automated Production* (1970). Much production was automated using electronics and information technology. The jet engine and containerization accelerated the interconnection of economies through faster trade. Widespread adoption of digital communications technologies (many enabled by the internet) allowed instantaneous information flow, facilitating international business.
- *Fourth Industrial Revolution – Cyber-Physical Systems* (2011). A fusion of technologies that blurs the line between the physical and digital. It is based not just on digitalization but on the integration of new and emerging technologies such as robotics, artificial intelligence, big data and 3D printing. These will combine into the 'Factories of the Future', which are wholly automated and use AI and machine learning to predict and adapt production demand, customization and methods.

These four phases are regularly referred to within academia, policy makers and industry to explain significant technological shifts and their impacts on the geoeconomy. While this phased approach can be critiqued – these stages are not universal at any geographical scale and former phases continue to operate as subsequent phases emerge – they do provide an indication of the trajectory of technological change. Within each of these stages, we find international businesses seeking to develop new innovations, or to commercialize innovations invented elsewhere, to capture new forms of value by considering the implications of the technological developments. Not all firms are interested in technological developments per se, but rather how new innovations can create economic and social value. For some firms, a disruptive innovation may not be that technological, complex or even innovative. The key is a company's ability to commercialize some form of change and to persuade consumers of the benefits that come from purchasing a new or modified good or service. Companies innovate by accident, by strategic investment, merger and acquisition, through strategic partnerships, copying and even by industrial espionage. One approach involves copying a product/service sold by another company in one country and developing a version that is targeted for sale in a very different territory. The product development process has been transformed by process and technological innovations. We now turn from discussing disruptive innovation to digitalization.

Where once a Formula 1 engine part would have been designed with plans drawn by hand, prototypes produced and modified and then the final part manufactured for use, it has now been many decades since this whole process was physical. The life cycle of a new innovation goes beyond the physical to embrace digital technologies. Change is more rapid. The innovation process is faster. New parts are designed using computer-aided design (CAD) software, a prototype 3D printing for testing (possibly in a wind tunnel using software to analyse the results), then the final product either printed or conventionally manufactured. Once in use, data is collected on the part to test its effectiveness, efficiency and longevity. A digital record of the part will be kept, including all the prototyping iterations, and the part may even have a 'digital twin' to compare modelled against real-world use.

The application of digital technologies to production processes has been heralded as the start of a new form of production system that is termed Industry 4.0. But these software solutions have existed for well over a decade. What is new about Industry 4.0 is the connection between different technologies and, for example, the integration of AI and machine learning into systems. This impacts our daily lives in visible and invisible ways. We are now accustomed to using chatbots as part of our interaction with businesses. AI-powered chatbots can handle basic customer inquiries, provide instant responses and assist with tasks such as order tracking, product recommendations and troubleshooting. They are available 24/7, reducing response times and improving customer service accessibility. Less visible to us as consumers are applications of AI and machine learning in supply chain optimization. Products may reach us sooner based on demand forecasting (analysis of our behaviours and preferences), warehouse control (stock controlled by deep-learning computer vision systems) and logistics and transport (algorithms assess and allocate the most optimal routes for transportation).

Digitalization is the use of digital technologies to change or create a business model and usually involves new value-generating activities. There are two key areas in which digital technologies are impacting on international business. First, by allowing greater intersection between firms across different geographies and industry enabled by the diffusion of digital transformation, providing new opportunities to connect new suppliers into new systems. This is not without complications, leading to cyber security issues (which is, again, a key focus of many national government strategies around digitalization). Second, by creating a more complex system of interrelationships between businesses as the 'rise of digitalization has produced alternative forms of value creation and value capture, such as ecosystems, platforms and technology systems' (Dilyard et al, 2021: 579). In the next section, we will examine platform economies before discussing a specific digital technology – 3D printing.

Platform economies

One of the defining ways in which international business has been transformed by digital technologies is through the development of platform economies. Kenny and Zysman (2016: 1) state that: 'platforms and the cloud, an essential part of what has been called the "third globalisation", reconfigure globalisation itself'. Srnicek (2016) cites household names Google, Facebook, Amazon, Microsoft, Siemens, GE, Uber and Airbnb as firms that have turned into platforms. They are businesses that provide the hardware and software for others to operate on. These powerful tech companies are transforming the global economy in a variety of ways. Srnicek (2016) argues that the problem for capitalist firms is that old business models are not particularly well suited to extract and use data. As data has increased significantly in volume (becoming cheaper to collect and store), a new type of firm has emerged: the platform. 'Platforms are characterized by providing the infrastructure to intermediate between different user groups, by displaying monopoly tendencies driven by network effects, by employing cross-subsidization to draw in different user groups, and by having a designed core architecture that governs the interaction possibilities' (Srnicek, 2016: 48).

There are five main types of platforms (Srnicek, 2016), capturing value in different ways:

1. *Advertising platforms* – where firms extract information on users, analyse it and use the data to sell advertising space. Examples include Google, Facebook, Instagram, YouTube.
2. *Cloud platforms* – where firms own the hardware and software of digital-dependent businesses and rent them out. Examples include Amazon, AWS, Alibaba, Oracle.
3. *Industrial platforms* – where firms which build the hardware and software necessary to transform traditional manufacturing into internet-connected processes that lower the costs of production and transform goods into services. Examples include Siemens, GE.
4. *Product platforms* – where firms generate revenue by using other platforms to transform a traditional good into a service and by collecting rent or subscription fees on them. Examples include Rolls Royce, Boeing, Spotify.
5. *Lean platforms* – where firms attempt to reduce their ownership of assets to a minimum and to profit by reducing costs as much as possible. Examples include Uber, Airbnb, Walmart.

As the five types of platform above suggest, platforms are not all about internet-based services, they include transformations in traditional industries. For example, in 1962, Rolls Royce introduced their groundbreaking 'Power by the Hour' programme. Instead of selling aircraft engines, Rolls-Royce started to sell comprehensive power solutions. Engines were supplied and maintained, and customers only paid when the engines were in use. The onus was on Rolls Royce to keep the engines operational. Competitors Airbus and Boeing also now have their own aftermarket service programmes. As the aerospace industry has become increasingly digitalized, these servitization models have developed into platforms, reliant on AI and other digital technologies. Aircraft are monitored in real time, supporting comprehensive Maintenance, Repair and Overhaul (MRO) services. These aim to keep aircraft operating at peak performance. Data analytics are used to collect and analyse the streams of data collected from aircraft. This enables the monitoring of aircraft performance, trends, alerts and to allow for predictive maintenance activities, eliminating unplanned downtime and extending the serviceable life of the aircraft (creating financial and sustainability gains). Boeing, Airbus and GE all use digital twins – a digital replica of the physical assets – which sit alongside the real-time performance data collected from aircraft sensors to detect anomalies in the system.

We can therefore observe how digital technologies are enabling firms to transform their business models and capture value in new ways. In the contemporary debates around platform economies, much focus is on the very largest platforms. This is due in part to the emphasis on 'network effects', that is to say, the more numerous the users who use a platform, the more valuable that platform becomes for everyone else. Also, platforms can grow quickly and rapidly expand internationally. If a platform wants to expand it does not need to build more factories or rent more retail outlets, it just needs more servers. Thus, platforms challenge some of the foundational international business theories. While still comparatively underexplored, it has been noted that platforms form, or replace, the 'ownership' advantage of Dunning's eclectic paradigm (Dunning, 1977), meaning that firms without an ownership advantage can internationalize (Nambisan et al, 2019). In addition, the 'location' advantage becomes an artefact and location is de-emphasized. Now digital infrastructure becomes a key location advantage (along with energy and water supplies to feed servers) and local labour may be relatively less important if advanced manufacturing (robotics, 3D printing, etc) are used. The networking effect of platforms is a core ownership advantage and is also one of the processes behind platforms becoming dominant. There are issues related to concentration and control and some types of platforms enabling other firms to internationalize – platforms can enable other firms to internationalize or can become dominant, restricting other firms from entering or flourishing in a marketplace. There is a tension, however, between platform internationalization and localization. A platform provides a framework that is applied to a territory and then alterations occur as the platform is replicated or stretched to include other territories.

We can therefore see significant implications for businesses that want to develop an international presence in terms of their ability to reach new customers through platforms. One could argue that place becomes irrelevant. Except that it does not. The geoeconomy is not an even playing field and distinct differences exist between places (see Chapter 8). Take, for example, the case of Uber in Germany. Uber entered the German market in January 2013 as part of its European expansion. Uber did not require drivers to have a commercial licence and faced legal action by the national taxi service Taxi Deutschland, who cited unfair competition. In 2014, the German court restricted Uber and in 2019, the Uber app was declared illegal (based on Uber bypassing registered and regulated taxi companies). Uber was banned or restricted at the same time in Barcelona, London and some other European cities. If you want to use Uber now in Germany, you can only do so as a regulated taxi service. Uber was not able to operate in these European contexts in the same ways it had done so in North America, having underestimated the regulatory power of European national governments and the power of the incumbent regulated taxi services (see Chapter 2).

In a final note regarding platforms, it is important to note that the development of platforms is not restricted to large tech firms located in countries like the US. The availability of AI and data analytics now makes it possible for start-ups across the world to develop platforms. This includes firms in the Global South, where technologies are being used to reach new customers, to better serve existing customers and to seek to solve economic and societal problems. This also includes copying and localizing innovations that have been introduced in one territory to another territory. Box 3.1 outlines the example of a Zimbabwean start-up firm developing an energy platform.

Box 3.1: NeedEnergy: a platform for remote energy management

International business as a field of study tends to draw on the experiences of international firms that are headquartered in advanced economies (typically the US, Western Europe and Japan). Early frameworks such as Hymer's internationalization theory and Dunning's OLI were conceived using data collected in the US and the Uppsala model was based on empirical observation of four Swedish small and medium-sized enterprises before the authors decided to test its applicability to international firms. The focus on the Global North has shifted over recent years, due in the main to the rise of the Asian Tiger economies and other economies such as India and Brazil. There is a large body of academic work on emerging market international firms, particularly from China (for a review, see Luo and Zhang, 2016) and attempts to better understand the Global South not just as the context in which international business happens, but also as the origins of international firms and innovation. It is clear, however, that there is still an imbalance and international business is starting to decolonize (Zagelmeyer, 2024), as contested as this process is.

Do our current theories, derived from the Global North, help us to understand the emergence and growth in the Global South? Clearly there are differences in the location factors both in terms of the context in which firms operate but also in relation to the markets they seek to serve (for more discussion of place-based differentials, see Chapter 7). Energy management is a global challenge, but it takes a particular form in different parts of the Global South.

NeedEnergy uses data intelligence to provide smart and clean energy solutions to meet Africa's growing energy demands. Founded in 2015, this Zimbabwean company has a vision to transform the African energy industry through a decentralized, smart and intelligent energy infrastructure that is independent, secure, financially inclusive and consumer controlled. NeedEnergy claim that over 600 million people in Africa do not have access to clean energy or power. Their goal is to provide energy access to 200 million people in the next 20 years using the platforms they are building for grids with minimum connectivity (edge-of-grid and off-grid). It uses AI-based technology to allow users to manage grids based on distributed energy resources, monitor energy and power consumption, generate energy, analyse data and more (NeedEnergy, 2024).

Energy supply in Zimbabwe has been challenging for several decades, with electricity rationing and frequent blackouts caused by drought (impacting on hydroelectricity generation) and regular breakdowns at ageing Zimbabwean coal-power plants. In consequence, many businesses use diesel powered back-up generators or are investing in solar panels. NeedEnergy see opportunities to also integrate battery storage technologies into these energy configurations, forming grid-connected microgrids that have solar panels, battery storage and diesel back-up generators (potentially removing the need for the latter). The company has developed Zimbabwe's first intelligent smart grid for LP gas. They are also running a pilot with microgrid operators that are providing renewable energy sources to remote regions in Africa. Finally, they are working on a project monitoring over 2,000 edge-of-grid smart meters in Australia to predict excess power and manage energy resources.

Co-founder Leyroy T. Nyangani stated that: 'we want to take our experiences from the African market to improve the global economy. So, we aren't just building things that help Africans, but things that could be adopted at a global level.'

The example of NeedEnergy illustrates how a company – still in the early stages of development with venture capital funding – can develop a platform and internationalize. The company has been able to enter the Australian market to capture data to assist with platform development in Southern Africa. This type of early internationalization (within a few years of the firm forming) would be much more unusual if the firm were a traditional firm, rather than a platform.

3D printing

Additive manufacturing, also known as 3D printing is a manufacturing process that uses layers of material (via a variety of different techniques including melting metal powders with a laser or extruded plastic) to create shapes that are impossible using conventional manufacturing techniques like injection moulding or milling. These 3D printing technologies have been classed as revolutionary, game-changing, disruptive and are claimed to be revolutionizing manufacturing. There is much hype around how these technologies could transform how and where products are made, with some heralding a new distributive era in which production and consumption are collapsed in time and geography (Johns, 2022). Over recent years, this hype has been tempered with more realistic assessments of the capabilities of the technology. The 3D printing technologies are not new – the first patent was passed in 1986 – and they still account for only 1 per cent of manufacturing. With 3D printing, you can design and produce more complex shapes, often using fewer materials (bringing gains in light-weighting that are critical in sectors such as aerospace and space applications). Innovation can be faster, products can be customized and small production runs are possible.

While 3D printing is not suitable for every application, there are some sectors such as medical devices, dental implants and hearing aids where 3D printing is now the dominant production method. For example, in 2000, Phonak, now part of Sonova, a Swiss firm providing innovative hearing care solutions, partnered with Materialise, a Belgian 3D-printing company. They were frustrated with the production of hearing aids. It was a labour-intensive process that could only be performed by a shrinking pool of highly skilled artisans and required a lot of manual retouching of the hearing aid before it was comfortable. Custom software and 3D printing creates a more comfortable, acoustically optimized hearing aid that can fit so deeply in the ear that it is nearly invisible to the outside world. The outcome is an alteration in value-in-use (see Chapter 5). Over 10 million customers have bought these 3D-printed hearing aids and the industry has been transformed – now around 99 per cent of the world's hearing aids are 3D printed.

In addition to changing how products can be made, 3D printing can also change the geography of production. This can impact on the geographical footprints of international businesses and cause them to reconsider their typically centralized modes of production (often in low–cost manufacturing locations in Asia, see Box 3.2). The flexibility and mobility of 3D printing, freed from the constraints of a tooled production line, means that decentralized and distributed models of production are possible – often shifting production closer to consumers. For international businesses, this may mean they are able to make costs savings regarding logistics and can support the life of their products through the quicker supply of spare parts.

Box 3.2: Shifting away from centralized production? Distributed manufacturing in remote locations

The contemporary global economy tends to be centralized, with high concentrations of economic activity in particular locations. In 2020, China, the world's global factory, accounted for 35 per cent of global manufacturing output. Its production exceeds that of the nine next largest manufacturers combined (OECD, 2023a). Services can also be concentrated, with advanced services clustering in global cities and innovation in locations such as Silicon Valley. Recent global events (financial crisis, environmental pressures, pandemic) have challenged global supply chains. Many international firms are reconfiguring their supply chains to reduce risk of rupture or failure. This includes reducing dependency on long supply chains, for example, from China. What does this mean for our theories of international business? We can observe a plethora of terms emerging to describe the 'return' of manufacturing back to advanced economies (reshoring or backshoring), to neighbouring countries (friendshoring), or to politically or culturally aligned countries (allyshoring).

There is less conversation about the broader shift away from centralized production to decentralized or distributed means of production. Decentralized production sees a movement away from highly centralized production locations to reliance on a larger number of smaller sites. Distributed manufacturing is a more flexible system, utilizing technologies to allow manufacturing to take place in a much wider range of locations and is underpinned by more peer-to-peer relationships rather than hierarchical supply networks. There is relatively little debate within international business about how distributed forms of organization could challenge the status quo, or enable more responsible business.

An example of distributed manufacturing is Fieldmade. They are a Norwegian technology company specializing in mobile 3D-printing solutions for defence, shipping, logistics and other manufacturing sectors. Fieldmade aims to revolutionize the supply of spare parts using digital inventories and 3D printing. This firm supplies customized mobile microfactories that can replace traditional warehousing, locating nearer the source of need. In the microfactory the spare parts are constructed using 3D-printing machines. Fieldmade microfactories are being deployed in a range of different contexts, reducing greenhouse gas emissions from energy production and shipping and making industrial production more cost-effective and less carbon-intensive. These include the energy sector. Onshore and offshore energy production often takes place in remote and/or challenging locations. To ensure optimal production in these locations, firms in sectors like oil and gas stockpile large and costly spare part inventories, ensuring backup in case of unscheduled maintenance or downtime. This creates costs (warehousing) and waste (many of the parts are never used). Fieldmade suggest that by adopting their digital inventory and 3D-printing solutions, operators in the energy sectors can reduce their spare part inventories by 10–25 per cent.

Another application is in defence as maintaining operability and combat readiness is the key to successful operations. Military logistics need to manage a complex flow of information, components and products through demanding supply chains. Field operations are often in rural areas, away from core logistics hubs, creating challenging supply chain requirements. Through the use of 3D printing, temporary parts can be manufactured to keep equipment operational while waiting for conventional parts to arrive (which can take weeks or months). Other defence contexts include ships and submarines. Fieldmade is operating in the context of several policies and projects by national defence agencies to create more resilience and flexible supply chains using digital inventories and the increased use of 3D-printing technologies.

Technological innovation has transformed the ways in which international firms organize, the value propositions they develop and the ways in which they engage with their customers and suppliers. The Fourth Industrial Revolution is less a revolution, more a reformation. This is because some elements of the previous 'revolutions' remain, creating an ever-increasingly complex mosaic of technological development, adoption and integration into the contemporary global economy. Some technologies, like 3D printing in distributed systems, involve a shift in supply chains, with greater focus on material supply chains as production takes place closer to the consumer. Technological innovation can also enable greater visibility of supply chains, which can help businesses be more transparent and encourage more sustainable models, such as circular economy approaches (see Chapter 4). The increase in interconnections in the geoeconomy have also accelerated processes of internationalization, creating firms that are internationalizing more rapidly. We explore these born global firms in the next section.

Early internationalization: born global firms

Born global theory explains how and why firms start operating in foreign markets at, or near, the time of their businesses being formed. This contrasts with traditional models of company expansion that see international expansion occurring more slowly and only after the firm is established in its home market. Born global firms are international in their perspective from the outset, with a global focus and commitment to international activities. Born global firms have emerged as a result of changes to the global business environment that have made conditions for internationalization more favourable (Johns, 2023). In many instances, born globals are enabled by widescale innovations in aviation, media and the movement of ideas between places.

The term 'born global' is generally applied to firms that enter overseas markets early in their establishment. It was first used in 1993 by the consulting firm McKinsey, and since then academics have worked to distinguish the characteristics of these born global firms. They have been defined as 'small (usually) technology-oriented companies that operate in international markets from the earliest days of their establishment' (Knight and Cavusgil, 1996: 1). Examples of born global firms include Skype, Spotify, Facebook, Google, Logitech, Twitter and Zara. These are the most commonly cited examples, but they are not the most typical. Their degree of success is extraordinary and most born global firms are more modest in their scale and scope.

Born global firms have benefited from significant advances in production, transportation and communication technologies, new market conditions where there is greater demand for specialized or customized products, the more sophisticated capabilities of the founders and entrepreneurs forming businesses, and the inherent advantages of small firms in terms of flexibility, adaptability and speed of response. Born global firms tend to enter new international markets within two or three years of formation and may enter new markets simultaneously.

The existence of born global firms raises some questions about the ability of existing international business theories to explain the *speed* and *range* of internationalization so early in the business life cycle. The process of firm internationalization is traditionally understood as an incremental process, by both Dunning's (1977) eclectic paradigm and the Uppsala model (Johanson and Vahlne, 1977). The notion of 'staged' internationalization has received criticism for some time – based on the failure of existing theories to account for differences in types of firms (for example, manufacturing versus services), failure to anticipate the actions of small, tech-intensive firms and the inability to consider multiple, concurrent market entry. Born global firms illustrate all these areas of critique.

Born global firms tend to be service firms but can also be found in manufacturing. They are not always high-technology firms, but do tend to utilize advance technologies. Born globals are most likely to be from countries where the market is limited, either by size (for example, firms like Skype from Estonia), or by market potential, where the firm is targeting a niche market. Box 3.3 introduces two born global firms from Latin America.

Box 3.3: Latin American born globals

Current academic literature focuses on high-profile, large born global companies. These tend to be from advanced economies. Greater attention should be paid to smaller born globals, particularly as these form the vast majority of the total population of born global firms. These firms that do not become very large multinationals still have important stories to tell about internationalization. They can have different strengths, including higher rates of profitability and may find it easier to act in responsible ways.

Latin America is a region rich in natural resources and minerals. Agriculture and mining are the dominant economic activities. Intra-region trade (between Latin American countries) is higher than trade with the rest of the world. Since COVID-19, Latin American companies have dramatically accelerated the adoption of advanced digital technologies. Cloud computing was the technology most used by companies in Argentina, Brazil, Chile, Colombia and Mexico in 2020 (55%), and was also the technology with the highest growth during the pandemic (26%), followed by big data and digital platforms (19% in both cases), the Internet of Things (18%) and artificial intelligence (16%) (OECD, 2023b).

Two Latin American born globals are Fiweex, a Wi-Fi management tool provider, and Platzi, an online educational platform. Fiweex was founded in Paraguay in 2015 and rapidly internationalized to neighbouring Argentina, then to Chile, Columbia and finally Mexico. The company's platform connects to the Wi-Fi network without asking for passwords by performing a brief connection process. It also provides a marketing and advertising solution, providing data on customers. The firm is still small, with 19 employees in 2024 and has funded its international expansion through investment rounds. In 2019, investment firm Cibersons contributed to Fiweex's seed money, and a move to Mexico was similarly funded. Platzi was founded in 2014, initially with offices in Mexico and Columbia. The co-founders moved to San Francisco after becoming the first Latin American company to be accepted on a start-up accelerator in Silicon Valley. It used start-up funds and networks to raise development capital. The platform delivers video and lesson content developed by Platzi in Spanish, English and Portuguese. In 2018 the firm expanded to Spain and Brazil. In 2019 the company had 119 employees.

These cases demonstrate that internationally competitive tech-based born globals are emerging from Latin America, and then internationalizing across continents. These firms have taken different approaches to the geography of their internationalization. Fiweex has focused on the Latin American region – due in part to the demand for password-less Wi-Fi access in the region (which has comparatively less internet connectivity than other global regions). Their potential competitive advantage outside the region is not certain due to the saturation of many advanced economies in relation to Wi-Fi. Platzi has a higher degree of internationalization beyond Latin America, including their move to Silicon Valley and market entry in Spain. The platform was initially developed in Spanish before extending to Portuguese (to attract users in Brazil) and English.

The born global concept is not without critique, with still much debate around whether this separate category is required. Is it a new concept or a rehash of an old phenomenon? There are some methodological concerns about how we research these firms given that many are small and medium-sized enterprises and examples are hard to find and research during their initial years. Contemporary research on born globals includes a focus on the organizational capabilities the firms require as they adapt, integrate and reconfigure their knowledge-based capabilities. We could learn more about how these firms collect information on the geoeconomy and develop this into internationalization strategies, often at rapid speed. Research could also take a longer-term view by considering firm internationalization after the initial market entries in the first three years, acknowledging that periods of rapid internationalization can happen later in the life of the company. Finally, greater attention could be paid to the entrepreneurs who set up these firms, their ability to secure venture capital and the values they hold and develop through the life of the firm. Internationalization is risky, especially rapid internationalization over multiple markets, and not all market entry initiatives succeed (Johns, 2023). Looking beyond the famous born global examples, we would benefit from more knowledge of failed born global firms as well as of born global serial entrepreneurs.

Conclusion

This chapter has examined the role of technology in the geoeconomy. It discussed the ways in which technological innovation has been conceptualized, focusing on disruptive and responsible innovation. These approaches are not incompatible, with the former seeking to understand disruptive business models and the latter providing a framework for business that is more responsible and embedded in stakeholder engagement. The chapter then outlined how technological progress has been retrospectively characterized into four industrial revolutions and noting the ways in which technological change has been politicized and the role of national government (see Chapter 2). More detailed discussion was made of two areas of disruption – platform economies and 3D printing. The ways in which digital technologies are impacting on firm internationalization and the ways in which firms configure their international supply chains are numerous. This chapter charts some of these processes of change from firm conception and early internationalization (including born global firms) through to how firms can use these technologies to create new business models and flexible and responsive supply chains.

The managerial considerations around technological innovation are numerous. Most broadly, the assumption that technological progress is inherently the 'best' way to advance business practices is being challenged. The prevailing narrative from most national governments tells us that technological progress is good. However, responsible businesses may wish to engage in more profound debate about how, and in which forms, technological innovation is part of firm value propositions and values in general. If technological innovation is considered central to the business, responsible managers will address the guidance around responsible innovation. They should consider how a technology innovates and what its societal impacts may be. Finally, firms could consider how being responsible could mean utilizing technologies to tackle big societal challenges. These include transitions to renewable energy and biotechnologies, increased resource efficiency using 'smart' digital tools and the adoption of circular economies, in which more extensive use is made of material recycling, repair, remanufacture and refurbishment. We address alternative values and circular values in Chapter 4.

Key terms

Born global firms – firms that internationalize within three years of their establishment. They tend to be small and technology-driven.

Digitalization – the use of digital technologies to change or create a business model and new value-generating activities.

Disruptive innovation – innovations that involve significant new technologies, changes in consumption patterns and enhanced benefits. According to Christensen (1997: xv), these innovations are 'typically cheaper, simpler, smaller and frequently more convenient to use'.

Platforms – businesses that provide the hardware and software for others to operate on.

Responsible innovation – a process that takes the wider impacts of innovation into account. It aims to ensure that unintended negative impacts are avoided, that barriers to dissemination, adoption and diffusion of innovation are reduced, and that the positive societal and economic benefits of innovation are fully realized.

Recommended reading

Christensen, C.M., Michael E., Raynor, M.E. and McDonald, R. (2015) 'What is disruptive innovation?', *Harvard Business Review*, 93(12): 44–53.

Srnicek, N. (2016) *Platform Capitalism*, Cambridge: Polity Press.

Stilgoe, J., Owen, R. and Macnaughten, P. (2013) 'Developing a framework for responsible innovation', *Research Policy*, 42: 1568–80.

References

Bihouix, P. (2014) *The Age of Low Tech: Towards a Technologically Sustainable Civilisation*, Bristol: Bristol University Press.

Bower, J.L. and Christensen, CM. (1995) 'Disruptive technologies: catching the wave', *Harvard Business Review*, 73(1): 43–53.

Chase, R. (2016) 'We need to expand the definition of disruptive innovation', *Harvard Business Review*, 7 January [online]. Available from: https://hbr.org/2016/01/we-need-to-expand-the-definition-of-disruptive-innovation [Accessed 18 August 2024].

Christensen, C.M. (1997) *The Innovator's Dilemma: When New Technologies Cause Great Firms to Fail*, Boston: Harvard Business School Press.

Christensen, C.M. and Raynor, M.E. (2003) *The Innovator's Solution: Creating and Sustaining Successful Growth*, Boston: Harvard Business School Press.

Christensen, C. M., Michael, E. Raynor, M.E. and McDonald, R. (2015) 'What is disruptive innovation?', *Harvard Business Review*, 93(12): 44–53.

Dilyard, J., Zhao, S. and You, J.J. (2021) 'Digital innovation and Industry 4.0 for global value chain resilience: lessons learned and ways forward', *Thunderbird International Business Review*, 63: 577–84. doi.org/10.1002/tie.22229.

Dunning, J.H. (1977) 'Trade, location of economic activity and the MNE: a search for an eclectic approach', in B. Ohlin, P.O. Hesselborn and P.M. Wijkman (eds) *The International Allocation of Economic Activity*, London: Macmillan, pp 395–418.

Gobble, M.M. (2016) 'Defining disruptive innovation', *Research-Technology Management*, 59(4): 66–71. doi.org/10.1080/08956308.2016.1185347.

Johanson, J. and Vahlne, J.-E. (1977) 'The internationalization process of the firm—a model of knowledge development and increasing foreign market commitments', *Journal of International Business Studies*, 8(1): 23–32. doi.org/10.1057/palgrave. jibs.8490676.

Johns, J. (2022) 'Digital technological upgrading in manufacturing global value chains: the impact of additive manufacturing', *Global Networks*, 22(4): 649–65. doi. org/10.1111/glob.12349.

Johns, J. (2023) 'Born global theory', in A. Mishra (ed.), *Sage Business Foundations: International Business.* London: Sage. https://doi.org/10.4135/9781071909041.

Kenney, M. and Zysman, J. (2016) 'The rise of the platform economy', *Issues in Science and Technology*, 32(3): 61–9.

Knight, G. and Cavusgil, S.T. (1996) 'The born global firm: a challenge to traditional internationalization theory', in S. Cavusgil and T. Madsen (eds) *Advances in International Marketing 8*, Greenwich: JAI Press.

Lepore, J. (2014) 'The disruption machine', *The New Yorker*, 90: 30–6.

Lubberink, R., Blok, V., Van Ophem, J. and Omta, O. (2017) 'Lessons for responsible innovation in the business context: a systematic literature review of responsible, social and sustainable innovation practices', *Sustainability*, 9: 721. doi.org/10.3390/su9050721.

Luo, Y. and Zhang, H. (2016) 'Emerging market MNEs: qualitative review and theoretical directions', *Journal of International Management*, 22(4): 333–50.

Nambisan, S., Wright, M. and Feldman, M. (2019) 'The digital transformation of innovation and entrepreneurship: progress, challenges and key themes', *Research Policy*, 48(8): 103773.

NeedEnergy (2024) 'Company overview' [online]. Available from: https://www.needenergy.io/ and www.youtube.com/watch?v=2eaaKLPgz4k. [Accessed 22 August 2024].

OECD (2023a) *Trade in Value-Added* [online]. Available from: https://www.oecd.org/en/topics/sub-issues/trade-in-value-added.html [Accessed 21 August 2024].

OECD (2023b) *Latin American Economic Outlook 2023* [online]. Available from: doi.org/10.1787/8c93ff6e-en [Accessed 22 August 2024].

Sandberg, B. and Hansén, S. (2004) 'Creating an international market for disruptive innovations', *European Journal of Innovation Management*, 7(1): 23–32. doi.org/10.1108/14601060410515619.

Srnicek, N. (2016) *Platform Capitalism*, Cambridge: Polity Press.

Stilgoe, J., Owen, R. and Macnaughten, P. (2013) 'Developing a framework for responsible innovation', *Research Policy*, 42: 1568–80.

Weeks, M.R. (2015) 'Is disruption theory wearing new clothes or just naked? Analyzing recent critiques of disruptive innovation theory', *Innovation*, 17(4): 417–28. doi.org/10.1080/14479338.2015.1061896.

Zagelmeyer, S. (2024) 'Moving beyond delinking, decoloniality and the pluriverse: reflections on the "decolonizing international business" debate', *Critical Perspectives on International Business*, 20(1): 71–93. doi.org/10.1108/cpoib-04-2023-0028.

4

Creating Value Responsibly?
Alternative and Circular Values

Introduction

Previous chapters have outlined the role of the state and technological innovation in the geoeconomy. This involved some consideration of how different actors in the contemporary global economy seek to derive value from economic activities, and how a diversity of approaches are taken by different international companies, entrepreneurs and national governments. Historically, greatest academic, policy-making and business attention has tended to rest with dominant practices. However, the intensification of pressures related to global challenges, particularly climate change, has fostered an environment in which alternative technologies, processes and practices are sought. Sustainable development has been a focus of policy-making for several decades, but the past decade has witnessed a plethora of policy-making initiatives at local, regional, national and supranational scales around circular economies. This focus acknowledges the potential benefits of finding means of production and consumption that have less impact on the environment. There are still some sizeable gaps in our understandings of how and why alternative values can be captured by international companies and how this can support responsible business. This chapter addresses the cross-cutting theme of value and discusses the building blocks of things, companies, intersections, intermediaries and innovation.

This chapter explores the concept of value in international business, moving beyond the traditional motivation focusing on solely financial metrics. It highlights the contrast between the motivation to follow a linear model of value creation, which is focused on maximizing profits through production and consumption, and alternative models based on circularity and resource efficiency. The chapter emphasizes the importance of considering multiple dimensions of value, including financial (profitability) and non-financial aspects (environmental impact, social responsibility) to better understand the generic value-creation process for a firm. The chapter also explores how the environmental, social and governance (ESG) framework can be utilized to measure motivation to create alternative values in international business. This framework enables stakeholders to make informed decisions based on a more comprehensive understanding of value creation.

Understanding value

In international business, the traditional concept of value has often been narrowly defined as maximizing profit or increasing sales. However, this perspective overlooks a broader range of considerations that are increasingly important for success in the international markets. This is where alternative values come into play. In the traditional sense, exchange value in international business is often defined from a company's motivation to focus on the profit-centric perspective. Exchange value in international business refers to the net benefit created by a company through its international operations (Macneil, 1980). This net benefit considers both financial and non-financial factors that contribute to the international company's success and sustainability in the global marketplace. The motivation of the financial perspective focuses on maximizing the financial gain that a company achieves through its international operations. Motivation to seek non-financial value that includes factors such as brand reputation, customer satisfaction, innovation, sustainability and stakeholder value is also valued by the international companies. Some key aspects of this exchange value definition include shareholder value as the primary motive is to generate return for stakeholders through increased sales, cost control reduction and ultimately, seeking to maintain or increase the company's profits. This often involves diversifying revenue streams, expanding into new international markets to access a wider customer base and potentially lower production costs. Exchange value focuses on achieving economic efficiency by optimizing resource allocation and minimizing waste in international operations. This involves strategies such as outsourcing production to countries with lower labour costs or negotiating favourable trade agreements to reduce import/export costs.

It is important to highlight that the concept of value in international business is evolving from a 'traditional' into a 'modern' perspective, which recognizes a more holistic approach to business practices and acknowledges an important role of alternative values. 'The issue of value is a pressing one because it exposes the tension at the heart of the social and political processes that render all things equivalent and comparable under a single measure of price' (Pitts, 2021: 1). Today, many companies are increasingly becoming motivated to develop broader motivations that reach beyond just profit, such as sustainability, since environmental and social responsibility are becoming more important factors in international business decisions. Companies are motivated – either by their own company values or through external pressures such as government regulations – to reduce their environmental impact and ensure ethical labour practices throughout their global supply chains. Stakeholder value is also becoming an important part of value as it is created by businesses for a wider range of shareholders, including employees and their well-being, local communities and the environment. While the traditional profit-centric definition of value remains a significant motivation in international business, a more holistic and 'modern' approach that considers broader societal, environmental motivations and responsible business practices is gaining traction. Pitts (2021: 2) argues that 'a leap must be made from economic to social theories of value'.

Alternative values

'Alternative values' challenge traditional solely economic motivations by prioritizing other types of values beyond their financial gains, such as social impact, sustainability, community well-being, ethical conduct, customer satisfaction, brand reputation or personal fulfilment (Patala et al, 2016). Alternative values emphasize the international business motivation to create value responsibly. Such value creation benefits society and the planet, even if this may not directly translate into immediate financial profits (Mehrotra and Jaladi, 2022). While motives to create alternative value might seem separate from motives to seek solely financial gains, they are often intricately linked. Non-financial value (or non-price values) may be reflected in sales price. That is, companies can translate their commitment to alternative values into a premium price for their products or services. Focusing on alternative values can lead to increased sales through other mechanisms. A strong brand reputation built on responsible practices can attract new customers. Additionally, employee satisfaction and focus on their well-being can improve operational efficiency and customer loyalty, ultimately boosting sales. Ignoring alternative values can have negative consequences. For instance, environmental damage, labour violations or ethical scandals can damage a company's reputation and lead to boycotts and lost revenue.

For example, Miniwiz, a Taiwanese social enterprise, shows how alternative values can challenge traditional economic motivations in international business. While financial gain is a motivation for business companies, Miniwiz prioritizes social and environmental impact alongside profit, demonstrating how these values can be intertwined for success and still remain financially sustainable. Instead of maximizing profits through conventional manufacturing practices, Miniwiz prioritizes upcycling waste materials into high-quality construction and consumer products. Such an approach minimizes environmental impact and promotes resource conservation. Their ability to create high-quality products from waste materials caters to growing international market segments that value sustainability.

Responsible businesses can be motivated to create alternative values. They can contribute to their business responsibly while enhancing brand reputation, reducing costs in the long term and driving innovation. Alternative values advocate for a closed-loop system where resources are kept in use for as long as possible, minimizing waste and maximizing resource efficiency (Ranta et al, 2020). Motives to create alternative value prioritize designing products for durability, reusability, repairability and recyclability, keeping materials in circulation and reducing environmental impacts. Some examples include 'product-as-a-service' models, that businesses which rent or lease products instead of selling them outright to their customers, encourage longer product lifespans and reduce material consumption. Another example refers to 'recycling and remanufacturing', that is processes to recover materials from used products to create new ones, reducing reliance on new resources and conserving energy (Adıgüzel and Donato, 2021). Box 4.1 introduces Schneider Electric multinational, which serves as an example for motivations to create alternative values to contribute to a more responsible global economy.

Box 4.1: Schneider Electric: linking alternative values and sustainability through waste minimization

Creating alternative value involves going beyond traditional profit maximization to consider the broader social, environmental and economic impacts of business activities. However, the debates in the literature suggest that implementing sustainable practices requires significant upfront investments in technology, infrastructure and training. In the short term, prioritizing sustainability and social responsibility may lead to lower profits and increased costs. Therefore, balancing the interests of different stakeholders, such as employees, shareholders, customers and the environment can be challenging.

Schneider Electric, a French energy management solutions business links alternative value with sustainability through waste minimization, creating value for society, the planet and its stakeholders. Schneider Electric prioritizes alternative values in their activities through minimizing their environmental footprint. For example, their 'Zero Waste in Manufacturing' initiative focuses on waste minimization throughout their global supply chain. This includes implementing closed-loop manufacturing processes where waste from one stage becomes raw material for another; designing products for disassembly and recyclability, extending their lifespan and reducing post-consumer waste, partnering with suppliers to implement responsible waste management practices.

Committed to innovation, the company invests heavily in research and development to find solutions to waste management challenges. They have developed innovative recycling technologies to process and reuse a wider range of materials from their production processes. The company is exploring ways to create more alternative values, for instance, how to incorporate recycled materials into their products, further reducing reliance on virgin resources.

We observe that, based on their activities, the company has achieved certain benefits. The company's waste minimization efforts have led to significant reduction in landfill waste and greenhouse gas emissions. This highlights two points. First, their commitment to sustainability resonates with customers and stakeholders, strengthening their brand image and attracting environmentally conscious consumers. Second, creating alternative values through waste minimization translates into cost savings through reduced waste disposal fees, lower resource consumption, and potentially streamlined production processes.

However, the company has some areas for improvement, including constantly changing regulatory challenges to ensure that it continues to adhere to sustainable practices. Despite its efforts to reduce emissions, the company's footprint remains significant due to its global operations and product manufacturing. Additionally, the company could explore more innovative circular economy models, such as industrial symbiosis. While Schneider Electric has engaged with various stakeholders, there is potential for even greater collaboration, transparency and more effective relationship management. By addressing these areas, the company can further strengthen its commitment to sustainability and create a more positive impact on the environment and society.

Although motivation to create alternative values challenges motivations to follow traditional linear economic models that prioritize short-term profit maximization and resource depletion, alternative values are not replacements for traditional profit-driven

Figure 4.1: Pathways of value creation in a circular economy

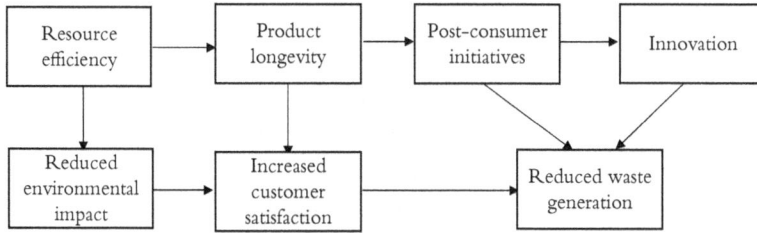

Source: Inspired by Sarpong et al (2023)

approaches in international business. They represent a broader definition of business motivations to create value that considers the long-term social, environmental and financial well-being of the company and its stakeholders. By being motivated to embrace alternative values, international businesses can achieve sustainable success and contribute to a more responsible global economy.

Circular economies

The circular economy offers an alternative pathway that focuses on creating value through continuous cycles (Kant Hvass et al, 2019; Ranta et al, 2020). In a circular economy, value creation happens through resource efficiency, product longevity and innovation (Sarpong et al, 2023) (see Figure 4.1). Circular economy aims to keep resources in use for as long as possible, minimizing waste and maximizing resource recovery through design, repair, reuse and recycling. By focusing on these core principles, companies can create economic value while minimizing environmental impact and promoting social responsibility. These alternative values resonate with an increasing number of environmentally conscious consumers, leading to a competitive advantage for businesses that embrace circular practices (Kennedy and Linnenluecke, 2022).

A firm could engage in all value-creation processes or only focus on one aspect. For instance, international businesses such as Philips adopted subscription models, where customers pay for the use of a product rather than for its ownership. This incentivizes Philips to create value in a circular economy by designing durable, long-lasting products and taking them back at end-of-life for refurbishment or recycling. Such circular models extend product lifespan by giving pre-owned items a second life, reduce demand for raw materials and create a secondary market for sustainable products. Vinted is a very good example of how fashion sale is redefined through a circular economy approach (see Box 4.2).

Box 4.2: The role of the Vinted app in circular economies

Circular economy models offer a promising approach to address environmental and social challenges when creating economic opportunities. The debates in the literature suggest that by shifting from a linear model (take-make-waste) to a circular one (reduce, reuse, recycle), businesses can reduce waste by minimizing landfill waste and pollution by extending the lifespan of products, conserve resources, mitigate climate change and offer social and economic benefits to local communities. The literature suggests that by adopting circular economy principles, businesses can contribute to a more sustainable and resilient economy while creating value for both society and the environment, especially in the context of the fashion industry (Bryson et al, 2024).

The fast-fashion industry is a significant contributor to global environmental pollution and resource depletion. Ongoing public debates raise concerns about emissions associated with production and transportation as well as local community development that brick-and-mortar second-hand local shops can offer in comparison to purchases made in the online environment.

Vinted, a leading mobile application in the pre-loved clothing market, offers a promising alternative and is a champion of a pathway to circular economy. By promoting the reuse and circulation of existing garments, Vinted demonstrates the route of value creation in the circular economy and offers a more sustainable approach to fashion with some caveats discussed at the end of this case study.

This highlights four points. First, Vinted contributes to alternative value creation in a circular economy in several ways. For example, Vinted creates a new marketplace for sellers to generate income and for buyers to access unique clothing at affordable prices. Vinted fosters a sense of community among users who share a passion for sustainable fashion and unique styles. By promoting second-hand clothing, Vinted contributes to a more sustainable fashion industry, society's well-being and reduces the environmental impact of clothing production, preventing them from ending up in landfills and contributing to a more sustainable clothing ecosystem.

Second, while Vinted offers a sustainable solution, challenges still remain. Authenticity of vintage items, ensuring good condition and logistics for deliveries require continued focus and innovation. Additionally, promoting ethical labour practices within the preloved clothing supply chains requires careful consideration.

Third, its cross-border logistics operations also have environmental implications. The transportation of items contributes to greenhouse gas emissions, especially if the items are shipped long distances. The use of packaging materials for shipping can generate waste. While Vinted offers convenience and a wider selection compared to traditional second-hand shops, the environmental impact of its logistics operation can be compared to local sourcing and reduced packaging.

Finally, the company needs to play a crucial role in facilitating transactions between buyers and sellers by managing buyer–seller relationships. When issues arise in purchase, effective management of buyer–seller relationships is essential to maintain trust and satisfaction. Although Vinted offers dispute resolution through mediation and proposes its customers to use purchase protection obtained for a fee, the platform needs to offer clear and fair return policies to address issues, such as sold incorrect items or unsatisfactory quality. The platform needs to provide an easily accessible customer support channel such as live chat, email or phone. However, as awareness of sustainable fashion grows, Vinted is well positioned to become a mainstream platform for conscious consumers seeking a unique and eco-friendly wardrobe.

Sharing platforms

The sharing economy and change in ownership are forms of consumption that aim to intensify the use of otherwise underutilized assets facilitating the reuse of assets. The sharing economies are varied in their definition and form and suffer from definitional vagueness. This is due to the fact that sharing is a relatively open concept, and we can question what is being shared, how and for whom. Belk (2007: 126) argues that 'sharing is an alternative form of distribution to commodity exchange and gift giving. Compared to these alternative modes, sharing can foster community, save resources, and create certain synergies.' The rise of the sharing economy and collaborative consumption plays a significant role in contributing to the circular economy by promoting resource efficiency, product life extension and waste reduction (Bryson et al, 2020; Bryson et al, 2024). Sharing economy and collaborative consumption focus on access over ownership. Resources, skills and services are shared between individuals or communities, maximizing their use before disposal.

Less emphasis on ownership leads to a decrease in the production of new items, lowering the environmental impact associated with resource extraction and manufacturing. Products in shared or rental systems are incentivized to be well maintained and repaired to ensure continued user availability, extending their lifespan and reducing the need for replacements. Redefining ownership does not negate the need for personal possessions entirely. The key lies in acquiring quality items built to last and prioritizing experiences over fleeting trends. By focusing on accessing the utility of products rather than just owning them, the circular economy promotes responsible consumption and contributes to a future where resources are used more efficiently and waste is minimized (Bryson et al, 2020).

By sharing existing resources such as clothes, tools or cars, the need to constantly produce new items decreases, lowering the environmental impact of resource extraction and processing. Platforms such as 'The Tool Library' allow individuals to borrow tools instead of buying them for occasional use. This reduces the number of tools sitting unused in garages and minimizes the need for manufacturing new ones. Sharing platforms incentivize owners to maintain their belongings in good condition to maximize their rental value. This promotes product longevity and delays the need for replacements. For instance, websites such as 'Turo' or 'Getaround' allow car owners to rent out their vehicles when not in use. This not only reduces the overall number of cars needed but also encourages owners to take better care of their vehicles to maintain their rental appeal.

Not all sharing economy practices contribute equally to the circular economy. Short-term disposable items might not be suitable for sharing models. The rise of sharing platforms presents logistical challenges such as ensuring product quality and responsible user behaviour. Addressing these challenges is crucial for the long-term success of a sharing economy and a circular economy.

Company ownership structure and its impact on value delivery

The ownership structure of an international business company has a significant impact on the value delivered by an organization, influencing how the company prioritizes its goals and allocates resources (Zahra, 2003). For example, private companies, owned by individuals or a small group, are often motivated by prioritizing long-term growth and stability over short-term profit maximization. They have greater flexibility in their decision-making and can take calculated risks for future gain. Private companies may be motivated by value creation that can be reinvested in the business for future expansion, research and development, or developing a strong brand reputation. They might prioritize employee satisfaction and long-term customer relationships to build sustainable growth. For example, a private international food company might prioritize sourcing high-quality ingredients and developing an innovative product, even if it means slightly higher prices but loyal customers.

The focus of cooperative companies is on mutual benefit and social impact alongside profitability as cooperatives are owned and operated by their members, who can be employees, customers or producers. Cooperative international businesses might be motivated by emphasizing fair prices for producers, employee ownership opportunities and community development projects (Novkovic, 2008). They often reinvest profits in ways that benefit members and the local communities in which they operate. For example, an international agricultural cooperative might prioritize fair trade practices, sustainable farming methods and reinvest profits into education and infrastructure projects in the communities where they source their products.

Listed companies with investors are owned by a diverse group of investors who are motivated by maximization of shareholder value through short-term profits and stock-price increases (David et al, 2010). They are under pressure to deliver consistent financial performance. Listed international companies might emphasize strategies such as cost reduction, increased sales and mergers and acquisitions to boost profits and stakeholder returns. They may be more focused on meeting quarterly financial targets than long-term investments that do not show immediate financial gains. For instance, a publicly traded international clothing company might prioritize outsourcing production to low-cost countries to reduce cost, even if it means compromising on quality or labour practices.

Each of the above-mentioned ownership structures has its own set of priorities, which can shape how the company defines and delivers value. The company's goals and values should be aligned with its ownership structure to ensure long-term success. The ownership structure defines which stakeholders are prioritized in value creation. Private and cooperative companies might prioritize employee and community well-being alongside shareholder returns, while publicly traded companies might focus primarily on shareholder interests. Companies need to take into consideration how their ownership structure can be leveraged to create and deliver value in changing circumstances.

Multiple-value dimensions and responsible value creation in international business

There is a host of non-financial values or alternative values that is important in international business. Value construct comprises several dimensions of value that an international company provides to its customers (Patala et al, 2016). These dimensions are explained in Table 4.1. Balancing these dimensions is an ongoing process and a challenge that requires careful consideration and strategic decision-making.

International businesses are motivated to create value for their customers through various ways, such as economic value (eg Aviva offers insurance services for iPhones

Table 4.1: Key value dimensions

Value type	Value dimension		Examples

Financial value	Economic value	• *Profitability:*
		  – Maximizing shareholder value through increased sales, reduced costs and effective resource allocation
		• *Revenue growth:*
		  – Expanding market share and increasing sales volume
		• *Financial stability:*
		  – Maintaining or increasing financial position to manage risks in the market
			Circular Electronics Partnerships combine Microsoft, Dell, Amazon and Google's forces to develop a new circular value for electronics by 2030. Developing energy-efficient products will create economic value by reducing production costs and potentially increasing their customer base and consequently, increasing sales.

Non-financial value	Social value	• *Social impact:*
		  – Improving working conditions (safety, fair wages, worker rights)
		  – Promoting fair trade practices
		  – Community development initiatives
		  – Philanthropy and social responsibility
		• *Ethical conduct:*
		  – Transparency and accountability
		  – Business ethics and anti-corruption practices
		  – Respect for human rights and labour standards
		• *Employee well-being:*
		  – Fair wages and benefits
		  – Safe working conditions
		  – Opportunities for professional development
			Nike implements sustainable sourcing practices and demonstrates social value by contributing to community well-being in Asian countries.

	Environmental or green value	• *Sustainability:*
		  – Environmental stewardship (minimizing environmental impact)
		  – Resource efficiency (reducing waste and energy consumption)
		  – Sustainable supply chain management
		  – Circular economy practices
			China invests in clean energy such as solar power, electric vehicles and batteries. In this way, it demonstrates environmental value by mitigating its ecological footprint.

	Customer value	• *Customer satisfaction:*
		  – Delivering value proposition that resonates with customers
		  – Building long-term relationships
		  – Ethical marketing and advertising practices
			Consumers are increasingly concerned about social and environmental issues. They are more likely to pay a premium for products that align with their values. Keurig Dr Pepper Inc. (fair trade since 2009) offers fairtrade coffee to its consumers as it supports sustainable farming practices and offers fair wages for coffee producers.

	Brand image	• *Brand reputation:*
		  – Strong brand image associated with alternative values
		  – Building trust with stakeholders
		  – Community engagement and social responsibility initiatives
			Chobani yogurt company is known for its commitment to supporting refugees and immigrants. They have a robust refugee resettlement programme, providing employment opportunities and training to refugees in the US. Chobani's social responsibility efforts are well communicated through their marketing campaigns and have a strong brand image, highlighting the positive impact on individuals and communities.

Source: Inspired by Patala et al (2016)

globally), social value (eg Fairtrade certified clothing protects workers from receiving unfair wages) or environmental/green value (eg timber companies plant trees to balance deforestation). These dimensions can be interconnected. For example, strong environmental practices (sustainability) can enhance a company's brand reputation and attract environmentally conscious customers. The relative importance of each dimension can vary, depending on the company's industry, target markets and overall company's strategy. Some companies may prioritize profit maximization, while others might place greater emphasis on social impact or environmental sustainability. It may be that a firm with a value proposition based on social or environmental impacts is able to increase its profitability – the two are not mutually exclusive and social and environmental initiatives do not always have cost implications. For example, minimizing waste can create savings in raw materials and waste-disposal costs. Understanding and prioritizing these various value dimensions is crucial as it allows companies to create a holistic approach to value creation that considers the needs of stakeholders and promotes responsible business practices.

Creating value responsibly

Creating value responsibly means businesses go beyond simply generating profit and actively consider the social, environmental and ethical implications of their actions. It is about ensuring their success benefits not just shareholders but also communities, employees and the planet. It is not just a moral imperative, it is also good business (Camilleri, 2022). Responsible value creation enhances brand reputation and customer loyalty as consumers are increasingly drawn to brands that prioritize sustainability and social responsibility that leads to improved competitive advantage. It also increases employee engagement and productivity as employees are more motivated and engaged when they work for a company that aligns with their values and makes a positive impact. Building sustainable value reduces risk and improves compliance as implementing responsible practices can help companies avoid reputational damage and legal issues. Creating value that benefits stakeholders contributes to a long-term financial sustainability as investing in sustainability and social responsibility can create long-term cost savings and lead to financial success. By adopting these strategies, companies can build stronger relationships with stakeholders, enhance their brand image and achieve sustainable success in the long term.

Figure 4.2 illustrates the value creation process for a generic firm, highlighting both positive and negative externalities. The left side focuses on maximizing shareholder value, while the right side considers a broader range of stakeholders and potential externalities.

The arrows in Figure 4.2 connect inputs, processes, outputs and stakeholders and represent the flow of resources and value creation. The emphasis on positive and negative externalities differs between two sides. Shareholder value focuses primarily on internal financial benefits, while wider values consider both internal and external impacts. It is important to note that the specific positive and negative externalities will vary depending on industry sector and company practices. Also, regulations and social pressure can influence the extent to which businesses consider externalities.

Figure 4.2: Value creation process for a generic firm

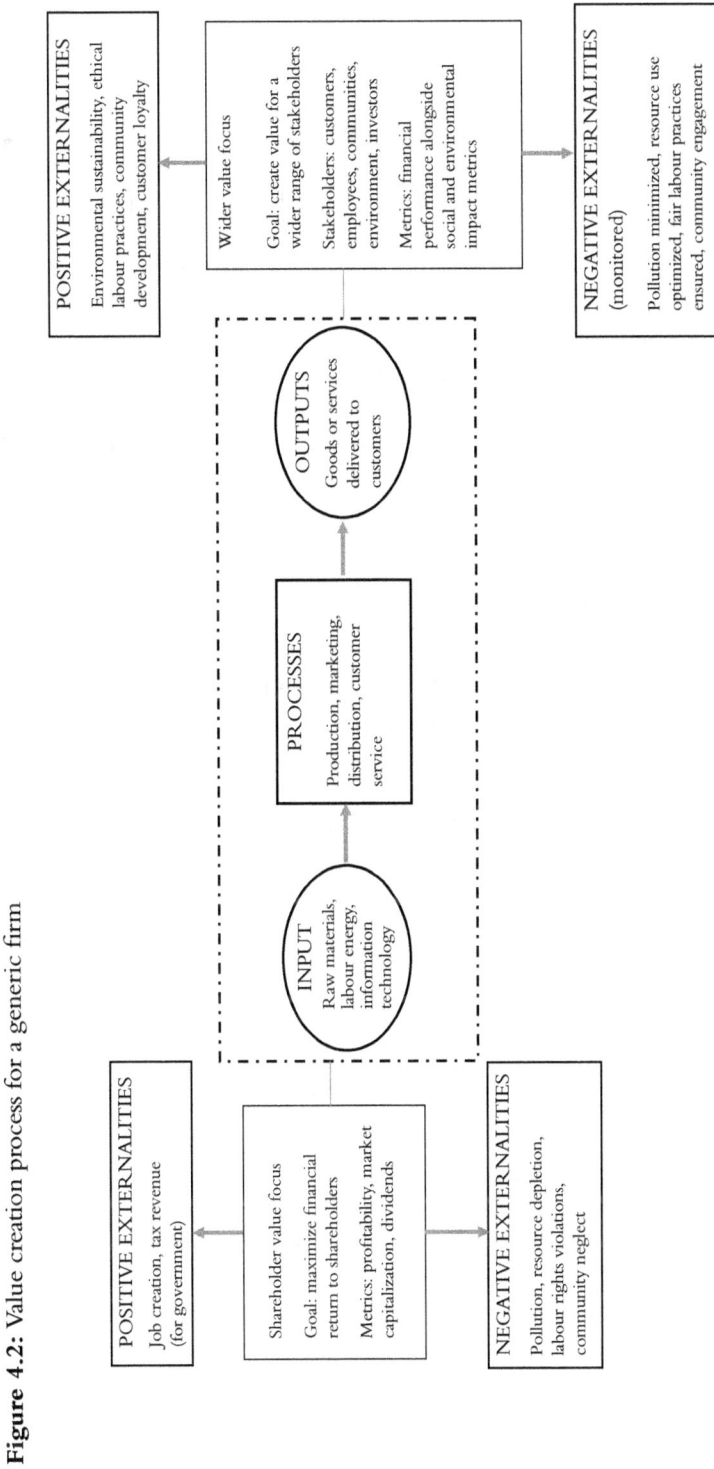

POSITIVE EXTERNALITIES

Environmental sustainability, ethical labour practices, community development, customer loyalty

Wider value focus

Goal: create value for a wider range of stakeholders

Stakeholders: customers, employees, communities, environment, investors

Metrics: financial performance alongside social and environmental impact metrics

NEGATIVE EXTERNALITIES (monitored)

Pollution minimized, resource use optimized, fair labour practices ensured, community engagement

OUTPUTS

Goods or services delivered to customers

PROCESSES

Production, marketing, distribution, customer service

INPUT

Raw materials, labour energy, information technology

POSITIVE EXTERNALITIES

Job creation, tax revenue (for government)

Shareholder value focus

Goal: maximize financial return to shareholders

Metrics: profitability, market capitalization, dividends

NEGATIVE EXTERNALITIES

Pollution, resource depletion, labour rights violations, community neglect

Businesses can prioritize shareholder value while considering the broader societal impact of their operations when making their business decisions. Responsible value creation is a journey, not a destination. It requires ongoing commitment, continuous improvement and a willingness to adapt to evolving expectation. By embracing this holistic approach, businesses can create a positive impact on society while ensuring their own long-term prosperity. Table 4.2 illustrates some key aspects that need to be considered when creating value responsibly.

By implementing these strategies, companies use responsible practices to support high margins through balancing profitability with positive social and environmental impact. This win–win approach builds trust with stakeholders, empowers communities and contributes to a more sustainable future for all. Motivation to create value responsibly is not simply extra work, but a fundamental shift of international business motivations in how international companies operate. It is important to highlight that the journey towards responsible value creation is unique for each company, and requires continuous learning, adaptation and collaboration. By staying committed to sustainable practices-related motivations, implementing these sustainable practices and engaging with stakeholders, international businesses can uncover the true potential of value creation for the benefit of their improved competitive advantage and their stakeholders.

Sustainable value propositions

Sustainable value propositions include a concern with creating, delivering and capturing value to consumers (Bryson et al, 2020) by extending the life cycle of products and materials (Bryson et al, 2024). This process is attributed to sustainable value proposition, which offers 'value provided to customers through the combination of direct economic benefits and derivative benefits of reduced environmental and social impacts' (Patala et al, 2016: 1). The approach benefits international businesses, society and the environment. Once positive outcomes are achieved, international businesses need to communicate their sustainable value propositions and their impact to their stakeholders.

A strong sustainable value proposition, communicated through effective positioning, captures consumer attention and resonates with their needs. In circular economies, positioning refers to the deliberate process of creating an image or perception of a company and its sustainable value proposition in the minds of international consumers (Casidy and Lie, 2023). Positioning is understood in terms of how a company envisions its brand to be distinguished from its competitors in the global marketplace in consumer minds about the international company's engagement in sustainable operations. Firms can position themselves based on social, environmental and/or economic benefits. By clearly communicating potential benefits to consumers, international companies can attract consumers who are a good fit for their value proposition (Patala et al, 2016), as well as build trust and loyalty with environmentally and socially conscious individuals who are willing to pay a premium for products and services that align with their personal values. Strong positioning can foster positive perceptions about a company's alternative values and lead to competitive advantages in international markets.

Similarly, engagement in a circular economy can contribute to gaining competitive advantage through unique selling propositions (USP) (Kant Hvass et al, 2019). It is a

Table 4.2: Key aspects and managerial implications for creating value responsibly

Key aspect	Managerial implications	Example
Defining a company's purpose	Companies can go beyond maximizing profits to articulate a purpose outlining how they contribute to a greater good (eg social development, or ethical practices)	Lego has a clear purpose to 'ignite the builders of tomorrow through joyful play, inspiring creativity and learning while fostering a positive and sustainable future for all'
Integrating sustainability into operations	Companies can create value responsibly by implementing sustainable practices across their operations, such as reducing resource consumption and investing in renewable energy (eg transitioning reliance from fossil fuels to renewable energy sources such as solar and wind power)	Dassault Systemes, a French multinational leader in 3D design software, emphasizes the creation of innovative solutions that consider environmental and social impact alongside economic benefits. Their purpose prioritizes responsible value creation that benefits stakeholders and the company's long-term sustainability
Innovating / introducing new products for good causes	Companies need to invest in R&D focusing on developing new technologies and processes that have a positive impact on society and the environment and use technology to improve efficiency, reduce waste and enhance access to essential goods and services	Tesla's electric vehicles offer a sustainable alternative to traditional cars, while its solar energy solutions help reduce reliance on fossil fuels
Prioritizing ethical sourcing and labour practices	Companies need to ensure ethical treatment of workers throughout their supply chain, including fair wages and better working conditions and transparency and accountability to stakeholders	Fairtrade International certifies products that meet strict ethical labour standards, ensuring fair wages and safe working conditions for farmers and producers
Combating corruption and bribery	Implement strong anti-corruption policies and ensure transparency in all business dealings	Ben & Jerry's company uses its platform to advocate for social justice issues and promote sustainable practices, while ensuring transparency in its sourcing and production process
Engaging with stakeholders	Actively listen to stakeholder concerns and incorporate their feedback into decision-making	Orsted, the Danish renewable energy giant, recognizes a broad range of stakeholders with diverse interests
Contributing to a circular economy	Companies may design products for recyclability or reusability, promote responsible consumption habits, and support recycling initiatives	Johnson Controls (JCI), a global leader in smart and sustainable buildings, contributes to a circular economy while manufacturing building automation systems with high durability and easy repairability, extending their lifespan and reducing waste
Measuring and reporting impact	Companies can develop metrics to track their environmental and social impact, such as carbon footprint reduction, community engagement initiatives, and employee satisfaction levels and publish reports on sustainability	Marks & Spencer, a British retailer, publishes annual reports detailing its environmental impact and efforts to minimize it, which encourages transparency and accountability

strategic approach that can give companies a significant edge in the marketplace. In saturated markets, differentiation of brands and services in consumer minds can be difficult. By adopting circular economy practices, companies can create USPs that resonate with socially and environmentally conscious consumers. For instance, Signify, a global leader in lighting solutions, offers 'pay-per-lux' lighting models. Instead of selling the light fixtures themselves, they charge customers on the amount of light used. This incentivizes the company to design energy-efficient lighting systems and take back old fixtures for refurbishment and recycling. Such a focus on circularity creates a win-win situation: reduced environmental impact for the company and lower energy costs for customers.

Consumers often lack information about the origin and life cycle of products. By embracing transparency and traceability throughout their supply chains (Kennedy and Linnenluecke, 2022), companies can build trust and create a USP around ethical and responsible production. For instance, Everlane, a clothing brand, is known for its radical transparency. The company shares information about their factory locations, worker wages and material costs on their websites. This commitment to transparency differentiates their company from competitors with less clear production processes and allows Everlane to attract socially and environmentally conscious consumers. There are several managerial implications regarding creating value responsibly. First, it can be difficult to estimate the potential market size and to identify customers.

Responsible value creation often involves products and services that cater to niche markets or specific customer segments with particular values and preferences. Consumer values and preferences related to sustainability and ethics can change rapidly, making it difficult to keep up with market trends. Also, fluctuations in consumer demand for responsible products can make market-size estimation more challenging. Companies face measurement challenges and quantifying the impact of responsible business practices on customers' preferences and loyalty can be challenging. Second, communication with customers is paramount as any value proposition based on social, environmental and/or economic benefits has to be able to demonstrate that the conditions imposed by the firm, and other authorities such as accreditation or standards agencies, are fully met. A strong value proposition must clearly demonstrate that the company's claims and promises are fulfilled. This requires open and transparent communication with customers addressing their concerns and providing timely updates on the company's progress toward its responsible business goals. Managers therefore have to develop strategies to collect and disseminate the relevant data across the business to avoid the value proposition being undermined. The companies need to track the company's performance against responsible business goals and identify areas for improvement. Companies also need to identify new opportunities to create value through sustainable practices and proactively address any issues or concerns that may undermine the value proposition.

Creating responsible practice through economic, environmental and societal value creation

Seeking a balance between economic goals, social and environmental responsibility is a complex but increasingly important challenge for international companies (Bryson et al, 2020). International companies have to be able to integrate their economic goals with social and environmental responsibility. In recent years, some international business companies have learnt how to integrate their economic, societal and environmental goals to deliver 'long-term value'. International businesses can create value by tackling global challenges such as climate change, poverty and inequality. Actively participating in solutions and implementing responsible practices enhances brand reputation and contributes to a company's competitive advantage (Haffar and Searcy, 2017). Patagonia, the outdoor apparel company that has introduced its '1% for the Planet' commitment, is another example of championing environmental conservation and ethical production practices, demonstrating how integrating social and environmental responsibility can create value for customers, employees and the planet.

Companies use certain strategies when seeking integration. For instance, they may embed social and environmental considerations into their core business strategies and not consider these as separate initiatives (Choi and Ng, 2011). Such an approach ensures these value dimensions are accounted for throughout the company's decision-making processes. To achieve integration, companies may proactively engage with stakeholders such as employees, communities and NGOs to understand their concerns and priorities. This fosters collaboration and helps identify mutually beneficial solutions but is not without challenges as there may not be alignment between the needs of all stakeholders. That is, managers need to develop more than a superficial understanding of the position of each stakeholder and use the motivations for alternative value creation to drive decision-making around which aspects to prioritize.

International businesses may experience a trade-off in the value-creation process. A trade-off occurs when pursuing one type of value creation comes at the expense of another (Haffar and Searcy, 2017). It can be difficult to navigate, as decisions often have ripple effects across all three dimensions. Some examples of trade-offs include using cheap, resource-intensive materials in manufacturing that might offer cost advantages but generate pollution and depletion of natural resources. Also, building a new factory might create jobs and boost local economy but it may contribute to increased air and water pollution. However, a growing body of research suggests that firms adopting sustainable practices can achieve a win-win situation by shifting from trade-off to synergy. Sustainable practices often lead to increased resources efficiency. Reducing waste, using renewable energy and optimizing production processes can lower costs and improve the company's bottom line. Also, sustainability often drives innovation in product design, supply-chain management and resource utilization. These innovations lead to new products, services and competitive advantages.

Measuring alternative value

Customers are increasingly motivated to support responsible or sustainable international businesses. However, such businesses have to effectively communicate their value proposition to new, existing or potential customers. They need to avoid claims of 'greenwashing' and find transparent mechanisms to accurately measure and report their sustainable business models and their corporate values. Where there is a need for improvement regarding social, environmental and economic goals, companies need to develop and utilize clear metrics to track the company's progress (Epstein and Roy, 2003). This data-based information will enable better decision-making and impact assessment and may be achieved through transparent external reporting practices.

Research suggests that measuring and reporting alternative values, alongside traditional economic metrics, is gaining traction (Epstein and Roy, 2003) as companies strive for a more sustainable and eco-friendly approach to international business. Companies can measure their performance by various means (Epstein and Roy, 2001; 2003). Moreover, rating agencies play an important role in this evolving landscape. They are creating frameworks to assess and score companies' performance on environmental, social and governance (ESG) factors. This framework provides a standardized approach to measuring alternative values, promoting comparability between companies. While still evolving frameworks such as the Global Reporting Initiative (GRI) and the Sustainability Accounting Standards Board (SASB) are providing standardization for ESG reporting. ESG ratings allow investors and other stakeholders to compare companies within the same industry based on their social and environmental performance. ESG ratings identify potential risks associated with a company's social or environmental performance, but they also highlight opportunities related to sustainable innovation.

The presence of ESG ratings and consumers using social media encourages companies to be more transparent and accountable regarding their social and environmental impact. Social media platforms provide a powerful voice for consumers to raise awareness about social and environmental issues related to company practices. Consumers can share their experiences with companies on social media, highlighting both positive and negative aspects of their environmental and social impact. Viral social media campaigns can significantly impact a company's reputation, pressuring them to improve their alternative value practices. Social media can be a valuable platform for consumers to share information about a company's social and environmental performance, supplementing data provided by rating companies. Consumers can debate and critique the methodologies used by rating agencies in their ESG assessments. Social media platforms can be used to verify or challenge claims made by companies or rating agencies through consumer experiences and investigative reports.

International business marketing managers need to communicate their responsible business practices throughout the product life cycle clearly; for example, highlighting the use of recycled materials, durable design and end-of-life options (repair, refurbishment, recycling). They are advised to showcase the environmental and social benefits of their sustainable products (Kant Hvass et al, 2019). The company can use impactful metrics to demonstrate reduced waste, water usage or carbon footprint compared to traditional options.

To prosper, international business managers need to attract investment (Dzwigol and Dzwigol-Barosz, 2020). They can do so by demonstrating how their responsible business practices contribute to their long-term financial stability and, ultimately, to circular economy. International companies can highlight reduced reliance on virgin materials, lower waste disposal costs and potential for recurring revenue streams from repair or take-back programmes. International companies can also emphasize how

Table 4.3: Unilever's ESG investment in a circular economy

Environmental	Social	Governance
Reduce raw plastic usage in packaging by 50% and increase the use of recycled plastic content in their packaging by 50%; to achieve net-zero emissions by 2030	Empower small farmers through promotion of *Fairtrade* practices to improve livelihoods in rural communities	Strive towards transparency and accountability to allow investors and stakeholders to track their commitment to responsible practices
Invest in sustainable sourcing for their raw materials to reduce their environmental footprint and ensure long-term resource availability	Promote diversity and inclusion within their workforce and throughout their supply chain	Integrate sustainability into their corporate governance structure, with board-level control and accountability for ESG performance
Reduce water usage per product by 50% by 2030	Engage with communities to address social and environmental challenges related to their operations	Manage risks associated with their operations, ensuring long-term sustainability

circular economy practices can mitigate risks associated with resource scarcity, volatile material prices and changing consumer preferences for sustainable products (Billio et al, 2021). International companies seeking investment could provide investors with clear data on the environmental and social impact of their circular economy practices. This could include life-cycle assessments and social-impact factors. Demonstrating how the company's responsible business model aligns with ESG investing principles can attract investors seeking socially responsible and sustainable investment opportunities (Billio et al, 2021; Boffo and Patalano, 2020). For instance, by integrating ESG investment principles with a focus on circular economy (Table 4.3), Unilever demonstrates a commitment to responsible business practices that benefit the environment, society and their long-term financial success. This makes them a leading example for other multinational corporations.

Unilever has made significant strides in its ESG commitments (see Table 4.3). However, as with any large corporation, its efforts are not without scrutiny or areas for improvement. While Unilever has made progress in improving supply chain transparency, there is still room for enhancement. Greater visibility into the sourcing and production processes of raw materials can help to ensure that sustainability practices are being adhered to throughout the value chain. Enhancing engagement with the Fairtrade international movement would improve the company's sustainability position regarding the social ESG dimension. Unilever has set ambitious targets for reducing waste and increasing recycling rates. However, achieving these targets may require more innovative approaches such as investing in advanced recycling technologies or partnering with waste-management companies.

International companies need to define measurable indicators that align with the chosen alternative values. Responsible companies readily provide information about their supply chain, sourcing practices, and labour standards in their published CSR reports detailing their social and environmental initiatives. Indicators could also include metrics for employee well-being, workforce diversity, community development or environmental footprint reduction. By proactively measuring alternative values through SMART key performance indicators (KPIs), international companies can better identify and possibly mitigate environmental and social risks. Clear and measurable KPIs ensure everyone in the company is working towards the same goal. Data gathered from measuring KPIs informs strategic decisions related to sustainability and risk management. KPIs provide a common language for communicating progress on alternative values to stakeholders. Aligning the company's KPIs with relevant industry standards or frameworks increases comparability. By incorporating alternative value metrics into their annual reports, international companies can create a more comprehensive picture of their impact (Epstein and Roy, 2001; 2003) and contribute to a more sustainable future for international business.

Conclusion

The international business motivation to follow the linear model of 'take-make-waste' is increasingly unsustainable. Instead, the business motivation to create alternative values, based on the principles of circular economy and responsible business practices, offers a more holistic approach. The multidimensionality of value recognizes the importance of both financial and non-financial motivations, including social responsibility and environmental impact. Surprisingly, the international business literature is silent on alternative values and motivated individuals who create alternative values, and this topic is further explored in Chapter 6.

For managers operating in the international business context, simply understanding alternative values is no longer optional. Consumers are increasingly demanding sustainable and ethical products and services while investors are increasingly focusing on ESG factors when making investment decisions. Companies that are motivated to prioritize alternative values cultivate stronger relationships with stakeholders and create a more sustainable and resilient business model for the future.

Key terms

Circular economy – aims to keep resources in use for as long as possible, minimizing waste and maximizing resource recovery through design, repair, reuse and recycling.

Effective positioning – contributes to the company offering's differentiation strategy regarding their engagement in sustainable operations and helps target specific customer segments. By clearly communicating sustainable value proposition, the company can attract socially and environmentally conscious customers who are a good fit for their value proposition.

Sustainable value proposition – international businesses create sustainable value propositions through a variety of mechanisms, such as economic value, social value and environmental/green value, and offer these to their socially and environmentally conscious consumers.

Recommended reading

Abreu, M.C.S.D., Ferreira, F.N.H., Proenca, J.F. and Ceglia, D. (2021) 'Collaboration in achieving sustainable solutions in the textile industry', *Journal of Business & Industrial Marketing*, 36(9): 1614–26.

Bryson, J.R., Sundbo, J., Fugslang, L. and Daniels, P. (2020) 'Business models and service strategy', in *Service Management: Theory and Practice*, London: Palgrave Macmillan (textbook), chapter 3.

Mehrotra, S. and Jaladi, S.R. (2022) 'How start-ups in emerging economies embrace circular business models and contribute towards a circular economy', *Journal of Entrepreneurship in Emerging Economies*, 14(5): 727–53.

References

Adıgüzel, F. and Donato, C. (2021) 'Proud to be sustainable: upcycled versus recycled luxury products', *Journal of Business Research*, 130: 137–46.

Belk, R. (2007) 'Why not share rather than own?', *Annals of the American Academy of Political and Social Science*, 611: 126–40.

Billio, M., Costola, M., Hristova, I., Latino, C., and Pelizzon, L. (2021). Inside the ESG ratings:(Dis) agreement and performance. *Corporate Social Responsibility and Environmental Management*, 28(5), 1426–45.

Boffo, R. and Patalano, R. (2020). 'ESG investing: practices, progress and challenges', OECD Paris, Available from: www.oecd.org/finance/ESG-Investing-Practices-Progr ess-and-Challenges.pdf [Accessed 6 April 2024].

Bryson, J., Sundbo, J., Fuglsang, L. and Daniels, P. (2020) 'Business models and service strategy', in *Service Management: Theory and Practice*, London: Palgrave Macmillan (textbook), chapter 3.

Bryson, J., Herod, J. Johns, J. & Vanchan, V. (2024). Localised waste reduction networks, global destruction networks and the circular economy. *Cambridge Journal of Regions, Economy and Society*,17(3): 667–82.

Camilleri, M.A. (2022) 'Strategic attributions of corporate social responsibility and environmental management: the business case for doing well by doing good!', *Sustainable Development*, 30(3): 409–22.

Casidy, R. and Lie, D.S. (2023) 'The effects of B2B sustainable brand positioning on relationship outcomes', *Industrial Marketing Management*, 109: 245–56.

Choi, S., and Ng, A. (2011) 'Environmental and economic dimensions of sustainability and price effects on consumer responses', *Journal of Business Ethics*, 104: 269–82.

David, P., O'Brien, J.P., Yoshikawa, T. and Delios, A. (2010) 'Do shareholders or stakeholders appropriate the rents from corporate diversification? The influence of ownership structure', *Academy of Management Journal*, 53(3): 636–54.

Dzwigol, H. and Dzwigol-Barosz, M. (2020) 'Sustainable development of the company on the basis of expert assessment of the investment strategy', *Academy of Strategic Management Journal*, 19(5): 1–7.

Epstein, M.J. and Roy, M.J. (2001) 'Sustainability in action: identifying and measuring the key performance drivers', *Long Range Planning*, 34(5): 585–604.

Epstein, M.J. and Roy, M.J. (2003) 'Making the business case for sustainability: linking social and environmental actions to financial performance', *Journal of Corporate Citizenship*, 9: 79–96.

Haffar, M. and Searcy, C. (2017) 'Classification of trade-offs encountered in the practice of corporate sustainability', *Journal of Business Ethics*, 140, 495–522.

Kant Hvass, K. and Pedersen, E.R.G. (2019) 'Toward circular economy of fashion: experiences from a brand's product take-back initiative', *Journal of Fashion Marketing and Management: An International Journal*, 23(3): 345–65.

Kennedy, S. and Linnenluecke, M.K. (2022) 'Circular economy and resilience: a research agenda', *Business Strategy and the Environment*, 31(6): 2754–65.

Macneil, I.R. (1980) 'Power, contract, and the economic model', *Journal of Economic Issues*, 14(4): 909–23.

Mehrotra, S. and Jaladi, S.R. (2022) 'How start-ups in emerging economies embrace circular business models and contribute towards a circular economy', *Journal of Entrepreneurship in Emerging Economies*, 14(5): 727–53.

Novkovic, S. (2008) 'Defining the co-operative difference', *Journal of Socio-Economics*, 37(6): 2168–77.

Patala, S., Jalkala, A., Keränen, J., Väisänen, S., Tuominen, V. and Soukka, R. (2016) 'Sustainable value propositions: framework and implications for technology suppliers', *Industrial Marketing Management*, 59: 144–56.

Pitts, F.H. (2021) *Values*, Cambridge: Polity Press.

Ranta, V., Keränen, J. and Aarikka-Stenroos, L. (2020) 'How B2B suppliers articulate customer value propositions in the circular economy: four innovation-driven value creation logics', *Industrial Marketing Management*, 87, 291–305.

Sarpong, D., Boakye, D., Ofosu, G. and Botchie, D. (2023) 'The three pointers of research and development (R&D) for growth-boosting sustainable innovation system', *Technovation*, 122: 102581.

Zahra, S.A. (2003) 'International expansion of US manufacturing family businesses: the effect of ownership and involvement', *Journal of Business Venturing*, 18(4): 495–512.

5

Business Models, Responsibility and Alternative Approaches to Monetarizing Value

Introduction

International business involves intersections configured around the coordination of value creation processes that stretch across international boundaries. In this chapter, our focus is on understanding the ways in which firms coordinate value-creation processes in a structured fashion. All forms of business are place-based and connected in complex ways to the ever-evolving geoeconomy. There are multiple ways in which value is created through configuring different approaches to organizing international business. These include export-based business models as well as extremely complex international businesses involving the coordination of multiple flows of money, data, people, raw materials, components, services and completed products across international boundaries. All businesses coordinate flows, and these include transactions that create multiple forms of value. A business may be price-driven with a focus on stripping out costs and enhancing profitability, but an alternative approach severs the relationship between the sale price of a commodity and its production cost. These represent two very different approaches to coordinating firm-centred wealth-creation processes. Process and/or technological innovations play an important role in opening new possibilities for businesses to configure innovative approaches to value creation. Many of these new approaches will be simple and often these approaches to value creation and realization appear to be obvious with the benefits of hindsight. Central to this process is commercial awareness or an individual's ability to identify a new business opportunity. This then leads to the development of a structure within which this new form of value creation and capture occurs. Such structures are known as hierarchies, firms, organizations and/or business models. A firm may form around a single business model with a business model defined as a coordinated approach to value creation and monetarization. Alternatively, a firm may be a form of business model conglomerate or have within it a complex array of distinct and intertwined business models.

In this chapter we explore different approaches to monetarizing value, and this includes a discussion and evaluation of conventional and alternative approaches to configuring business models. The approach begins by defining business models and their characteristics and then places this discussion within an established debate on the theory of business. It then provides the foundations for the analysis of business models and responsible business. This part of the discussion explores the elements of a business model and how these relate to the practice of international business. The final part of the chapter explores complex business models or multisided business models. The chapter has two cross-cutting themes. The first theme involves providing a business model informed approach to international business that begins to bring the various themes outlined in this book together. Thus, a business model is developed to exploit or engage with different places within the evolving geoeconomy. These business models are underpinned by process and technological innovation and represent solutions to creating and monetarizing different forms of value. Second, the chapter highlights that there is no one approach to configuring a business model, but there are multiple alternative approaches. These alternatives come with different characteristics that reflect some of the driving principles or motivations that drive value creation processes and their monetarization. It is important to differentiate between value creation defined as the generation of social and environmental values intended to provide a solution to some societal problem or consumer need and the monetarization of these values. This is to differentiate between values-in-use, or use values, and exchange values, with the latter focusing on the translation of values-in-use into revenue. This process comes together under the term 'strategy'; however, the strategy debate has become one founded upon discussions of business models. But what is a business model?

Business models defined

The term 'business model' describes the ways in which a firm engages in business activities (Chesbrough and Rosenbloom, 2010) or describes the processes by which firms try to create value (Wirtz, 2011). This term has entered the lexicon of managers, consultants, academics and journalists. It was first used in an article published in 1957 that developed a business-simulation game designed for executive training (Bellman et al, 1957). The focus was on modelling business. In 1960, the first academic paper that used the term in both the title and abstract was published and this provided an account of business models in the context of information systems (Jones, 1960). Much of the early literature on business models developed accounts of business modelling. It is only in the 1990s with the emergence of e-commerce and the dot-com boom that the term gained wider applicability (Teece, 2010; Zott et al, 2011).

From the 1990s, the term was initially used to describe innovative ways of practicing or doing business with an emphasis on information communication technologies, the internet and e-commerce. Thus, much of the early literature on business models highlighted the relationship between process and technological innovation and the emergence of new business model forms. This early literature has been supplemented by an ongoing debate in which the business model approach has become a central element of the business and management toolkit. The term is now used to describe the basic choices a firm makes regarding approaches to business including revenues and costs. A business model can be considered as a type of formula for making money. Within a given industry, for example, automotive or management consultancy, different business models coexist. This is also the case within firms. A firm may have an overarching business model but may also have many coexisting business models.

A business model provides structure to a business as it is the outcome of a set of core decisions regarding the firm's approach to creating all types of value. A business model may be designed carefully or may emerge as individuals come together to develop and implement solutions to creating value which is then monetarized. It is important to note that a business model may not be the outcome of a process of careful debate, discussion and design, but may emerge by default. Nevertheless, a business model is continually adapted to changing circumstances. This might include business model innovation in which there is a critical alteration in a firm's approach to business. New disruptive business models are created by start-up firms and established firms adapt and experiment with new approaches to configuring their business models. There are, however, processes at work that restrict business model innovation, and these include regulations and institutional constraints, accepted sector and consumer conventions and even cultural constraints.

Fundamentally, every business is configured around some purpose, or driving motivation, and this then is reflected in the firm's business model, or models. Cutting across these models are business activity systems that reflect Chandler's three pillars of corporate form: management, marketing and production (Chandler, 1977). The practice of management involves defining objectives or purpose, decision-making, coordination, evaluation including measurement and motivation. Chandler makes a distinction between coordination and monitoring by market and price mechanisms as is the case of a single-unit business compared to internal monitoring and coordination by firms that consist of many units located in different locations. These multiunit and multisite businesses employ a 'hierarchy of middle and top salaried managers to monitor and coordinate the work of the units under its control' (Chandler, 1977: 3). The dramatic growth in this type of international business reflects the development of new approaches to management and business models that are configured around internalizing the activities of many business units located in many different locations.

Management is about choices, and this includes decisions regarding the prioritization of investment options and business model configurations. Within an industry, there may be many coexisting business models and managers must decide which one to adopt. This could be an explicit or implicit decision as dominant approaches to configuring a business model will exist in an industry or economic sector. An important point to remember is that firms are complex, and this is especially the case for an international business that coordinates the production and sale of many different lines of goods and/or services. Each unit, division or even product line might have a different business model. This is to acknowledge the complexity of international business combined with inter- and intra-firm diversity.

The business of international business

All businesses have an explicit or implicit business model or what Drucker termed 'a company's *theory of the business*' (1994: 96, italics in the original). According to Drucker, a theory of business has three parts. First, there are assumptions made by a firm about the environment within which the business operates. This includes the current structure of society, market structures and conditions, customers, and technology (see Chapter 7). Second, there are assumptions made about the organization's mission (see Chapter 4). These missions might be modest or ambitious. Third, assumptions are made about the firm's core competencies that are required to facilitate or enable the firm's mission. These three assumptions work together as:

> the assumptions about environment define what an organization is paid for. The assumptions about mission define what an organization considers to be meaningful results, in other words, they point to how it envisions itself making a difference in the economy and in the society at large. Finally, the assumptions about core competencies define where an organization must excel in order to maintain leadership. (Drucker, 1994: 100)

These assumptions must be aligned, but also must avoid, for example, greenwashing, as a company's mission should reflect its actual or real operations and the ways in which it engages with customers. To Drucker, the theory of a business must be explicit and be understood throughout the organization. It is important that it is never taken for granted and is continually challenged, tested and refined. Some of these theories of the business last for decades, but they all eventually become obsolete – the implication being that a firm must continually renew its theory of business, as failure to do so threatens an organization's future. A key point is that at the first signs of a theory of the business becoming obsolete, a firm should reconsider its environment, mission and core competency assumptions – the point being that 'patching never works' (Drucker, 1994: 101) and radical change or innovation will be required. Here it is important to consider business failures and companies that have engaged in processes of radical restructuring. In 2013, Microsoft, for example, implemented the 'One Microsoft' strategy. This was a major restructuring event aimed at unifying the firm's operations and culture with a focus on breaking down traditional silos to promote collaboration and innovation. Prior to this, there had been a more piecemeal or patching approach. To support this type of radical change process, an organization must engage in an ongoing systematic diagnostic process of its theory of the business.

The debate on the theory of the business has become one positioned around business models. Nevertheless, central to the theory of a business, and the business model approach, must be an appreciation of an organization's goals or mission or, in other words, the question to ask is: What is the business of the business? In 1970, Friedman provided one answer to this question when he proclaimed that the only social responsibility of business should be a focus on maximizing profit (Friedman, 1970). Profits are then distributed to a firm's owners or shareholders, and they can make decisions about charitable donations. This emphasis on profitmaking as a firm's only mission was echoed by Levitt, who argued that 'the function of business is to produce sustained high-level profits' (Levitt, 1958: 44). Moreover, this process requires 'variety, diversity, spontaneity, competition – in short, pluralism' (Levitt, 1958: 44). Levitt then argues that the debate on business and social responsibility is associated with the danger of removing diversity creating corporations with 'all-embracing duties, obligations, and finally powers' and one outcome would be businesses that are '*not narrowly profit-oriented enough*' (Levitt, 1958: 44, italics in the original).

The debate on the business of business has moved on since the 1970s. Business can still be profit-oriented whilst pursuing hybrid goals configured around creating profits and social goods. This shift towards businesses with missions constructed around the delivery of double or triple bottom lines does not have to imply that a firm is not sufficiently focused on creating profit. A distinction must be made between how a business is organized compared to what a firm does. On the one hand, managers must focus on cost control combined with profit generation by applying conventional management techniques that include outsourcing, offshoring/reshoring, best shoring and automation. This is all about productivity and how the outcome of a theory of the business or business model is delivered. On the other hand, managers must be concerned with what a business seeks to achieve. This includes how the firm's products and services are differentiated from competitors. It also includes the relationship between a firm's mission and how this is related to attracting and retaining highly talented individuals. The implication is that profitability can be enhanced by business models that include an emphasis on social responsibility. There is no tension between profitability and social responsibility; acting responsibly may lead to sustained high-level profits. There is an important caveat to consider; sustained high-level profitability is only possible when a business is engaged in an ongoing process of business model adaptation and sometimes this requires radical change.

Some would argue that managers must make decisions regarding trade-offs between creating social goods and profitability (Nilsson and Robinson, 2018). This can include an ongoing discursive formation of profit and value that is used to balance the tensions that exist in a business model formulated around balancing a double or triple bottom line (Bryson and Buttle, 2005; Bryson and Lombardi, 2009). Such trade-offs will occur for some businesses, but not all. One of the dangers is in isolating the creation of social goods from profit-making activities as this sets up a trade-off scenario. In some business models, profit generation is intertwined with social responsibility to such an extent that these two processes are inseparable. In these types of business model, any notion of a trade-off evaporates. There are two approaches to consider. On the one hand, managers can configure a business model in which there is no distinction between acting responsibly, or doing good, and profitability. On the other hand, managers can configure a business model in which the primary focus is on profit generation, but subsequently profit is extracted and allocated to doing good. A trade-off emerges in this type of business model between how much is invested back into the business, allocated to owners or shareholders or 'invested' in doing good. Central to this distinction between these two approaches is how a business model is defined. In the first approach, doing good and creating profit cannot be separated, whilst in the latter approach doing good is an afterthought. These are not mutually exclusive approaches, as a firm following the first strategy might also decide to allocate some profits to create additional social goods. It also might be the case that a business will have a unit with a business model configured around the first approach and units that follow the second approach.

We now need to explore business models in greater depth, but an important point to reflect upon is diversity of approaches. It is possible to argue that there are as many ways of running or configuring a business as there are businesses. This would be an extreme argument, but all businesses have their own peculiarities or idiosyncrasies. A business model approach provides a framework that can be applied to compare different businesses and also a tool to inform the process of creating and adapting a business model. However, it is important not to fall into the trap of trying to copy an existing business model or business. Any attempt to copy will come with problems as it is impossible to develop a complete replica. For example, Chowdeck, the Nigerian food delivery company, was established by Femi Aluko based on his experience of rapid food deliveries during a work trip to Dubai (Kene-Okafor, 2024). He decided to replicate the same service levels in Nigeria, but this required experimentation to create a new optimized local food delivery model that would minimize discounts and would only partner with the best restaurants. This business relies on geotagging and applying and enforcing strict regulations on vendors and riders; vendors must accept orders within a five-minute window, with failure leading to order cancellation and Chowdeck reducing the vendor's prioritization level on the platform. This is to highlight the complexity that is hidden within a business model as it is operationalized with much of this complexity remaining hidden even to those who are working for the company. The business model approach, or applied theory of business, is operationalized by people. In this process, people add additional layers of complexity that come from culture, tradition, irrationality, politics and power dynamics.

Business models and responsible business

The attraction of the 'business model construct arguably lies in its holistic approach' (Foss and Saebi, 2015: 1). This includes understanding the development of a compelling value proposition for customers by a network of stakeholders and some mechanism for capturing a proportion of that value (Leih et al, 2015: 24). A value proposition is some type of solution that has been developed to solve a need, or a problem being experienced by a customer or society (Figure 5.1). According to Teece, 'the concept of a business model lacks theoretical grounding in economics or in business studies. Quite simply there is no established place in economic theory for business models' (2010: 175). This difficulty reflects the focus in economics and business studies on price. Similarly, Zott et al (2011) noted that there is no widely expected language to examine business models and that there is a diverse set of business model definitions.

The term 'business model' is used in four ways in the literature. First, in many instances the concept is used to frame an empirical analysis without being defined (Zott et al, 2011). Second, business models are often directly related to firms that typify a particular type of approach to business – the Apple business model compared to that of Samsung (Baden-Fuller and Morgan, 2010: 157). Third, there are scholars who

Figure 5.1: Value propositions

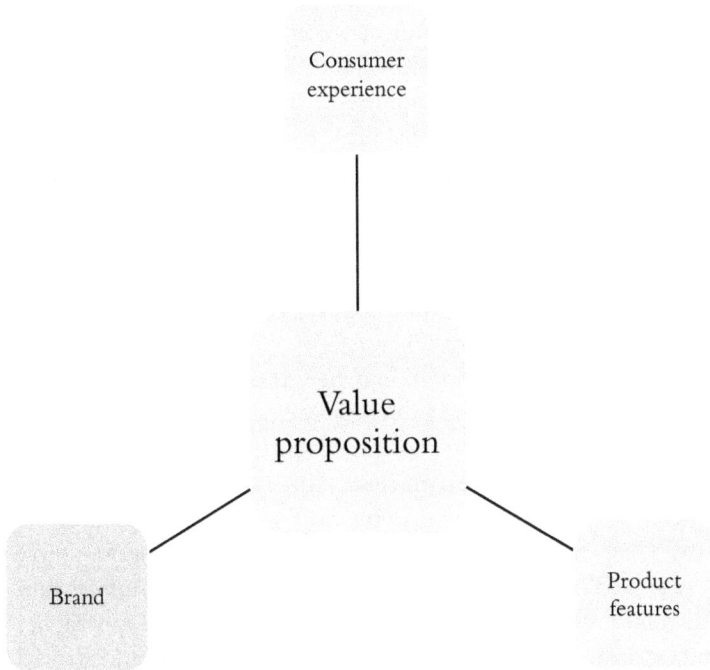

relate the business model concept to debates over strategy informed by the adoption of new technology (Zott and Amit, 2008). Fourth, a more recent approach is to adopt the construct to develop a comparative approach to understanding business behaviour and performance (Teece, 2010; Baden-Fuller and Morgan, 2010).

A business model contains many different elements; these include: governance; a set of products and services; a firm's resources and capabilities; the organization of a firm and its activities; the revenue generation model; the investment model; customer engagement; value delivery; target market segments and monetization or the value proposition that is provided or offered to customers; the firm's network with external organizations that support value creation; and the organization's strategy, including motivations. It should not be assumed that profit is the central motivation behind the activities of all firms. Many firms are satisfiers and are not driven by a desire to grow; a firm may also blend a search to create profit with other forms of value.

A business model may apply to a complete company and take the form of an overarching model. Nevertheless, a large and complex international business may include many different business models. This is to argue that a business model may exist at the level of a business unit, profit centre or product line rather than at an organizational level. For some firms, every business unit or every subsidiary may have its own value creation logic and approach to value capture. Within a large firm, discrete business models that exist within different business units may be complementary and this occurs when 'two businesses managed by the same company are complements if the performance of each of them increases the returns of operating the other' (Casadesus-Masanell et al, 2015: 74).

A business model may work well in one context – for example, in the home or domestic market – but might face major challenges in foreign markets (see Chapters 6 and 7). International businesses must appreciate that the successful internationalization of a business model requires the capability to adapt the model by retaining non-location-bound firm-specific advantages (FSAs), whilst adapting location-bound FSAs to the target foreign market (Figure 5.2). This requires identifying and considering the role of home- and host-based contingencies and also what are termed 'exo-contextual antecedents' or 'environmental contingencies' (Evers et al, 2023). These exo-level factors reflect economic, political, legal, social, cultural and technological differences between countries (see Chapter 2).

Traditionally, business model innovation is viewed as static, but newer work focuses on business innovation as dynamic and as an ongoing process. Business model innovation can involve subtle changes. These are not always disruptive (see Chapter 3). The primary focus of the existing literature is on profit-making (Amit and Zott, 2012) and there is a relative paucity of work examining value creation and appropriation beyond profit generation (see Chapter 4). New digital technologies play an important role in business model innovation. These include whole new product and service lines emerging based on digital innovation as well as the application of digital approaches to existing processes and services. This includes applying platform-style solutions to accessing new markets and the identification of new digital channels. Companies can offer new digital

Figure 5.2: International business and value propositions

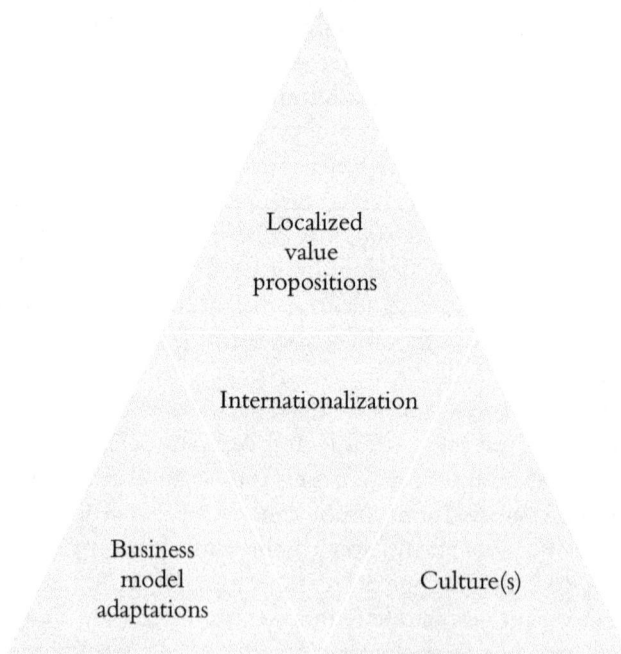

Localized
value
propositions

Internationalization

Business
model   Culture(s)
adaptations

products or digitally enabled products. There are two linked processes at work here. On the one hand, there are new digital products and services being developed. Some are new to the world whilst others substitute a digital solution for one that had been analogue. On the other hand, digital solutions are altering existing business processes, and this applies to all business activity areas; for example, accountancy, order-tracking and supply-chain coordination.

When applied alongside digitalization, there is no universally accepted robust conceptual framework that can assist businesses, practitioners and academics to understand the constructs of digitalization, digital transformation and business model innovation. There is much debate about the relationship between digital transformation and business model innovation. It can be argued that digital transformation involves the creation of a new business model, or that a digital transformation is about more than using a technology as it should involve the development of a digital strategy, or that new business models lead to improved business performance. In short, there is no clarity about what business model innovation involves, or what the consequences of the innovation might be, particularly in the case of digital business model innovation. This creates a challenging environment for international businesses wishing to innovate their business models using digital technologies. Managers may also have to consider if their business has one business model, or in fact multiple business models, and how these operate across different geographical territories (see Chapters 7 and 9).

Business models and practice

A business model provides the link between a firm's strategy, or theory of doing business, and its business processes and practices that are required for strategy execution (Evers et al, 2023). Every business model includes three related elements that form a value or profit-creation process (Figure 5.3). First, the *value proposition*, or *transaction content*, is the distinctive contribution made by an organization in the value creation process. This includes the types of solutions provided or promised by the organization to its customers or beneficiaries. The value proposition is configured around the identification of an opportunity to craft and use values that can be monetarized.

The second element involves the identification, creation, coordination and management of a *value network* of interconnected relationships that form a nexus of interactions or a value chain (see Chapter 9). The value network configures the processes, financing and revenue and inter-firm relationships required to deliver the firm's value proposition. The competitiveness of a value proposition may be founded within the composition of the value network. A core firm practice is thus the ability to configure and coordinate the value network related to each product or service creation and delivery process. This transfers competition from the arena of the firm to the identification and coordination of a value network that has been assembled to deliver or manage a project. The shift from firm to network reflects the ability of the network to access sources of financial capital, to spread the risk across the network, access specialist expertise and draw upon established private–public sector relationships. In practice, the value network created by new firms may form around the founders' friendship networks.

Figure 5.3: Business model elements and structure

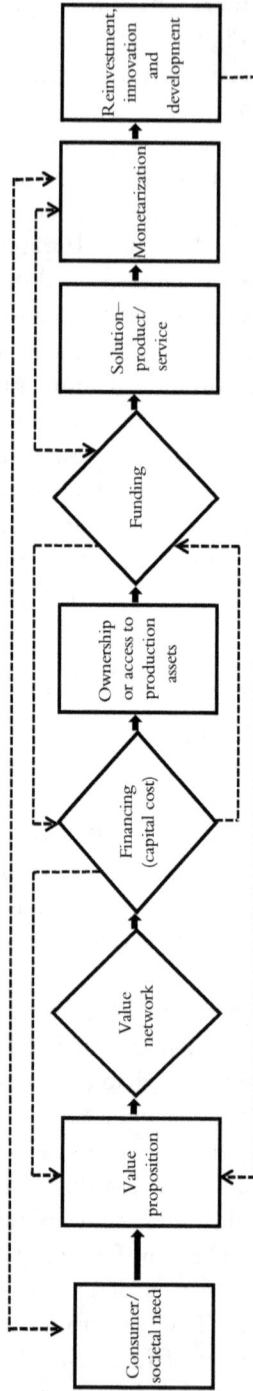

A value network consists of at least three types of agent (Ehret and Wirtz, 2015). First are *network architects* that oversee the identification, coordination and integration of the value network. The composition of the network is an outcome of decisions regarding financing, funding and yields. Second, are *hybrid contributors* who add to the value network by developing and providing related or supporting products and services (software, cybersecurity, project management). Third, are *product providers* specializing in the development of intermediate products to enable the delivery of the value network.

A business model's third element is *monetization*, often labelled as a 'value-capturing mechanism' or 'revenue model'. The revenue model describes the various ways in which a network architect intends to monetize the value proposition. Associated costs include the initial financing of the capital works combined with the costs of operations, maintenance and refurbishment. There may be multiple revenue streams as monetization can take many forms, and this includes selling products and services, but it can also include renting products. Additional revenue may come from repairs and servicing and even from product recycling. Monetization also includes financialization (see Chapters 1 and 6), or the ways in which firms manage their money to generate financial or investment returns. For example, in March 2022 Apple had US$202.5 billion in cash and investments, Alphabet held US$169.2 billion and Microsoft US$132.3 billion. In 2014, Apple had US$158.8 billion in cash and cash equivalents, whilst the US government only had US$48.5 billion (Shvartsman, 2024). The configuration of a firm's value propositions is the central driver behind all business models, and this includes monetarization of products and services combined with returns on financial investments.

Value propositions and responsibility

There is a danger in being too focused on the relationship between monetarization processes and transactions within business. Whilst these are important, the central driver behind all business models is the creation and delivery of some type of value proposition for customers. The nature of this value proposition, or transaction content, and how this is received by customers unlocks the monetarization process. Too often business practitioners, consultants and academics become overly distracted by understanding and optimizing how a product or service is created rather than exploring the essence of the value proposition that a business model is configured to deliver. The global value chains (GVC) approach focuses on transaction governance (see Chapter 9), and in the configuration of networks of firms and their intergovernance. The GVC approach sidelines and even overlooks the configuration of the value propositions that are developed by a business model.

Value propositions can be configured in many ways. It is useful to apply a segmentation approach to value propositions based on identifying products and services that have value propositions with similar characteristics. A firm may sell products in the same range, with each product having a slightly different value proposition. A value proposition may be price-based with the good or service sold solely on price. In this case, there is a clear relationship between production costs and the selling price.

Alternatively, there may be no relationship between the selling price and production costs. In this case, a firm has crafted a value proposition around a product's unique selling proposition (USP) that may produce excess profit, or supernormal profit, or profit that is greater than a normal return on capital. Value propositions that create excess profit come from investment in innovation and brand development. They also may emerge based on a business model in which value propositions are configured around product scarcity and the creation of things that become coveted objects.

A value proposition emerges from a firm managing the convergence of different business processes. These include the design of a good and service including packaging, marketing and post-consumer initiatives. An excellent example is Tony's Chocolonely. This Dutch brand's value proposition is founded on the idea of making '100% slave-free' chocolate. The company works directly with cocoa growers in Ghana and the Ivory Coast and pays them a premium on top of the Fairtrade price for cocoa. This value proposition is reflected in the design of their chocolate bars. Thus, their 180g bars are divided into unevenly sized chunks to remind consumers that the profits that come from the chocolate industry are unfairly divided. In addition, the bottom of this company's chocolate bars represents the Equator and the chunks above, the Gulf of Guinea.

Some aspects of a product's value proposition may be related to the business models transaction structure, governance or GVC. This may include place-based associations. In 1953, Neil Borden outlined the concept of the marketing mix to explore the ways in which companies differentiate themselves from competitors when marketing their products or services. In this analysis, Borden identified 12 interrelated factors that are central to the relationship between firms, customers and competitors (Borden, 1964). These factors were grouped by McCarthy (1960) into four categories: Product, Price, Place and Promotion. The four categories are known as the fours Ps and are central to the ways in which a firm configures a product's value proposition.

For international business, place-based product associations may matter. On the one hand, high-value products, and those with high margins, may benefit from place-based associations as 'a significant proportion of the value of such products is entwined in place-based symbolic relationships and this enables firms to compete on other product qualities apart from price' (Rusten et al, 2007: 143–4). The point being that linking products to places and places to products is to create a value proposition that draws upon a named location's economic, cultural, social and political values. This is to accept that with international business, national constructions of identity still matter and that part of this national construction or projection of identity comes from products with value propositions that are marketed by drawing upon place-based symbolism. To many companies and customers, where a product is designed matters (Box 5.1). There are numerous examples of value propositions that include place-based associations. A hand-rope winch, for example, purchased in 2024 and produced by Einhell, the German tool manufacturer, is marketed as 'Einhell Germany AG, German Designed Quality'. This label appears in four places on the product's packaging and yet the actual place of manufacture is listed in a much smaller font and on the underside of the box as 'Made in P.R.C.' (People's Republic of China).

This product's value proposition is clearly configured around German design rather than Chinese manufacturing.

Box 5.1: Value propositions, place and sustainability: Penguin biscuits and Tim Tams

Value propositions are created by people and reflect a combination of ideas developed in the past and a company's existing approach to managing a business. Can a value proposition be copied or is each firm's value proposition unique? The answer to this question is that they can be copied, but that a direct copy is impossible. Context is all-important and this includes every company's organizational and historic context and place. A value proposition is much more than a product. Copying a product/service will result in adjustments and ideally the outcome will be the development of a very different product/service. For example, Tim Tam is an Australian brand of chocolate biscuit that was first sold in 1964 by the Arnott's Group, an Australian producer of snack food and biscuits that was founded by William Arnott in 1865. During 1958, Ian Norris, the then Arnott Director of Food Technology went on a world tour to seek design and taste inspirations for the development of new products. This highlights the important role that learning from other places plays in new product development. A product developed and sold in one market can be identified and used to inspire a new product development process, and the outcome might be a brand new product. A localization process might produce a very different product rather than a copy. In Britain, Norris discovered the Penguin biscuit that had initially been developed by MacDonald Biscuits, a Glasgow-based biscuit company, in 1928. Penguin is now a McVitie's brand. But the Penguin biscuit had originally been inspired by a biscuit that MacDonald Biscuits had found on sale in Antwerp. Thus, there is a trail of place-based design inspiration that commenced in Antwerp and then led to Glasgow and onwards to Australia and elsewhere.

Norris liked the Penguin biscuit, which consists of two biscuits with a chocolate-cream filling that is then covered in chocolate, but he decided that it was possible to make a better version. In 1964, Arnott's introduced the Tim Tam biscuit, which consists of two malted biscuits separated by a hard chocolate filling and coated with a thin layer of textured chocolate. The name 'Tim Tam' was inspired by another travel experience; Ross Arnott had attended the 1958 Kentucky Derby and Tim Tam was the name of the winning horse. Tim Tams are made in Australia, with the packaging proclaiming that this is 'Australia's Favourite Cookie'. Arnott's began exporting them to the US in 2008 and officially to the UK in 2024. Prior to 2024, they were only available in the UK through specialist shops.

There are four different varieties of Penguin as its producer has sought opportunities to develop linked value propositions that take the form of brand stretching. Arnott's have applied a similar strategy. From the 2000s, different Tim Tam varieties have been produced, including limited editions. These varieties include dark chocolate, white chocolate, caramel, dark chocolate mint, honeycomb and choc orange. Additional product localization has occurred. In 2011, a cheese-flavoured variety was developed for the Indonesian market. Penguin and Tim Tam biscuits highlight the importance of value propositions and their monetarization. Producing product variants is one way of extending a product's reach and this includes developing products that are targeted at specific international markets. For Arnott's, a core challenge that has been set by the company is to ensure that by 2040, Tim Tams are produced by a net-zero emissions production process. For one of their Australian factories, this required the installation of 10,000 solar panels. The shift towards greener Tim Tams has multiple targets: 2040 – net zero in Arnott's own operations; 2050 – net zero across its value chain; and 100 per cent sustainable sourcing of key ingredients by 2035.

A copy then is rapidly integrated into a company's existing strategy and place-based settings and this process results in modifications to that which was copied and the emergence of a new value proposition, product and/or process.

An international business can be extremely complex as many different types of products and services can be created. A firm may have an overarching set of clearly articulated values, ethical principles or even a stated philosophy. These statements may underpin all the firm's value propositions or they may be comparatively disconnected from the products and services that are provided to customers. This type of disconnect reflects higher level and overarching ethical statements that may be difficult to directly relate to the firm's value propositions. Thus, a firm that claims that it always does what is right or what it promises might be difficult to hold to account as to who decides what is right or what has been promised. Einhell, for example, provides an account of the company's philosophy under the strapline 'Einhell – The high-performance Enablers'. The company then asks the question: 'But what does this mean?' (Einhell, 2024). The answer is: 'Whether it is for our customers in the product development or in the service or for our employees regarding flexibility and loyalty or for us as a company when we're working with our sales partners – we thrive to do our best to enable everything, so that everyone can participate in enjoyment and freedom.' This is a high-level philosophy that covers customers, employees and the company. For customers, it includes designing products that focus on customers' needs that includes 'customer-friendliness and a stable pricing policy'. For employees, this is defined as 'a company that stands for good work-life balance, fair compensation, employee development, flat hierarchy and a collaborative leadership style'.

Value propositions, sustainability and circularity

Sustainability is becoming increasingly important for consumers and businesses. Existing firms are shifting the configuration of their business models to include a concern with sustainability (see Box 5.2). New firms are forming with business models configured around value propositions that place sustainability at their core. These new forms of sustainable business models have value propositions that aim to craft sustainable solutions that make positive environmental, social and economic contributions. Value propositions are critical here as these include a very different approach to companies that are creating solutions in which sustainability is an afterthought or in which only some aspects of sustainability are incorporated into the value proposition.

Box 5.2: 'Alternative' value propositions and Framework Computer

Managing a business is all about balancing the tension between change and stability. A value proposition must alter in response to internal and external pressures. New value propositions can be added to an existing company with the outcome being some form of value proposition segmentation. Alternatively, new firms can be formed around what might initially be perceived to be radically alternative or disruptive value propositions. However, if these are successful, then they will be copied by others.

People matter in international business. New international businesses are being formed daily around the values of their founders. In January 2020, Nirav Patel established Framework Computer in San Francisco to produce laptops. This company's value proposition is configured around its commitment to the electronics right to repair movement and to designing products that last. Framework laptops are designed to be easily disassembled with the design and related value proposition prioritizing repairability and upgradability. The company also promotes open-source principles with its laptops designed around an Expansion Card system that is used to add features including USB ports. Every module within a Framework laptop has a QR code that provides access to support information, guides and replacement parts. Framework also provides a Marketplace where users can purchase replacement parts, and the tools required to repair and upgrade its laptops. Framework encourages an ecosystem to develop around its products that encourages partners to develop and sell modules that are compatible with its laptops. The company's value proposition is based on the understanding that the best approach to reducing the environmental impacts of electronics is to extend their life. In addition, Framework laptops are made from 50 per cent post-consumer recycled aluminium and around 30 per cent recycled plastic. Product packaging includes no single-use plastics. Individual components are purchased from different contract manufacturers predominantly located in Asia and transported to the main assembly site in Taiwan. Framework does not own manufacturing or fulfilment centres, and all these functions are outsourced.

Product obsolescence is central to all conventional business models as the expectation is that consumers will need to replace products that remain functional. Product obsolescence encourages products to be discarded and they may become waste. An alternative approach is for products to be designed for repairability, with repairs and upgrades producing additional revenue streams. Thus, there are different approaches to configuring business models. These include circular economy business models that are configured around designing out waste and designing for circularity or closed loops (Du et al, 2025). An alternative is based on developing a product platform that is modular, and this provides opportunities for consumers or other companies to repair and upgrade products.

Framework does not claim to be sustainable as it notes that no electronics device maker is sustainable. The company is aware that many consumer electronics firms have developed alternative value propositions and failed, but that a company's success is founded upon its products. In the language of business models, value propositions matter and the evolution of these value propositions is critical for a firm's long-term sustainability. Nevertheless, this is a company that is trying to develop an alternative approach to designing electronic devices.

Here it is important to reflect on change and value propositions. Thus, what constitutes a new or alternative value proposition? When does an alternative value proposition become conventional? How does an alternative approach change consumer behaviour and also impact on other company strategies?

Value propositions unlock three forms of value. First, there are use values or values-in-use that are unlocked that are directly related to the solution provided by the value proposition. Second, there are exchange values that are the outcome of a monetarization process of the value proposition's use value. Usually there is a direct relation between these two forms of value, with profitability representing a return on invested capital. Third, a value proposition may include what are termed non-monetary values or non-price-based values (see Chapter 4). These can include place-based associations as well as speed of availability, repairs and the availability of spare parts, recyclability and sustainability. Nevertheless, the literature here is confused as these non-price-based or non-monetary values may be directly linked to the price and/or a product's USP or value proposition. In other words, these non-monetary values can be monetarized and may be a critical dimension of a company's market positioning.

Every business model is unique, with different business models implementing very different approaches to sustainability. It is worth noting that a business model is dynamic, and this includes alterations to the value proposition and to product design, manufacturing and GVC configuration (Box 5.2). There is a tendency in the international business literature to isolate business processes. This can include focusing the analysis, for example, on sustainable international business model innovation, but framed within the context of international marketing (Chabowski et al, 2025). The difficulty here is that a sustainable value proposition requires the configuration of an approach that cuts across all aspects of a business. The starting point for a company should be the value proposition and a value proposition should not be equated with marketing. A truly sustainable or responsible business must be simultaneously sustainable in all business activity areas. A concern with applying some version of circular economy principles and practices could be part of this everyday enactment of responsible business practice. Nevertheless, circularity is only one approach to sustainability.

Business models and alterity

There is an important literature on alterity or alternatives to profit-centred approaches to configuring economic practice. In 1996, Gibson-Graham developed the case for alternative economic and political practices when they argued that: 'one must represent economic practice as comprising a rich diversity of capitalist and non-capitalist activities and argue that the non-capitalist ones had been relatively 'invisible' because the concepts and discourses that could make them 'visible' have themselves been 'marginalized and suppressed' (Gibson-Graham, 1996: xi).

This led to a rich body of literature that explores alternatives in the social economy, financial services, retail, work, exchange and employment spaces, lifestyles and the diverse economy (Fuller et al, 2010). Much of this debate highlights that there is no single approach to realizing solutions to societal challenges. In the language of business models, this is to acknowledge that value propositions can have very different configurations, with each configuration reflecting particular approaches to business practice. These different approaches may reflect the concerns of individual entrepreneurs and business owners. The key point is to accept that there is no single current way of practising business, but many alternative approaches coexist with one another. Alternative business practices include business models that are configured around circularity. Nevertheless, an innovative approach to configuring value propositions will initially appear to be simultaneously innovative and alternative but may eventually become a conventional approach.

Alternative business models include different approaches to ownership. An international business might be privately owned, a partnership, a private or public limited company, a not-for-profit organization or a cooperative. Cooperatives can be extremely innovative. For example, Stanford Federal Credit Union was established by a group of Stanford University employees in 1959. In 1994, this was the very first financial institution to offer online banking services. There are large worker cooperatives that are also international businesses. The Mondragon Corporation, for example, is a workers' cooperative with its headquarters located in the Basque region of Spain. This company has over 70,000 employees and has sales in more than 150 countries and operates in four areas: finance, industry, retail and knowledge. SACMI, the Italian multinational group, is another example, with this company manufacturing machines and complete plants. The company has branches in 28 countries. Worker cooperatives can also focus on local provision, with one of the best examples being the Uralungal Labour Contract Co-operative Society (ULCCS), which is the oldest worker cooperative based in India. This company was established in 1925 and is a total solution provider (TSP) for infrastructure development and management.

Multisided business models, financialization and alternative forms of monetarization

Business models constructed around circularity are designed to reduce waste and to ensure that any discarded materials retain value (Du et al, 2025). This is to avoid the production of waste. The 'waste' from one production process is the raw material input of another process. This is to highlight the importance of what are termed 'multisided business models'. These business models involve identifying two or more potential customer groups and designing and delivering goods or services that connect these two groups. There are two forms of such business models.

First, all business models have production processes that create waste; for example, heat, cold or materials. There are different approaches to dealing with waste. The most important is based on developing resource-efficient production processes that include a focus on lean production. Where waste is produced it can be discarded at a cost. An alternative is to convert discarded outputs into value by selling them to other customers and developing a market for production processes' waste products. These may be a form of indirect multisided business model as there is no direct connection between the two client groups.

Second, there are multisided platform business models, in which a company facilitates interactions between two distinct user groups with the platforms operating as intermediaries. In these business models, the platform tries to develop a relationship with two consumer groups and tries to make money from this combined process. Search engines are classic examples of such multisided platform business. Google, for example, provides free search services for all, but this search process creates data streams. Google monetarizes these data streams by obtaining revenue from targeted advertising and retailers. These are multisided business models as there are two sides to the model: producer-to-consumer relationships and producer-to-customer or client in the form of a commercial relationship with a retailer or advertiser. Consumers access these free services by donating their time and use of the platform to the platform's owner. Google then collects data from this process, and this is transformed into products/services that create additional revenue streams for the company.

There are different forms of multisided business model. Another type is based around financialization. This term describes a particular form of financial capitalism characterized by globalization, neoliberalism and the ascendancy of shareholder value. At the centre of financialization is a focus on the effective and efficient management of an organization's finances. At an extreme level, the financialization argument is that a company's dominant business model is configured around a value proposition, in which finance becomes an end in itself rather than an input to create innovative solutions to societal challenges (Epstein, 2005). One account of financialization argues that: 'American firms today make more money than ever before by simply moving money around, getting about five times the revenue from purely financial activities, such as trading, hedging, tax optimizing, and selling financial services, than they did in the immediate post-World War II period' (Foroohar, 2016: 5). Financialization is a central feature of international business as such firms have the opportunity and ability to generate financial returns on the configuration of cross-border transactions. Ultimately, financialization highlights the growing importance for some firms of profit accumulated through financial channels rather than from trade and commodity production. This can include a company setting aside a proportion of their profits to fund a share buy-back scheme with the outcome being an increase in the company's share price without any increase in the firm's productive capability or capacity. It also includes holding and investing profit offshore as part of a tax optimization strategy.

A company engaging in financialization develops a finance-focused business model that is configured around generating returns from the application of financial engineering. This can include engaging in land or property speculation as well as setting up departments that specialize in generating revenue from financial activities. One consequence from financialization is that there is a shift in the balance of non-financial firms' returns that accrue from financial initiatives. This includes firms investing in financial assets including land, stocks and bonds rather than solely focusing on investing in non-financial assets that are directly related to enhancing productive capability.

Ultimately, financialization can transform a firm's value proposition to one configured around investment returns. In 2005, Yahoo, the web service provider headquartered in California, acquired a 40 per cent stake in Alibaba in a deal valued at just over US$4 billion. Of this, US$1bn was in cash and Yahoo also added its China assets to the deal that were valued at US$700 million. This was a financial gamble as core elements of the Alibaba business were loss making in 2005. Nevertheless, the investment became one of the technology sector's most strategic investments with this stake valued at over US$80 billion in 2016. The problem for Yahoo was that its stake in Alibaba rapidly became more valuable than the firm's own struggling web business. Moreover, the company was faced with a major challenge as the sale of its stake in Alibaba would generate a substantial tax bill. For Yahoo, there was a paradox to solve in that the value that could be realized from selling its Alibaba stake in a tax-efficient manner was worth more than the financial returns being generated from Yahoo's core business. Yahoo had transitioned from being an innovative provider of web services to being a financial investor with one dominant asset.

Conclusion

All businesses have an explicit or implicit applied theory of business, business model or set of linked business models. A business model is driven by a set of motivations, and these may alter over time. New firms have formed around founder-defined approaches to sustainability or responsible business and extant businesses are adapting to consumer, government or sector concerns over sustainability. One of the cross-cutting themes that emerges in all discussions of business models and international business concerns the requirement for constant adaptation. This takes three forms. First, micro-foundational day-by-day adjustments, with many of these remaining invisible. These incremental adaptations may transform a business through a process of compound adaptation. Second, more strategic adaptations that are planned and intended to enhance the geographical reach and/or efficacy of a firm's business model. This might include operational adjustments or layering financialization initiatives on to a firm's existing product/service lines. Third, business model adaptation in response to plans to enter another host or foreign market. This is a complex process as all that might be required is an adjustment to a product's labelling. Alternatively, fundamental alterations might be required to a firm's product/service offering.

There have been two overarching cross-cutting themes explored in this chapter. On the one hand, the focus has been on developing a business model informed approach to international business. This highlighted some of the decisions that managers must make as they engage in business model innovation and adaptation. On the other hand, the analysis has highlighted that there is no one dominant business model, but that there are multiple alternative approaches to business model configuration. Part of this analysis has highlighted that a business model might be designed, or might emerge, from a set of linked decisions with the outcome being a business model that works in practice. Here it is important to differentiate between an academic debate on business model innovation and internationalization compared with the everyday practice of managing an international business. In the world of business practice, the only rules that apply to business model innovation are extremely general. A firm should have clarity regarding its motivation or fundamental driver and should also be aware that what works in one location might not work in another. Thus, place might matter and place-based adjustments might be required (see Chapter 7). The use of the word 'might' highlights that in some cases place will have no significant impact on the internationalization of a business model. In many other cases, understanding place and place-bounded consumers is the first challenge faced by a firm that wants to internationalize into a new market. All this means that establishing and running an international business is an exercise in the applied practice of contingency. In other words, effective international business management is contingent upon understanding the specificities of place and how these relate to a company's firm-based advantages and capabilities (see Chapter 6 and 7). Place, contingency, adaptation and firm-based advantages are all foundational elements in international business theory, and we now turn our attention to exploring these theories.

Key terms

Business model – describes how a business creates, delivers and captures all types of values.

Multisided business models – business models that are configured by indirectly connecting different customer or client groups together.

Value proposition – the unique offer that a business model provides to customers.

Recommended reading

Chabowski, B.R., Gabrielsson, P., Hult, G.T.M. and Morgeson III, F.V. (2025) 'Sustainable international business model innovations for a globalizing circular economy: a review and synthesis, integrative framework, and opportunities for future research', *Journal of International Business Studies*, 56: 383–402.

Evers, N., Ojala, A., Sousa, C.M. and Criado-Rialp, A. (2023) 'Unraveling business model innovation in firm internationalization: a systematic literature review and future research agenda', *Journal of Business Research*, 158: 113659.

Nilsson, A. and Robinson, D.T. (2018) 'What is the business of business?', *Innovation Policy and the Economy*, 18: 79–106.

References

Amit, R. and Zott, C. (2012) 'Creating value through business model innovation', *MIT Sloan Management Review*, 53(3): 41–9.

Baden-Fuller, C. and Morgan M. (2010) 'Business models', *Long Range Planning*, 43: 156–71.

Bellman, R., Clark, C., Craft, C., Malcolm, D.G. and Ricciardi, F. (1957) 'On the construction of a multi-stage, multi-person business game', *Operations Research*, 5(4): 469–503.

Borden, N.H. (1964), 'The concept of the marketing mix', *Journal of Advertising Research*, 4(2): 2–7.

Bryson J.R and Buttle M. (2005) 'Enabling inclusion through alternative discursive formations: the regional development of Community Development Loan Funds (CDLFs) in the United Kingdom', *The Service Industries Journal*, 25(2): 273–86.

Bryson, J.R. and Lombardi, R. (2009) 'Balancing product and process sustainability against business profitability: sustainability as a competitive strategy in the property development process', *Business Strategy and the Environment*, 18: 97–107.

Casadesus-Masanell, R., Ricart, J.E. and Tarziján, J. (2015) 'A corporate view of business model innovation', in N.J. Foss and T. Saebi (eds) *Business Model Innovation: The Organizational Dimension*, Oxford: Oxford University Press, pp 74–84.

Chabowski, B.R., Gabrielsson, P., Hult, G.T.M. and Morgeson III, F.V. (2025) 'Sustainable international business model innovations for a globalizing circular economy: a review and synthesis, integrative framework, and opportunities for future research', *Journal of International Business Studies*, 56: 383–402.

Chandler, A.D. (1977) *The Visible Hand: The Managerial Revolution in American Studies*, Cambridge: Harvard University Press.

Chesbrough, H. and Rosenbloom, R. (2010) 'The role of the business model in capturing value from innovation: evidence from Xerox Corporation's technology spin-off companies', *Industrial and Corporate Change*, 11(3): 529–55.

Drucker, P. (1994) 'The theory of the business', *Harvard Business Review*, September–October: 95–104.

Du, B., Bryson J.R. and Qamar, A. (2025) 'Aspiring towards automotive circularity: a critical review and research agenda', *Journal of Environmental Management*, 380: 125150.

Ehret, M. and Wirtz, J. (2015) 'Creating and capturing value in the service economy: the crucial role of business services in driving innovation and growth', in J.R. Bryson and P.W. Daniels (eds) *Handbook of Service Business: Management, Marketing, Innovation and Internationalisation*, Cheltenham: Edward Elgar, pp 129–45.

Einhell (2024) 'Our philosophy' [online]. Available from: www.einhell.com/einh ell-germany-ag/philosophy/ [Accessed 14 February 2024].

Epstein, G.A. (2005) 'Introduction: financialization and the world economy', in G.A. Epstein (ed.) *Financialization and the World Economy*, Cheltenham: Edward Elgar, pp 3–16.

Evers, N., Ojala, A., Sousa, C.M. and Criado- Rialp, A. (2023) 'Unraveling business model innovation in firm internationalization: a systematic literature review and future research agenda', *Journal of Business Research*, 158: 113659.

Foroohar, R. (2016) *Makers and Takers: The Rise of Finance and the Fall of American Business*, New York: Crown Business.

Foss, N.J. and Saebi, T. (2015) 'Business models and business model innovation: bringing organization into the discussion', in N.J. Foss and T. Saebi (eds) *Business Model Innovation: The Organizational Dimension*, Oxford: Oxford University Press, pp 1–23.

Friedman, M. (1970) 'The social responsibility of business is to increase its profits', *New York Times Magazine*, 13 September.

Fuller D., Jonas A.E. and Lee R. (eds) (2010) *Interrogating Alterity*, Farnham: Ashgate.

Gibson-Graham, J.K. (1996) *The End of Capitalism (As We Knew It): A Feminist Critique of Political Economy*, Oxford: Blackwell.

Jones, G.M. (1960) 'Educators, electrons, and business models: a problem in synthesis', *Accounting Review*, 35(4): 619–26.

Kene-Okafor, T. (2024) 'Nigeria's YC-based Chowdeck', *Tech Crunch* [online]. Available from: https://techcrunch.com/2024/04/30/chowdeck-hopes-to-scale-notoriously-tough-food-delivery-market/ [Accessed 19 September 2024].

Leih, S., Linden, G. and Teece, D.J. (2015) 'Business model innovation and organizational design: a dynamic capabilities perspective', in N.J. Foss and T. Saebi (eds) *Business Model Innovation: The Organizational Dimension*, Oxford: Oxford University Press, pp 24–42.

Levitt, T. (1958) 'The dangers of social responsibility', *Harvard Business Reviews*, 36(5): 41–51.

McCarthy, E.J. (1960) *Basic Marketing: A Managerial Approach*, Boston: Prentice-Hill.

Nilsson, A. and Robinson, D.T. (2018) "What is the business of business?", *Innovation Policy and the Economy*, 18: 79–106.

Rusten, G., Bryson, J. R. and Aarflot, U. (2007) 'Places through products and products through places: Industrial design and spatial symbols as sources of competitiveness', *Norsk Geografisk Tidsskrift – Norwegian Journal of Geography*, 61(3): 133–44.

Shvartsman, D. (2024) 'Apple Inc: facts and statistics, investing' [online]. Available from: www.investing.com/academy/statistics/apple-facts/ [Accessed 19 September 2024].

Teece, D. (2010) 'Business models, strategy and innovation', *Long Range Planning*, 43: 172–94.

Wirtz, B.W. (2011) *Business Model Management: Design – Instruments – Success Factors*, Wiesbaden: Gabler Verlag.

Zott, C. and Amit, R. (2008) 'The fit between product market strategy and business model: implications for firm performance', *Strategic Management Journal*, 29: 1–26.

Zott, C., Amit, R. and Massa, L. (2011) 'The business model: recent developments and future research', *Journal of Management*, 37(4): 1019–42.

6

International Business Theory and Responsible Business Practices

Introduction

Every business is engaged in a process that involves developing its own applied theory of business (see Chapter 5). These applied theories are taken for granted and informed by combinations of different types of learning. This includes academic and experiential learning. Nevertheless, these taken-for-granted theories would never be classified by academics as theories. However, it is important to remember that a theory should enhance understanding of some event or process. Applied theories are saturated with tacit knowledge. In business, practitioners are often unable to explain why a decision was made in a particular way. This is part of a process of reading a business that is intuitive; often, instinct is involved, but sitting behind instinct is tacit knowledge, or learning that is impossible to codify and transfer easily between people (Bryson et al, 2004) (see Chapter 1). Tacit knowledge is required to understand and produce explicit or codified knowledge. Thus, 'the ability to identify the most important information or to judge a bad idea from a good one requires tacit knowledge' (Bryson et al, 2004: 43).

International business theory has emerged as an important corpus of knowledge regarding the management and coordination of cross-border economic transactions. Applying this theory in practice is extremely challenging. These international business theories have been developed to understand a precisely defined business challenge, but the problem is that in the real world of business practice there are no precisely defined business challenges. All business decisions require an understanding, appreciation or awareness of likely impacts on other business processes and initiatives. A theory is a simplification of something that is inherently complex. This process includes assumptions that are made to simplify the theory development process, but such assumptions can never be applied in the real world of business practice. In Chapter 1, we emphasized that understanding a business is similar to reading. The experienced business practitioner will understand the vocabulary of business and its grammar and much of this understanding will take the form of tacit knowledge that has been informed by a combination of academic learning and experience. Every international business theory contributes vocabulary and grammar to understanding business, but applying these ideas in practice is much more challenging compared to discussing a case study. Our approach to reading a business developed into a framework consisting of four cross-cutting themes and eleven building blocks divided into three types: things, processes and facilitators (see Chapter 1). In this chapter we map this framework on to international business theory to identify intersections, gaps and opportunities. Our aim is not to provide a detailed review of these theories but to explore the contributions they make to understanding international business practice, and the challenge of applying them in practice. There is an important caveat to make. International business theory should never be considered as a corpus of best practice or even good practice. Applying this type of approach to business theory is far too restrictive. Many international business practitioners make decisions that involve hundreds of millions or even billions of dollars without any reference to academic theory. Some of these decisions result in failure and some would be considered counter to existing theory. Occasionally, new business practices emerge that challenge existing theory. This is an important point; theory is always backward-looking as it has been constructed upon research that has been undertaken in the past. There is, as we have argued in Chapter 1, timeless theory, but even these timeless theories might be rendered obsolete by business process innovations or radical alterations in consumer behaviour.

Frameworks and international business theory

Our framework outlined in Chapter 1 identifies four cross-cutting themes that underpin all business activity. This framework can be applied to all businesses, but our current focus is on applying this to international business. In this section, the framework's cross-cutting themes are mapped onto international business theory to identify the many contributions that have been made by this theory to understanding international economic transactions. However, we are also interested in gaps or areas where international business theory has nothing yet to contribute to understanding international business as practice and framed within a concern for responsibility. Our framework, whilst being very general, also seeks to provide an integrated approach to understanding international business.

Before we begin this process, it is important to set out some parameters for assessing theory. It is far too easy to criticize a theory for failing to enhance understanding of a process that falls outside the parameters set by the theory. Thus, the first question to ask of any theory is: What is the problem that the theory is trying to understand? This then should be followed by other questions that include:

- How does the theory relate to other theories and perspectives?
- When and where was the theory developed and does this impact on applicability?
- What assumptions are made by this theory?
- What is the theory's key contribution or contributions?

- In what ways does the theory support the practice of business management?
- In an applied sense, what are this theory's advantages and limitations?

There is a well-developed academic debate on international business and it includes a corpus of what can be labelled classical international business theory. There is an important critique of this literature that has questioned whether this research agenda is running out of steam (Buckley, 2002; Buckley and Lessard, 2005) or alternatively highlights difficulties with exploring big questions or grand challenges (Buckley et al, 2017). Part of this critique highlights the importance of learning new lessons from emerging economies (Anand et al, 2021) or alternative forms of international business, including criminal multinational enterprises (Buckley et al, 2024). One issue is that a form of conceptual path dependency has emerged with international business theory that tends to stifle innovation. Our concern in this book is with exploring the intersections between practice and theory but framed within an appreciation of responsibility. Responsibility goes hand in hand with accountability, but this raises the question of accountability to whom? Is this accountability to all stakeholders or to some subset? The relationship between accountability and responsibility depends on context and this includes regulation as well as place-based differences in stakeholder expectations. It also includes differences in the ways in which competing firms read context. Context always matters.

In the business and management literature, context is central to the contingency approach or theory (Child et al, 2003; McAdam et al, 2019). Contingency theory suggests that 'the performance of two companies with identical sets of objectives will be determined by the quality of their adjustment to prevailing contingencies' (Child, 1975: 25). This is to distinguish between the universal applicability of theories compared to the particular or the ways in which one firm reads and responds to situational variables. Contingency theory includes environmental contingencies that are external to firms and internal contingencies, and these include the ability of a firm to respond to context based on factors such as size, governance structure, motivation, strategic partnerships and existing assets.

Our international business framework is not a theory but instead is meant to outline the core building blocks and cross-cutting themes that are involved in everyday business practice. Theory then is overlaid onto our framework to identify how this informs understanding of international business and business practice. There is a caveat here in that an international business theory may enhance understanding of a business process, but it does not necessarily have to support business decision-making processes. Our view is that business theory, and international business theory, highlights some relationships or intersections that practitioners should consider, but such theory does not offer solutions. This is to differentiate between the role theory plays in informing understanding and the context within which decision-making processes occur. Thus, international business theory alerts practitioners and students to the questions and issues that need to be addressed, but any solution is context dependent. The contextual nature of the business decision-making process offers opportunities for innovation to occur and sometimes this might be disruptive innovation. One of the most important aspects related to context is motivation and this is the starting point for our approach to understanding international business practice.

Motivation

Our framework begins by identifying four cross-cutting themes that we now map onto international business theory. The first is motivation. Motivation is initially an internal state that is configured around the goal-directed behaviour of an individual. The concept of motivation is used to explain why people initiate, continue, engage with, or end some type of behaviour at a particular time. Motivation is influenced by experience, background, education, personality, time and place. Peer pressure contributes to an individual's motivation. Socialization processes are also important, founded upon agents who play an important role in the ways in which individuals learn and internalize cultural norms, beliefs and behaviours (Morawski, 2014). These agents include family, friends, education, media and religious institutions. Socialization is a lifelong process that commences at birth and ends with death. There are many types of socialization, with primary socialization occurring in childhood with the emphasis being on learning societal norms, values and behaviours (Crisogen, 2016). There is also positive socialization, which involves processes that encourage individual conformism to a group or society. In addition, there is adaptive socialization based on an individual acquiring the personal capabilities to enable social participation. Resocialization involves the process of abandoning existing roles and learning new roles. For business and management, primary socialization provides the foundations that result in the challenge of managing across borders or managing individuals that have been socialized into very different ways of engaging with the world. Understanding differences in primary socialization outcomes, including motivations, is a core challenge for international business managers. However, it is important not to overlook organizational socialization or the processes by which new employees learn attitudes, behaviours and values required to become effective members of the group – the company – they have joined. The employee selection process is one that seeks to map an individual's motivations and learnt social norms and values onto those of the organization.

International business theory has very little to contribute about primary socialization, but does indirectly engage with organizational socialization in theories that explore 'internalization' or the processes by which information is transmitted within organizations. This is an interpersonal process involving the creation of an enabling and supporting organizational culture. Thus, Buckley and Casson argued that 'there is special reason for believing that internalization of the knowledge market will generate a high degree of multinationality among firms. Because knowledge is a public good which is easily transmitted across national boundaries, its exploitation is logically an international operation' (Buckley and Casson, 1976: 45). This is an important issue as a core international business challenge involves cross-border organizational socialization to try to ensure that employees follow similar motivations. In the world of everyday management practice, enhancing cross-border internalization involves common recruitment and training processes, developing and sharing common traditions, heritage and history as well as temporarily relocating people between branch offices/plants. Thus, international businesses relocate employees around their branch networks as part of this organizational socialization process (Bryson and Rusten, 2008).

This training is an important part of developing individuals with the potential to occupy senior management positions within an international business. There is an added complication to consider. These are the organizational challenges that come from employing non-native speakers. Language is central to communication. English has emerged as one of the most important business languages. The implication being that many non-native speakers must learn to cope, and even more than cope, with working and living through the medium of a second language (Śliwa and Johansson, 2014; Couper and Piekkari, 2025). There are implications here for recruitment and training and also for individuals as they learn to adapt to the challenge of being a non-native speaker.

Motivation is indirectly dealt with by international business theory. This is unfortunate, but then motivation is a complex psychological phenomenon. In John Dunning's eclectic paradigm of Ownership, Location and Internalization, or the OLI, motivation is considered as a group or firm-level issue. This is understandable as most international business theory, including the OLI, focuses on understanding firms or organizations rather than people (Casson and Li, 2022). Here it is important to remember that firms do not make decisions, but rather decisions are made by people employed by firms. People have very varied motivations. Thus, a manager may be driving a new product development process or entry into a new market to support their career ambitions rather than to support the long-term interests of the company. There is often a hidden misalignment between individual motivations and the group, or collective motivation. This is to highlight that decision-making is always a culturally, politically, and individually inflected process.

Dunning's Ownership, Location and Internalization (OLI) paradigm is an important framework for identifying and evaluating the factors that influence all types of foreign direct investment (FDI) (Dunning, 1988). Here it is important to appreciate that this paradigm is very limited in scope as the focus is only on understanding processes that sit behind a company's decision to enter foreign markets. This is called the 'eclectic paradigm' as Dunning's motivation was to bring different theories together. The OLI has a very restricted engagement with motivation. The reality is much more complex as a business seeks to become international as it is motivated by a desire for market expansion, diversification, to access resources (talent, government subsidies), to enhance the firm's competitive advantage, to achieve some type of optimization, for learning, responding to client demands, in response to government incentives, or in response to sector or global trends. In addition, there might be a desire for a company to enhance its status by becoming an international business. All these are very standard business motivations that are driven by a search for additional profits, and this includes optimization with a focus on stripping out costs.

An alternative international business theory is the Uppsala model, which is a staged model, intended to explain how companies expand internationally based upon learning from experience or experiential learning (Johanson and Vahlne, 2009). Thus, a company becomes international through configuring a sequence of investments in other countries. This sequence is explained by a firm gradually acquiring increased market knowledge that is then related to increased market commitment. Sitting behind the Uppsala model is a concern with understanding a company's internal characteristics and its motivations to invest in other countries. This approach distinguishes between the most rational decision – which would be for a company to invest in a country with the most favourable conditions – compared with a decision that reflects bounded rationality. The outcome is that a company seeks initially to invest not in the best location, but instead in the location that best meets the company's existing learning and characteristics. This then is a pragmatic theory based on the application by firms of a step-by-step approach to internationalization. Here it is important to appreciate that companies internationalize at different speeds as they transition from exporting to establishing facilities in target foreign markets.

Value

The second cross-cutting theme in our framework is value. In this book, we devote two chapters to exploring all types of conventional and alternative values and international business (see Chapters 4 and 5). To us, value is everything and is a fundamental driver behind all business decisions. There is a paradox here in that international business theory has very little to say about value. Value is too often assumed with the implicit definition being one based around profit maximization and reflecting approaches to value developed in neoclassical economics (Cairns and Śliwa, 2017). There is a major research gap in international business theory that revolves around how this literature treats value. This is especially important as international businesses seek to engage more explicitly with configuring practices deemed responsible and which engage with ongoing environmental, societal and governance (ESG) concerns.

Some readers might disagree with our analysis of the strange omission of a concern with value in international business. However, let us take three examples. In 1988, Dunning published a restatement of the eclectic paradigm (Dunning, 1988). The term 'value' occurs 16 times in this paper. It is never defined, with this word being used in two ways. First, there are six mentions of 'value-added'; for example as in value-added chain or low or high value-added activities. These remain undefined and there is no indication of what these value-added activities might be and what differentiates one from the other. The term value is then used in a very general manner; for example as in 'once the value of the relevant parameters is known' (Dunning, 1988: 14). Second, a paper published in 1999 explores if the eclectic framework is descriptive or normative. This paper uses the term 'value' only three times and only to describe the 'value' of quantitative measures (Brouthers et al, 1999). Third, a paper published in 2022 explores complexity and international business theory (Casson and Li, 2022). This paper argues that international business is inherently complex given that it involves managing across many countries, products and technologies, the complexities related to international transport and communications, cultural and political diversity and speed and unpredictable change. However, the paper only uses the word 'value' once.

Managing international business involves explicit decisions about value and also implicit assumptions about value. These decisions regarding value are enveloped by motivation. The practice of international business as responsible business is one that hinges around a discussion that sits at the intersection between a debate on motivation and one on value. It is unfortunate that the international business literature has very little to contribute to this discussion. The key point to reflect on is that business managers have choices, and these choices include those related to implementation. A manager, even a chief executive officer, may inherit a firm's existing aims, mission statement and motivation and may have limited ability to alter these. However, the key issue revolves around how a firm's motivations are implemented. This is an important issue for all readers of this book to reflect upon.

Practice and conventions

Managing an international business involves strategy that is enacted through routines, practices, processes and conventions. International business theory tends to ignore these. There is a new concern with what are defined as micro-level processes, and practice as a bottom-up process. These processes include practices of bricolage or improvisation (Vale et al, 2021). The argument is that the business model literature has focused on conceptualizations and descriptions of business models rather than on understanding how new business models emerge and are implemented. This process of emergence and implementation has much to do with micro-level processes rather than strategic planning. There is much in common here with evolutionary economic geography that has emphasized the importance of understanding routines and the ways in which these act as constraints on companies, but also how changes in micro-level processes can transform businesses.

A routine is an everyday practice, and such practices might be prescribed by an organization and supported by explicit rules and conventions and this includes training. Alternatively, a routine may be a business micro-level process that has emerged from employees improvising and adapting or developing firm-level practices to support delivery of a company's values-in-use. Routines take many forms and include those that are known by management, those that are known by management but are not acknowledged as official or prescribed practice, and those that are unknown or hidden from management. The important point is that these routines and practices may experience trivial and non-trivial changes and, combined, such changes over time can result in transformational change. There is an important point to reflect upon, in that this type of bottom-up process might challenge a company's current approach concerning responsible business or corporate social responsibility.

A routine or practice is coupled with resources and capabilities. Organizations compete on the basis of routines, and these include those that relate to managing internationalization and the challenge of working across borders. Hidden behind international business theories like the OLI, Uppsala and the Springboarding approach are a host of routines, and it is differences in routines and practices that differentiate one firm from another. These micro-level differences can explain international business failure based on a company's inability to alter routines to fit the needs of a specific context. This can be considered to engage with international business theory that focuses on internalization or the 'I' in the OLI (Buckley, 1988). Nevertheless, internalization tends to be treated as a meso-level process rather than as an outcome of micro-level processes, but there are some exceptions. Weeks and Galunic (2003), for example, argue that a company's internalization, or shared identity that emerges across employees working for a firm, develops by members of the firm learning routines that are part of the firm's behaviour or approach to everyday practice. This bottom–up micro-level process includes practices that support the development of a shared intra-firm cultural mode of thought that includes ideas, beliefs, assumptions, values, interpretative schema and know-how. These everyday practices are critical for ensuring that attitudes and approaches to enacting responsible business as an everyday practice are shared between employees.

These micro-level processes or routines are defined as 'settled and repeated patterns of behaviour that may both enable and constrain firm behaviour. Routines that constrain may prevent firms from innovating and replacing or modifying existing routines. Some routines become a form of mindless or passive behaviour in which existing procedures prevent a firm from learning and innovation' (Bryson and Ronayne, 2014: 472–3). Routines and practices are path dependent with decisions made in the past influencing and often determining behaviour in the present with the implication being that 'routines may prevent change and lead to firm failure through path dependency' (Bryson and Ronayne, 2014: 475). All international business practitioners must be sensitive to understanding how routines and the everyday enactment of international business practice support the development and implementation of a firm's international ambitions. Routines and practice really matter, but these micro-level processes are not well understood by international business theories that tend to focus on the level of the firm rather than with understanding the interactions between macro- and micro-level processes.

Conventions are another form of practice. Sector conventions emerge that reflect isomorphic pressures for firms within a sector to enact business in a similar manner (see Chapter 1). Such conventions may be in response to government regulation or expectations set by the finance sector (Mulhall and Bryson, 2014). Financial services play an often unacknowledged role in shaping sector conventions. An excellent example comes from the role played by insurance companies who set, regulate and limit sector- and economy-wide practices regarding acceptable levels of risk (Billing and Bryson, 2019). Insurance conventions regarding risk can limit innovation and inhibit change.

Change/evolution

The fourth cross-cutting theme in our framework is change/evolution. The geoeconomy is always changing being the outcome of the interactions between things, processes and facilitators (our building blocks). As each of these are dynamic, the geoeconomy can be characterized as always being in a state of becoming. This presents challenges for academics and practitioners. Academics seek to understand the global economy by developing theories to 'read' it and this includes frameworks that are created to understand and explain the actions of firms and other actors. Practitioners are less concerned with total explanation, rather focusing on collecting and analysing current information to inform decision-making and strategy. A key concern for both, however, is how to do either of these things while the object of study is changing and evolving.

Dunning's (1988) eclectic paradigm is a core international business framework. It seeks to explain the conditions under which a firm will leave its home market, identifying location, ownership and internalization factors. This theory has been widely applied within international business (see Chapter 7) but is not without critique. One of the primary areas of criticism is around the static nature of this theory. It understands only a single moment of time in a firm's history, isolating instances of internationalization in which the firm is a single, bounded rational entity searching the global for an internationalization opportunity. While it does provide a basis for understanding internationalization motivations, it does not help us understand what happens after the initial internationalization event, nor explain disinvestment or multiple forms of market entry that happen concurrently. The theory does not claim to do this for us, but as we try to understand international business as a whole, a more dynamic approach is needed.

Emerging from a critique of Dunning's eclectic paradigm, Johanson and Vahlne's (2009) Uppsala model explicitly attempts to integrate change into internationalization. Based on initial observation of Swedish small and medium sized enterprises, the model has since been applied to international firms. The model focuses on learning within firms, acknowledging that internationalization is a process through which firms gain knowledge and expertise. Their 'establishment chain' plots out the incremental stages that a firm may go through as it develops its internationalization strategy – typically starting with exporting, then other market entry forms such as strategic alliances before conducting FDI in overseas markets. The Uppsala model also incorporates a geographical dimension, suggesting that firms are more likely to internationalize to geographically or culturally proximate locations before entering more distant markets.

The response of international businesses to change and evolution is to learn. Knowledge acquisition and strategy development become central to responding to uncertainty. These factors are implicit in Dunning's eclectic paradigm – considered in the internalization factor in terms of how firms configure their supply networks; in the ownership factor through consideration of how firms are positioned versus domestic firms; and in the location factor through which locations (typically countries) hold particular resources and opportunities. Thus, firms collect knowledge, but in Dunning's framework that knowledge is applied in a singular moment in time to one market entry. For practitioners the reality is likely to be very different with knowledge acquired over time and through a series of new market entries. The Uppsala model allows us to understand the sequential accumulation of knowledge over time, although there is increasing evidence of firms developing strategies to 'leap forward' in their learning (see, eg, born global firms). What is currently absent from the contemporary international business literature is a complete framework to understand how firms, and the practitioners of which the firms are composed, learn and enter new markets over time. The literature is also relatively silent on overlapping internationalization (entering several new markets at the same time), multiple internationalization (using multiple market entry methods in one new market) and disinvestment from markets.

Building blocks

Our framework identifies three sets of buildings blocks: things, processes and facilitators that must be considered in the context of the cross-cutting themes that we have just explored. We now explore these building blocks by initially focusing on things.

Things

Companies/firms

All academics, policy makers and practitioners interested in firms apply either an implicit or explicit definition of a firm. There are many alternative ways of defining firms. International business theories that are influenced by neoclassical economic theory tend to define firms as being goal-directed, profit-searching and profit-driven entities (Cairns and Śliwa, 2017). This includes an emphasis on optimization. Thus, the OLI is all about assessing the interactions between three processes – ownership advantages, locational advantages and internalization or intra-firm processes – with the objective being for firms to make the best decisions defined as those that will create the most profit. Similarly, Buckley and Casson's internalization theory includes the postulate, or assumption, that firms try to maximize profits in a world of imperfect markets (Buckley and Casson, 1976). There is nothing inherently wrong with assuming that a firm will seek to maximize profits, but the reality is very different. There are many different firm-level approaches, and these include alternative definitions and measures of business performance (see Chapter 4). These include companies that are focused on capital appreciation rather than revenue generation and also boards of directors who focus on share price and this includes the application of a form of financialization that involves share buy-back schemes (see Chapters 1 and 5). Buying back shares increases share prices, but has no impact on productivity, operations or production processes.

There are many ways of defining a firm. In 1937, Coase developed an answer to the question of 'Why do firms exist?' His answer was based on the costs related to acquiring information to inform decisions regarding production processes (Coase 1937). Thus, to Coase, firms exist because there are costs related to market-based transactions and when these costs exceed the cost of intra-firm production then a firm, or the internal hierarchy of an organization, will in principle be used to undertake this activity. This market-versus-hierarchy approach led to transaction cost economics or a concern with understanding when outsourcing versus insourcing approaches are applied by firms.

One way of defining firms is to identify their characteristics (see Bryson et al, 2022: 5). These include:

- profit-seeking and this might include attempts to maximize profit;
- companies that follow a triple bottom line with a concern for creating positive environmental and societal impacts or with limiting negative impacts;
- decision-making under uncertainty;
- rules, rituals, routines, habits and conventions;
- learning, knowledge creation and transfer, and innovation;
- employee recruitment, training and performance management;
- corporate activity systems – operations management, sales and marketing, accounts, human resource management, procurement, supply chain management, corporate governance, etc;
- improvisation under uncertainty;
- bounded rationality and information asymmetry;

- path dependency linked to sunk costs; and
- managing risk versus reward.

Firms are also legal entities that can negotiate written and unwritten contracts and can also initiate and be recipients of legal challenges. Firms are also legal structures, and this defines the boundaries of any one firm for legal and tax collection purposes. Of course, taxation leads to appreciating how firms engage in financial engineering to minimize their exposure to taxation, including strategies involving cross-border manipulation of profits.

An alternative approach is to place people at the centre of any definition of a firm. In this approach, this includes the exploitation of others, including those working for firms being directly or indirectly involved in modern-day slavery, or the severe exploitation of other people for commercial gain, including sexual abuse and sexual harassment and other types of discriminatory and exclusionary behaviour. A people-centred definition of firms involves understanding the ways in which people come together for a temporary period to control and coordinate assets. This includes negotiating and enforcing contracts and coordinating intra- and inter-firm relationships with people and other organizations. Central to this type of approach is understanding how a collective works together to achieve some type of shared purpose. But how is this purpose defined and implemented? The emphasis in international business theory is very much driven by profit motivations, and yet profit is not everything in the world of business and it is not even mostly everything as there are many other motivations behind business decision-making processes.

Motivation is of critical importance for business practitioners and scholars. Thus, the primary role of 'a firm' is to 'direct and align perception, understanding, and evaluation by the people connected with it' (Nooteboom, 2000: 71). Profit-seeking is downplayed in this definition, but this statement raises important questions for the coordination of perceptions across an international business. This then links to the OLI and this approaches concern with intra-firm processes. Definitions matter and should be explicit.

For practitioners, there are some firm characteristics that must be central to an applied definition of a firm. One such definition is that:

a firm is in a continual process of becoming, adaptation or evolution – it never becomes – and this process involves the temporary ownership or control of a bundle of assets by a group of individuals to coordinate tasks leading to the production of products/services. This places operational dynamics at the center of our definition, whilst acknowledging that firms have bounded rationality and are simultaneously cultural, social, political and knowledge processing entities. (Vanchan et al, 2018: 100)

People and their capabilities are central to this definition, including constraints on decision-making processes and an appreciation that all companies are in a continual state of change and transition.

Money

International business theory heavily engages with money, and ultimately, the pursuit of profit and profit maximization drives the activities of international business. In international business, money is perceived as a critical tool for facilitating global trade and achieving profit maximization. Money serves several functions. Money allows companies to exchange goods and services across borders efficiently. It provides a standardized unit of value that is universally accepted, making transactions easier and more transparent. Money can be saved and accumulated over time and then can be used to make future purchases or investments. This enables companies to plan for future growth and expansion. Money serves as a common unit of measurement for valuing goods, services and assets. This allows companies to compare prices, calculate profits and losses and make informed business decisions. Money can be invested in various financial instruments, such as stocks, bonds and currencies. This allows international companies to generate returns on their capital through financialization and expand their international business operations. Although money is a fundamental tool in achieving their financial goal by enabling companies to efficiently conduct transactions, manage resources and invest in growth opportunities, it is important to note that while profit maximization is a key objective for international business companies, it is not the only factor that international businesses need to consider. Other factors that we emphasize in Chapter 4, such as social responsibility and long-term sustainability play a significant role in decision-making processes by people who work for these organizations. All international businesses must consider the interests of various stakeholders, including employees, customers, consumers, suppliers, communities and the environment. A narrow focus on profit maximization can neglect these non-financial factors. For these reasons, a holistic approach is essential for successful and responsible international business practice.

Too often money, however, is the invisible presence in international business theory. By this, we mean that money as a core shaper of corporate decision-making processes is overlooked or even ignored. Decisions over money, its flow and its intersection with territory and place really matter. Both the OLI and springboarding approaches (Luo and Witt, 2022) make no contribution regarding money and decisions regarding money (but see Hu et al, 2025). Yet in the world of international business, money is not everything, but, for all decisions involving internationalization, it is almost everything. Money matters, and also intersects with territory. For example, in 2024, Superdry, the British clothing company, argued that Shein, a core rival, was being allowed by governments to compete based on a strategy that enabled it to 'dodge tax', and that this provided Shein with an unfair advantage (Harris, 2024). Shein's business model highlights that corporate strategy, or business model innovation, involves the simultaneous alignment of multiple business activity areas. This type of alignment is not covered by existing international business theory. Thus, Shein's fast fashion business model includes drop-shipping direct to consumers. Superdry is charged import duties on the clothing that it imports in bulk into a country like the UK whilst Shein avoids such duties. For the UK, this means that Shein can ship clothing directly to consumers with each parcel being worth less than £135 and both Shein and its consumers avoid paying import duties. A company like Shein can then develop a billion-pound turnover business in the UK without paying any UK tax. Shein is an excellent example of a new type of business model based around configuring a different relationship between the company, production and consumers.

International business theory must pay much more attention to tax and trade tariffs. There are many issues for practitioners to consider. These include decisions regarding a company's registration, or the place where its effective management is located, as this has implications for where a company pays corporate income tax. Companies can make decisions regarding locating in a tax-friendly jurisdiction. There are also tax and tariff loopholes that can be exploited.

In January 2025, Donald Trump was inaugurated as the 47th President of the United States. One of his actions has been to stop low-value products being shipped tax-free to the US under the so-called *de minimis* exception. This exception allowed international exporters to ship packages worth less than US\$800 inspection and duty-free into the US. The *de minimis* provision was introduced in 1938 and was intended to ease trade and reduce the burden on consumers, but the threshold increased over the years. This exception 'evolved from a measure intended primarily to promote fiscal efficiency for the benefit and convenience of the U.S. Government to one that was also intended to promote trade for the benefit and convenience of businesses, consumers, and the US economy' (Casey, 2025: 6). Between 2013 and 2023, the number of *de minimis* entries to the US increased from approximately 120 million to 685 million. It was estimated that there had been more than 1 billion *de minimis* shipments to the US in 2024 (Casey, 2025). Trump's alteration to *de minimis* impacts the business models of companies like Temu and Shein. One consequence would be goods delayed in customs and additional costs for consumers. One response would be for these firms to expand their US warehouses and to export goods in bulk to the US. Customers would still have to pay import taxes, but more jobs would be created in the US.

People

International business theory has developed as a firm-centred set of theories in which the object of study is firms rather than people. In many theories, decision-makers are assumed, overlooked or considered to be rational decision-makers making informed decisions. This reflects theories that are influenced by neoclassical economics that assumes that businesses seek to maximize profits, that consumers make rational decisions that are driven by a concern with maximizing utility, and that people make decisions based on being able to access perfect information defined as all the relevant information required to make an informed decision (Cairns and Śliwa, 2017). Neoclassical approaches assume that investors will seek to maximize their investment returns and this is assumed to be responsible behaviour as long as profit-maximizing firms are law abiding. Subsequently, an investor can decide to allocate part of their investment returns in line with their views on socially responsible investment behaviour (see Chapter 5).

International business theory tends to overlook or even ignore human resource (HR) functions, and this includes exploring cross-culture or cross-border employee engagement practices. These include approaches to on-boarding, training and staff development and appraisal, and these processes must be placed within territory-specific regulations and conventions. HR professionals apply and impose approaches to managing people that play a central role in international business. Nevertheless, approaches to HR practices developed in a firm's home nation may inform practices throughout the company. Some firms outsource defined HR activities to intermediaries, and this includes, for example, internship and graduate recruitment programmes, as well as the recruitment of very senior employees through subcontracting this task to companies that specialize in executive search or head hunting.

One of the issues with international business theory is the lack of clarity regarding who within an organization should be responsible for decision-making. The challenge is that decision-making occurs at different levels and ranges from micro-level everyday operational decisions to strategic decisions that shape the future direction of a company. A key issue then is who should take a decision and where they should be located. Should decision-makers be centralized or decentralized? The decision-maker is the most granular level of analysis and it is also the one that is most overlooked in debates on international business theory. The danger is that the international business literature tends to 'assume that firms and not people are the principal actors in IB' (Casson, 2018: 386). This assumption highlights that international business theory's focus is not to inform everyday practice within firms but instead is intended to inform a more academic debate on international business.

International business theory, whilst being heavily influenced by neoclassical approaches, does relax some of these assumptions. Hymer's seminal work on multinational enterprises (MNEs) shifted the research focus away from a concern with international exchange or trade to one based on understanding MNEs as the 'institution for international production' (Dunning and Rugman, 1985: 228). In this account, Hymer relaxed two neoclassical assumptions. Thus, the 'MNE is a creature of market imperfections' (Dunning and Rugman, 1985: 229), and this also includes replacing assumptions regarding being able to access free knowledge with an appreciation that decision-makers will have access to proprietary knowledge.

It is important to return people to the centre of international business theory and this is especially the case in discussions regarding the relationship between such theory and the practice of responsible business. There are two points to consider here. On the one hand, there is the well-known complication of managing across borders. This includes the emphasis that the Uppsala model places on firm-level learning regarding foreign territories and psychic distance. Psychic distance includes cultural, economic and to some extent geographical distance and the ways in which these are understood and perceived between decision-makers located in a firm's home market compared to a target foreign market (Johanson and Vahlne, 1977). On the other hand, international business theory is too concerned with profit maximizing behaviour and tends to overlook that individual decision-makers have multiple motivations and concerns. These include varied interpretations of applied corporate social responsibility. In addition, primary socialization is a place-inflected process, and this explains many of the challenges related to managing across borders.

There are important intersections between people, things, territory and culture. This includes dynamics or evolution as some of the dimensions of this intersection can change rapidly. The international business as responsible business framework that was outlined in Figure 1.1 does not explicitly highlight the importance of culture. Culture could be included as another cross-cutting theme; culture is place- and people-based and can be conceptualized within territory. Place-based differentials matter, and these include differences in lifestyles, the projection of individual and group identity and the ways in which individuals relate to one another. Social media can alter group dynamics as subgroups can rapidly form that seek to set new agendas and it can also alter consumer behaviour. It is important to appreciate that rapid change can occur; classical international business theory tends to ignore this type of rapid change that can alter some of the dynamics of the intersections between people, place and international business. Such a moment of change can represent a discontinuity that represents a break with the previous 'normal'. An excellent example is the Chinese Guochao movement (Pattinson, 2023). This word can be translated as 'national trend' or as 'Chinese chic' and reflects a shift in Chinese consumers preferring Chinese brands that promote and celebrate Chinese cultural identity (Danziger, 2023). This highlights the important relationship that can exist between product or service design and place (Bryson and Rusten, 2011) with place-based associations being inscribed in physical goods and services (Rusten et al, 2007). Alternatively, this could be conceptualized as a form of deglobalization or reverse globalization or as a form of economic nationalism or economic patriotism. Nevertheless, 'guochao' is associated with Chinese consumers seeking products and brands that reflect their Chinese identity. This preference has been promoted through social media, on live streaming platforms and by influencers and this has supported the development of a shared sense of national unity and patriotism. Chinese brands and companies have risen to the challenge and guochao brands have increased their market share.

The guochao movement highlights that products, and product design processes, are central to all businesses, but that international businesses must pay attention to the importance of localization processes that can respond rapidly to alterations in place-based consumer behaviour (Rusten et al, 2007). In response to the guochao wave, international businesses who have been selling in China have had to enhance product and service localization (see Chapter 7) (Danziger, 2023). This includes incorporating Chinese elements into their products and services and related marketing campaigns. Companies have introduced regional-specific features that highlight localized aspects of Chinese culture and have also provided localized services. This also includes partnering with Chinese celebrities.

There are many ways of conceptualizing the guochao movement. One way is to consider this as a localized product/service development process that enhances a product's unique selling proposition. It also increases a product's values-in-use and removes or dilutes any liability of foreignness that might be associated with a brand. An alternative perspective is to consider this as a form of distributed product development process that comes with opportunities for learning to spread around a company's geographic footprint (Bryson and Rusten, 2011). Thus, a product alteration developed for the Chinese market might have value in other territories. This type of hybridization design process that blends local Chinese culture with international aesthetics represents an opportunity for Chinese firms, and also for foreign firms selling in China, to develop a new design idiom. The outcome might be a wave of guochao-inspired products that are sold internationally. The guochao wave highlights the intersection between people, products and place, and it is to place that we now turn our attention.

Place

Despite many international business activities being predicated on the exploitation of differences between places, place is often implicit rather than explicit in theories and frameworks. Dunning's eclectic paradigm does highlight location as one of its three central tenets, but this is arguably the least developed relative to ownership and internalization. Dunning treats place as a variable in his conditions for internationalization, viewing nation-states as the containers of resources that firms are seeking to access and exploit. Places may provide markets for goods, and/or the resources needed to produce them. Much attention has been paid to developing Dunning's ownership advantages, with scholars differentiating between different types of ownership advantage. That debate has been well-developed, but there has been only a simpering discussion of geography and place with regard to the location factor.

International business has increasingly acknowledged the importance of geography, primarily with regard to the broader context in which economic activities are located. International business scholars have engaged in some dialogue with economic geographers (see, for example, Cook et al, 2018), primarily through their observation of two geographical shifts in the global economy. First, the emergence or revitalization of clusters of activities and second, the increased global dispersion of activities conducted within value chains and coordinated by multinational firms (Cantwell, 2009). International business theory has begun to acknowledge that local contexts continue to retain their distinctive differences and that international firms face growing challenges in managing the complexity of their interactions across space or between places (Meyer et al, 2011). This has been increasingly apparent in how innovation processes are understood (see Cano-Kollmann et al, 2016, and the innovation building block in this chapter). Still though, this work views the firm as the primary unit of analysis, examining how firms must balance their interconnections within their own firm network with external connections to host markets. This reflects the preponderance of international business to focus on international firms through their headquarters and subsidiaries.

One key area in which international business theory does make a series of distinctions between firms based on place is through the categorization of markets. Adopting broader framings of markets as 'emerging', 'developing', 'advanced', 'developed' or 'transitioning', international business theory has paid particular attention to emerging market multinational firms. The historical dominance of large multinational firms originating in North America, Western Europe and Japan has shifted, resulting in increasing attention being paid to emerging multinational enterprises (EMNEs) by international business (Luo and Witt, 2022). This distinction serves to highlight the rise of international firms from markets such as China, Japan and Brazil. Thus, we can observe that international business has paid some attention to place, insofar as the international scope of firm operations provides the raison d'être for the subdiscipline to exist. This has rarely translated into the development of a deeper understanding of the complexities of space and place in conceptual terms, or of the multiple scales over which we can observe firms interacting with place. We explore place-based differentials in Chapter 7.

Territory

We can also understand firm operations occurring over territories. These are more defined spaces that are specific, bounded geographical spaces (compared to the more fluid nature of space and place). Territories are owned and governed by particular actors (typically governments of different scales, but this can include other actors such as the military, a religious body or private individuals). International business does not typically examine territories, using the term 'place' when it does consider spatial dynamics. Dunning's eclectic paradigm overlooks territories, focusing instead on the nation-state as the container of location advantages. Economic geography offers some insights into the role of space and place in shaping the transformation of firms and industries and the impact of firms on places. Dicken and Malmberg (2001) observe the mutually constitutive relationships between firms and territories, which they term the 'firm-territory nexus'. This views firms, industrial systems and territories as three major dimensions of this nexus, which is itself embedded in the overall macro-dimension of governance systems. The term is increasingly used to examine territorial resilience in the face of external shocks, with Simmie and Martin (2010: 29) viewing territorial resilience as an adaptive capacity that is specific to a territory as, 'It is the differential ability of a region's or a locality's firms to adapt to changes and shocks in competitive, market, technological, policy and related conditions.' Thus, we can see that outside the subdiscipline of international business, dynamic perspectives are being used that acknowledge the multiple actors involved in territories and the capacity for firms and territories to evolve. We explore this further in our discussion of firms in place in Chapter 7 and in relation to global value chains in Chapter 9.

Nation-states can collude with one another, and this can be informal and formal. Collusion is an attempt to advance the interests of a territory and group of territories. Such collusion is overlooked by international business theory and includes, for example, governments deciding to work together to advance a common objective. Such common objectives can include trade with the establishment of a trading bloc or some type of military or defence alignment.

There are different forms of territory. One of the most important conceptual developments has been the varieties of capitalism literature that reveals that 'despite numerous claims of growing convergence and the "globalization" of managerial structures and strategies, the ways in which economic activities are organized and controlled ... differ considerably' (Whitley, 2000: 3). These differences are reflected by territory, with territory being equated with nation-states. In this perspective, each nation-state has a different formation of capitalism or a different variety. Capitalism is not uniform, but rather is variegated (Hall and Soskice, 2001). Thus, every country has its own variety of capitalism, and this reflects differences in governance and institutional structures (see Chapter 2). There are territories in which governments seek to regulate, coordinate and oversee everything whilst an alternative approach involves governments playing a much lighter role. Differences in varieties of capitalism are reflected in approaches to taxation and law. An excellent example comes from the difference between territories that adopt common versus civil law. Common law originated in England in medieval times and is based on case law and precedent, whilst for civil law codes and statutes are created by the legislature and are the primary source of law. Countries like the UK, US (except Louisiana), India (except Goa) and Canada follow common law, whilst countries like Germany, France, Indonesia, Japan and China follow civil law. China's approach to law was influenced by European civil law.

The case of Louisiana and Goa highlights that nation-states are not homogeneous territories. International business theory and the varieties of capitalism approach assume that nation-states are homogeneous. By this we mean that these theories overlook the importance of subnational place-based differences. These differences really matter. For example, common law has many advantages over civil law as regulation follows innovation rather than existing codes constraining innovation. The case of emerging global financial centres is an excellent example as countries seeking to establish new global financial centres tend to create special economic and legal zones. Thus, for example, Astana International Financial Centre, Kazakhstan, and Dubai International Financial Centre (DIFC) have been isolated from these countries' national legal systems and instead come under common law jurisdiction. For Dubai this means that the DIFC is independent from the Dubai court system. These subnational differences really matter and are overlooked by international business theory. The point being that even at the level of a nation-state, subnational differences really matter. A nation-state should be considered as a mosaic with each element of this mosaic having a different set of characteristics, including resources.

Within international business theory, a concern with understanding emerging market multinationals (EMNEs) had developed. This includes Hennart's (2012) early work on EMNEs, in which he argued that the OLI suffers from the basic flaw of assuming that country-specific advantages (CSAs) are freely available to all firms operating in a territory. Some CSAs cannot be accessed by non-local firms or local firms have an unfair advantage over access. To Hennart (2012), emerging economy firms can access firm-specific advantages that they lack through mergers and acquisitions or strategic partnerships. A classic case is Lenovo's purchase of IBM's laptop division, and Grupo Bimbo, the Mexican multinational food company, purchase of Sara Lee's North American Fresh Bakery division.

A new strand of international business theory emerged with the springboarding perspective developed to explore EMNEs (Luo and Tung, 2007; 2018; Luo and Witt, 2022; Hu et al, 2025). The springboarding approach seeks to explain how EMNEs internationalize by acquiring strategic resources that have been developed by other companies in other territories and their acquisition is intended to reduce the 'institutional and market constraints' experienced by EMNEs in their home market (Luo and Tung, 2007: 481). Springboarding continues to evolve and now includes double-loop springboarding in which an EMNE initially acquires resources from developed market economy businesses to enhance their business as a form of inward investment (the first loop) and then a second loop based on outward internationalization emerges that 'works either in parallel to or in separation from the primary springboard loop' (Luo and Witt, 2022: 774). This includes the upward spiral model that argues that EMNEs develop by self-improving positively reinforcing multi-stage processes including learning and acquisition of strategic resources to compensate for their capability voids.

Springboarding does enhance international business theory, but there are three problems with this approach. First, like most international business theory, this approach is silent on how this occurs in practice (but see Hu et al, 2025). Second, springboarding overlooks subnational differences within territories. Third, there is no conceptual and empirical justification for suggesting that 'springboarding' is only applicable to EMNEs. Thus, many developed market enterprises engage in springboarding through acquisition and strategic partnerships. For example, Stripe, the Irish–American multinational financial services and software company, acquired Recko, the Indian fintech company involved in buying payments tracking and automation. This is an example of a developed market economy business acquiring capabilities that it did not have, and in this case these revolved around acquiring expertise in assisting internet businesses with automated payment reconciliation. Similarly, in 1994, Volkswagen, the German multinational conglomerate, acquired Škoda Auto, the Czech automotive manufacturer. In 1994, Czech was an emerging economy and Volkswagen acquired capabilities that it did not have, and this includes the Škoda brand, heritage and production facilities. This led to the transformation of both Škoda and Volkswagen.

Processes

Things are embedded in processes, and it is to a discussion of these processes that we now turn our attention.

Governance structures

The structure and characteristics of a firm's approach to corporate governance impacts on decision-making processes as these relate to internationalization choices (Strange et al, 2009). Decisions made about corporate structure reflect considerations regarding how a firm should be governed to enhance efficiency and effectiveness. Nevertheless, many firms inherit their corporate governance structure and there are limited opportunities for major change. The international business literature highlights two governance characteristics: ownership and the board of directors. Ownership impacts on decision-making processes, and this includes managers of publicly listed firms being forced to focus on short-term profitability. The composition of a board of directors, including its diversity, has important influences on shaping decision-making processes. Boardroom diversity is required for effective oversight of an international business, and this includes directors who have experience of working and managing in different territories. There is another dimension of corporate governance that is critical. This focuses on understanding inter-firm governance and alternative contractual relationships. These include different forms of strategic alliance and outsourcing relationships (see Chapter 9).

Too often the firm is taken as the 'phenotype' or the smallest unit of analysis and this is the case with international business theory. There are complications here. Thus, for a complex international business, the phenotype might not be the firm, but some subunit – for example, a division or subsidiary – and this might include a focus on investments made in one or more territories. It is important not to confuse research undertaken at the plant, division or subsidiary with the complete firm. All this reflects the challenge of defining the firm, but for practitioners the core challenge is with developing appropriate governance structures. For international business, governance structures may include an overarching board and then boards that oversee specific investments. A distributed governance structure is commonly based on a tiered set of boards, and related company structures, being created to take control of a set of assets, but within a governance structure overseen by a company's main board. These subsidiary boards develop their own mandates but framed within the context of the overall firm. There are different approaches. On the one hand, these subsidiary boards might be able to set and control their own destinies and might be granted considerable independence. The independence of these subsidiary boards might be one way of responding to geopolitical tensions regarding the ownership of business assets and concerns over data geopolitics. On the other hand, the subsidiary boards may only be responsible for operational decisions with investment decisions made by the overarching board.

There is a real danger in assuming that all firms are the same. This is not the case. Different governance and ownership structures are associated with different motivations. For example, Mars, the American multinational manufacturer of confectionery, pet food and other food products, is one of the largest privately held companies in the world. This ownership structure means that Mars can adopt a long-term perspective on investment and corporate strategy as the management team is removed from shareholder concerns with quarterly earnings. A company like Mars will operate in a very different manner to a publicly listed company. There are many companies like Mars, for example Aldi (Germany), Auchan Holdings (France), ByteDance (China), Hermès (France), Huawei (China), IKEA (Sweden), LVMH (France) and Nippon Life Insurance (Japan). Some of these are listed companies – for example Hermès and LVMH – but ownership or control is still vested in a family. Thus, the Arnault Family Group control 46.84 per cent of LVMH stock and 63.13 per cent of voting rights. There are a multitude of smaller international businesses that are owned and controlled by their founders or current owners. These firms might be managed to reflect the interests of their owners, and these might be rather idiosyncratic and not be aligned with the stress placed in neoclassical economics on profit maximization.

It is important not to overlook state-owned enterprises (SOEs). These are companies that are owned or controlled by a government, and this includes national, regional or provincial governments. These firms may be government owned as they are involved in providing essential or critical public goods and services. Alternatively, government ownership or control may reflect a particular variety of capital based on the state being directly involved in economic activity. SOEs are increasingly becoming international businesses. According to the World Bank 'collectively, state-owned investors, including public pension funds and state owned banks, have become the third-largest holders of financial assets globally, after only banks and insurance companies. As a result of this internationalization process, commercial enterprises in one country may be controlled—partially or totally—by the state of a different country' (World Bank, 2023: xvi). One concern with SOEs is that they may represent an unfair form of international competition as they may have access to cheap and even unlimited government funding. This is considered by the World Bank to be an important distinction between SOEs and private enterprises as the 'former often face a softer budget constraint' and also experience 'more advantageous regulatory treatment' (World Bank, 2023: xviii). Another issue concerns the lack of transparency that can exist with some SOEs. SOEs include joint stock companies, limited liability companies and partnerships limited by shares. China has more SOEs than any other country. Chinese SOEs initially were established to enact national goals, and their financial performance was of limited importance. SOE reform in China, however, has led to a situation in which Chinese SOEs are encouraged to engage in profit-seeking behaviour as this increases the value of the Chinese state's assets.

There is an important issue to consider concerning corporate governance and the application of artificial intelligence (AI) to boardroom decision-making. For corporate governance, there are important issues to consider. Companies that are incorporating AI into their businesses must develop and implement an overarching AI governance framework. This must ensure that the company has sufficient oversight and accountability for the AI that is being applied. Roles and responsibilities should be defined. An ongoing evaluation process is required and an approach to governance developed that includes a risk and incident management strategy. Training is part of this process to ensure that all are aware of the possibilities and risks that come from AI adoption. AI must be aligned to an organization's intended mission and the danger exists that a misaligned AI system would develop that seeks to pursue some other mission. This alignment problem is a well-known corporate governance challenge as companies develop mechanisms that are intended to ensure that managers continue to act in the interests of shareholders rather than in their own interests. For AI, the governance challenge is to ensure that systems are controlled, regulated, and evaluated to ensure that they remain aligned to the company's mission. A board would have to be extremely careful to ensure that it does not become too over-dependent on AI. Over-dependence could result in automation bias, or the propensity for humans to favour suggestions from automated decision-making systems and to ignore contradictory information even when this is correct.

The automation of administrative tasks raises the question of effectiveness and the need for monitoring. AI should not be permitted to make strategic decisions, but to inform decision-making processes. There are major risks here; how many board members or managers understand algorithmic decision-making processes? Many board members will not have the capabilities to understand these processes, and this adds another layer of corporate risk and uncertainty. All board members, and members of a management team, must appreciate that humans are notoriously bad at monitoring algorithms and thus may fail to identify an emerging AI alignment problem.

One of the problems with AI is that it is trained on historical data. AI makes decisions based on learning about the past. There are two challenges here. First, a company that does not continually train their AI systems on recent data will have systems that will support outdated decision-making. Second, continually training an AI system with new data may result in AI bias emerging with the outcome being some type of alignment problem. The first duty of a board remains unchanged by AI. A board must ensure that it is aligned to the company's mission which should reflect shareholder/owner and wider societal interests. AI has a supporting and enabling role here, but the board's primary responsibility, as far as AI is concerned, is to ensure that appropriate corporate governance is in place to reduce the company's exposure to the many risks associated with AI adoption.

Decision-making

Within a firm, there is a small group of people involved in strategic decision-making, a much larger group involved in decisions related to everyday operations and an even larger group that is removed from having any significant input to organizational decisions. Firms are established by entrepreneurs who are decision-makers who are risk takers. There is then a gradual transition as entrepreneurs are replaced by managers who are concerned with organizational reproduction and transformation. Decision-making processes are more informal as a firm is established and then are rapidly formalized. It is important to differentiate between firms in which decision-making is still dominated by an entrepreneur and/or owner and those that operate like publicly listed corporations with a board of directors. With the former, decision-making processes represent the interests, desires and motivations of the entrepreneur or owner. With the latter, a board of directors with executive and non-executive members takes ownership of overseeing the governance structures that support the company's strategic decision-making process. This includes holding fiduciary responsibility to stockholders. Publicly listed MNEs, governed by boards of directors balancing diverse stakeholder interests, face stringent demands for transparency and ethical conduct. These pressures often slow decision-making but also shape strategic planning, risk management and international growth, highlighting governance's critical role in cross-border operations.

Family-owned firms often operate under centralized, value-driven governance tied to the founding family, enabling rapid decision-making but this then may come with accountability, transparency and succession challenges. These dynamics highlight the need for international business theory to account for the agility and risks inherent in family governance. SOEs, on the other hand, blend commercial goals with socio-political mandates, reflecting government priorities. This dual focus often creates governance complexities, such as balancing profit motives against public policy objectives, illustrating how governance mediates firm behaviour where economic and political agendas overlap.

These variations show that governance is not one-size-fits-all; each model uniquely influences how firms behave. The rights and responsibilities of a board are circumscribed by law, and this includes responsibilities related to due diligence, risk management and preventing the reckless use of company assets. Nevertheless, company boards can still act recklessly and irresponsibly. It is worth noting that employees play a very limited role in shaping major strategic decisions, but there is an important compounding effect that comes from the accumulation of decisions made by individual employees. This compounding effect can result in mission creep.

It is important to remember that too often international business theory assumes a boardroom view, and this includes overlooking the fact that decisions made by a company's board are constrained by sector and investor conventions and expectations as well as by firm-level decisions that have been made in the past. People as decision-makers cannot be isolated from their place, time and corporate context. It is important to remember that there are three sides to a decision made by people working for a firm: the decision in context, implementation in context and evaluation as a process to inform continual adjustment. All this must be placed within an appreciation of who is making these decisions and their individual and collective motivations. There is an important politics to decision-making processes that reflects ongoing power politics as groups or individuals influence the outcome of a decision-making process. This comes back to how firms are defined. A firm may be defined as a collective of individuals who come together to achieve some common purpose by taking temporary ownership or control of a set of assets. This highlights that a firm's motivation or mission might change in response to alterations in the company's leadership.

Facilitators

Things and processes are enabled by facilitators, and these support outcomes. These facilitators highlight that international business practice is complex as it involves intersections between place, territory and business activity systems (processes and things involved in processes).

Intersections

Intersections in international business refer to the points where different elements of economic activity converge. These can include different points such as cultural, economic, legal, political or technological intersections. For example, economic intersections refer to the conditions of different countries that significantly impact international trade. International business theory, due primarily to its focus on the firm as the analytical unit, has not paid attention to points of intersection in the global economy. International business scholars observe the firm and make some consideration of the context in which its activities take place (see the place and territory building blocks), but there is no broader framework to examine intersections with other actors and processes (our building blocks). As such, the subdiscipline of international business has to look beyond its own theories to understand the intersection between, for example, the economy and politics, as exemplified by the semiconductor sector (see Chapter 2). Another intersection is with innovation and technological change (see Chapter 3). In these chapters we demonstrate how insights from other disciplines are necessary to observe and understand these intersections, such as political economy and innovation studies. In Chapter 9, we examine social science perspectives such as global value chains which make explicit consideration of the intersections between actors and geographical scales, in the global economy. The configuration of intersections in international business can be complex, involving multiple stakeholders and institutional contexts. Intersections are points of possible collaboration and conflict (sometimes concurrently), with stakeholders having conflicting priorities. We therefore require dynamic frameworks for analysis that give space to understanding the multiple intersections between companies/firms, people, places, territories, things and money.

Intermediaries

Intermediaries such as trading companies, agents and merchants have always played a key role in international business. Despite the growing importance of understanding the phenomenon of intermediaries, there are misperceptions and confusions regarding the concept and value of intermediaries, which result in disconnected and fragmented research findings (Virtanen et al, 2023). The understanding of intermediaries in the international business literature is narrow – focusing on the individuals or organizations that facilitate the exchange of goods and services between buyers and sellers across borders (but see Hu et al, 2025). The subdiscipline has considered many dimensions of the activities of these intermediaries, expounding on the 'principle-agent problem' and considering the factors of success or failure in these international relationships. Distributors are companies that purchase goods from foreign suppliers and resell them to domestic customers. They often have a network of retailers or wholesalers to distribute products. For example, Alibaba, while primarily known as an online marketplace, also acts as a distributor for many international products. It connects manufacturers from China and other countries with buyers around the world. Alibaba provides a platform for these manufacturers to list their products, and it often acts as a broker in facilitating transactions between buyers and sellers. Alibaba helps to connect international suppliers with domestic customers.

Contemporary perspectives on intermediaries should consider them in more expansive terms, considering other types of intermediaries beyond companies. These include states (see Chapter 2), who play an intermediary role for firms, for example, in trade negotiations and technologies (see Chapters 2 and 3), including the internet and AI. In Chapter 7, we discuss the problem of integration versus responsiveness that firms face when organizing their international operations. This illustrates the ways in which intermediaries can constrain or enable business activities – firms are connecting to other actors beyond their headquarters and subsidiaries. They are using intermediaries including people (their employees and suppliers), technologies (for communication) and institutions who create the contexts in their home and host environments (regulation, incentives, etc, outlined in Chapter 2). The narrow view of intermediaries from international business shows us that by leveraging their expertise and local knowledge, intermediaries can help companies overcome the challenges associated with doing business in foreign markets and to achieve their internationalization goals. They can help reduce the costs and complexities associated with international trade and facilitate market entry for companies. A broader perspective allows us to see a wider set of intermediaries, many of whom may connect to firms with responsible business agendas, but not necessarily in positive ways.

Innovation

The central role of innovation in driving change and development in the global economy has led to this process receiving substantial academic attention (see Chapter 3). International business theory focuses upon the interconnections between innovation processes and internationalization and the increased significance of the knowledge-seeking motive for international firm networks (Cantwell, 2016). International businesses link localized innovation systems to international knowledge exchange, and Cantwell (2016: 41) notes that 'the shift of techno-socio-economic paradigm in the information age is associated with a shift in the character of IB [international business] and innovation, with critical implications for IB theory and concepts'. Cano-Kollmann et al (2016) highlight the foundational importance of Dunning's work for understanding innovation-driven multinational enterprises, due in the main to the inclusion of location factors in the eclectic paradigm. This may give too much credit to Dunning's work as it does not explicitly identify innovation as a key factor in internationalization. Innovation is implied in Dunning's ownership factor, through the development of unique or more advanced products and services providing competitive advantage. One could also consider innovative capacity and resources to be considered in the location factor, but this is not specifically highlighted by the eclectic paradigm. Indeed, as Cano-Kollmann et al (2016) suggest, integration of insights from other disciplines, particularly economic geography and innovation studies, allows acknowledgement of the co-evolution of firms and territories (see building blocks on companies/firms and territories) and spatially dispersed yet connected innovation processes.

The innovation processes driven by international firms continuously alter the nature and composition of firm activities at the global scale. The need for interdisciplinary approaches is echoed by Anand et al (2021) in their examination of innovation in and from emerging economies. They draw on work from innovation and development studies to better understand the ways in which societies are reconfiguring their institutions and networks to improve their knowledge resources. Thus, we can see that the need to adopt co-evolutionary approaches to understanding firms in their contexts, implies that international business theory must draw on work from outside the international business literature.

International business theory and responsible business practice

The usual way to explore what is often termed mainstream international business theory is to review and outline each approach. This type of review can show how each theory builds on that which has gone before. The reviewers of our book proposal had some reservations regarding this book's structure and approach to 'mainstream' theory as our book does not follow the convention that has been developed by other international business texts. It is important to remember that this book is intended for taught postgraduate students, and it is not our aim to provide an overview of what is a set of well-known theories. We also do not want to critique these theories for what they never set out to achieve. Each theory has a well-defined focus and set of assumptions. It is important to remember that theory is meant to inform understanding, but that all theory must be a simplification of a much more complex reality. Our framework is not a theory but rather seeks to identify the vocabulary required to read international business. Understanding the grammar of international business comes from engaging with theory and some of this is defined as international business theory.

Our review of our framework's cross-cutting themes and eleven building blocks (see Figure 1.1) has gone some way to mapping our approach onto existing international business theory with a focus on relating existing theory to practice and responsible business. The outcome is Table 6.1 that maps the framework's cross-cutting themes and building blocks to international business theory, practice-related challenges and responsible business challenges (Table 6.1). Our approach highlights both the major contributions that have been made to understanding international business, but alongside an appreciation of the limitations of any one theory. It is important to differentiate between academic understanding versus applied practice. In the world of the classroom, a case study of an international business can be discussed and many learning points identified and suggestions made regarding business practice. All this, however, is about exploring a real firm that has been translated into a business case and then the analysis and discussion is more about a virtual rather than an actual firm. The point being that in the classroom any learning point or business recommendation will have no impact on people. People include employees and those who work for subcontractors and across a company's value chain, consumers and those who benefit from the tax revenues paid by a firm.

The world of real management practice has direct, indirect and induced impacts on people and these impacts matter. A decision to automate a process throws people out of work, whilst a decision to offshore might reduce product price or enhance margins, but at the expense of redundancies in the firm's home market and possible labour exploitation in other territories. This is to highlight that any corporate decision has multiple impacts and these impacts may be simultaneously positive and negative. This is a critical point. International business theory, and theories of innovation, overemphasize the positive impacts and often completely overlook the negatives (Gardner and Bryson, 2020). Hymer's theory of international business, which is considered to be the first international business theory, is one based on a company

Table 6.1: International business theory and practice and responsible business challenges: revisiting the framework

Building blocks	International business theory	Practice challenges	Responsible business challenges
Companies/Firms	Companies as the object of study	Complexity of decision-making processes, including trade-offs, overlooked by theory	How is a concern with responsible practice diffused throughout an international business? Isomorphism
Money	Money assumed or the focus is on profit generation	Opportunity costs, sunk costs and trade-offs	Maximizing profit and accountancy logic might dominate
People	Largely invisible	Recruitment, training, incentivization and productivity	Incentivization and monitoring; isomorphism and socialization
Things	Ill-defined and often assumed	Opportunities, limitations and challenges	Constraints on acting responsibly
Place	Place-based differences important but imprecisely defined	Opportunities and complexities	Tensions
Territory	Overemphasis on territory but ignores subnational differences in, eg institutions	Complexity, cross-cultural opportunities and problems	Adjustments to different territorial structures and implications for responsible business; transparency
Governance structures	Often assumed or theory focuses on one type, for example smaller firms	Complexity	Constraints that force conformity to a less than responsible sector norm
Decision-making processes	Assumed as there is no attempt to explore who, where and how decisions are made	Politics, tensions, culture	Conflicting values and motivations
Intersections	Often assumed but can include a focus on learning and knowledge and intra-firm interactions	Configuration, coordination of formal intersections and an appreciation and understanding of the informal	Contextualization including ensuring that all involved with a company are following the same approach to responsibility
Intermediaries	Overlooked, but some approaches highlight the actions of non-firm actors	Identification, selection, monitoring, motivation and evaluation; value for money	Constraints imposed by intermediaries
Innovation	Often seen as the backdrop for a theory	Trade-offs, opportunity costs, sunk costs	Positive and negative contributions to enhancing a firm's responsibility

(continued)

Table 6.1: International business theory and practice and responsible business challenges: revisiting the framework (continued)

Building blocks	International business theory	Practice challenges	Responsible business challenges
Cross–cutting themes			
Values	Value – either ignored or defined around profit	What and whose values? Value or values	Profit versus other values; practices that align to acting responsibly
Motivation (individual and collective)	Assumed that this is based on maximizing profit and this includes cost control	What and whose motivation?	Motivation configured around an appreciation of responsibility
Practice and Conventions	An emerging area, but overlooked in mainstream theory	Awareness of existing routines (ostensive and performative) and the constraints imposed, change management, employee engagement	Existing practice and conventions and their alignment with a firm's values and motivations
Change/evolution	Often theory is focused on one event, but there are theories that explore phases or stages	Gradual, but compounded and also revolutionary or rapid change; awareness of change opportunities and potentials and the strengths of existing practice; employee engagement	Responsible business and how this is integrated into a firm's change and evolutionary processes
Overall: international business as an integrated practice	Each theory focuses on a well-defined business challenge or practice; thus, theory is siloed	Must consider all business areas that impact on a decision, and which will be impacted; there are no silos in the real world of business practice; each building block and cross-cutting theme is interdependent	Tensions, trade-offs, dominance of a profit maximizing logic; the need to apply an integrated or holistic approach

configuring a monopolistic advantage founded on articulating and exploiting place-based differentials and firm-specific advantages (Dunning and Rugman, 1985). This type of monopolistic advantage is considered as a positive advantage for a firm, but the reality is one that local firms are destroyed, countries and consumers may become too dependent on a foreign supplier and people are made redundant as their employers must respond to what could also be considered to be an unfair advantage held by a competitor. However, we must remember that a monopolistic advantage is usually a short-term advantage.

Dunning's OLI emerged as an attempt to develop an overarching theory of why and where firms internationalize. There is no question that this was a path defining conceptual contribution as it highlights trade-offs that are made by companies between location, company assets and company processes. International business used to involve direct ownership of assets and resources, and this explains the OLI's emphasis on FDI. However, times have changed and there are many pathways towards international business and many firms are involved in configuring all pathways – from exports to FDI to a host of different partnership arrangements. Ownership becomes supplemented or even replaced by the ability of an individual or group of individuals – a firm – to gain access to resources owned by others. The limitations of the OLI are well known and reflect this theory's emphasis on understanding the initial internationalization stage. The Uppsala approach shares an interest in a common research or business problem with the OLI. Nevertheless, Uppsala adds some additional decision-making complications involving place-based learning as well as appreciating that internationalization is not a single event in the life of a firm, but part of a sequence of decision-making processes. This is an important point.

International business theory does assume that there is something special about the intersections between a company and its home nation, or territory. There is often an omission in these sequence-orientated approaches. Thus, a large international business may emerge from one host location, but rapidly its link to this location may dissipate. These are firms that think internationally and may eventually sever their emotional attachment to their country of origin. A more common practice comes from acquisitions, and these could be defined as a form of springboarding. There are many examples. The well-known American store brand, 7-Eleven, was originally headquartered out of Dallas, Texas, but is now owned by a Japanese company. Holiday Inn was originally headquartered out of Memphis, Tennessee, and is now owned by a UK company. Hellman's mayonnaise was originally headquartered out of New York, but is now owned by Unilever, a UK company. Hellman's is an excellent example of the complexity of product, company and place intersections. Its founder, Richard Hellmann, was born in Germany and his product innovation was to develop a version of French mayonnaise for the American market.

The practice of managing within international business is not well understood and not covered explicitly by international business theory. Further complications come from asking questions regarding responsible business practice. This raises the question regarding responsible business practice for whom. Is this intended for shareholders/owners, managers, employees, subcontractors, consumers and/or the governments within whose territories a business operates? If responsible business practice covers all stakeholders, then this has major implications for managerial practice. For practice, the important point to appreciate is that a decision-maker has choices, and these choices come with different degrees of responsible business outcomes. Nevertheless, no decision is unconstrained as all decisions are influenced by a firm's history and context(s). Context includes ownership, motivations, governance structure, sector-based conventions and expectations. Often corporate decision-making is constrained by decisions made by insurance companies regarding the degree of risk they will insure for a premium. The best corporate decision might come with unaffordable insurance premiums. Ultimately, this chapter has highlighted the ways in which eleven building blocks and four cross-cutting themes impact business decision-making. A core discussion point to consider is the multiple trade-offs that the responsible business practitioner needs to consider. Trade-offs are central to the OLI but focused predominantly around balancing three processes. The real world of business practice is so much more complex, involving multiple trade-offs and this includes considering opportunity costs, or the loss of other alternatives once one alternative is selected over another. Of course, opportunity costs might also include sunk costs, or costs that have already been incurred and cannot be recovered and which would have to be written off, as an investment might be coupled with a disinvestment.

Theory is meant to simplify matters. Another way of describing theory is to compare it to a searchlight which illuminates one area whilst placing other areas in complete darkness. The OLI and springboarding are very modest theories as both seek to illuminate a well-defined business decision-making problem. Both provide guidance on factors that should be considered when making a management decision. Neither approach provides everything needed to inform a decision. This raises the question regarding what the omissions or gaps in these approaches are. The answer to this question is that a theory provides general or universal guidance but is unable to take cognisance of the particular. The particular includes all the factors that must be considered that reflect the context of any one corporate decision. Sitting behind this context lies motivation, or an individual's or collective's overall mission. This might be framed around profit-seeking behaviour focused on maximizing profits or alternatively motivation might be configured around values that intersect with ongoing debates on responsible business practice (see Chapter 4). The word 'ongoing' in this sentence alerts us to the fact that definitions and perceptions of what is responsible business practice are fluid and change over time. What is considered to be responsible business behaviour today might be defined as irresponsible tomorrow. Decisions must always be understood and explored with reference to time and space, or in other words to the context within which they were made. Thus, responsible business practice varies between territories or nation-states and even between sectors.

Mapping practice and responsible business on to existing international business theory does highlight that this theory has enhanced understanding, but the focus has not been on practice and responsibility (Table 6.1). Applying a practice perspective that is informed by a concern with responsible business identifies points for discussion and reflection. These include how an organization's values are diffused throughout a complex international business. Perhaps this is not required as a conglomerate organizational structure would not demand the application of a common set of values or even approach. There is an employee engagement challenge that takes a different form for international business. Employee engagement is a critical aspect of change management and cross-cultural alignment within the context of an international business. There is a well-developed literature that develops a site-level approach to employee engagement, but a much less-developed literature on international business, employee engagement (Boccoli et al, 2023), recruitment, training, incentivization and productivity. One challenge is that much theory focuses on firms, yet managing firms requires engaging with people with diverse characteristics, including cultural and gender diversity, and neurodiversity.

Conclusion

The framework presented in this chapter highlights the complexity and challenge of managing international businesses. Our approach includes four cross-cutting themes, but Table 6.1 highlights that there is another type of less visible cross-cutting practice challenge. This involves tensions and trade-offs that managers working for international businesses must consider either explicitly or implicitly. One outcome of this chapter is a modification to our framework approach that we outlined in Chapter 1. This modification is outlined in the last row in Table 6.1. This recognizes that the practice of international business is one that requires the application of an integrated approach. Every international business theory is siloed as there is a well-defined focus on a business challenge. But the everyday practice of international business cuts across silos and requires decision-makers to consider the feedback loops that will form as a result of a decision being made and implemented. These feedback loops are saturated with tensions and trade-offs and some can be known, but some remain unknown. Failure in international business is sometimes due to an inability or reluctance of decision-makers to understand and adjust to some type of place-based context (see Chapter 7). Failure also comes from failing to identify and mediate against negative feedback loops. In many instances, failure seems to reflect stupidity, but this is to ignore the difficulties decision-makers experience related to unequal power dynamics, power politics, rapid alterations in circumstances and information asymmetry as this relates to bounded rationality. Failure is never planned, but should always be anticipated and strategies, practices and routines adjusted. Not all failures can be avoided, but all involved with failure should learn from this experience and improve their processes, procedures and practices.

It is important to reflect on the essential elements that must inform responsible international business practice. This includes being very aware of differences between territories and places and/or cross-cultural differences. This includes being aware of subnational differences that are too often overlooked. It must include a focus on reducing or even removing waste and this includes waste as it is related to labour exploitation. The following chapters explore this in different contexts – Chapter 7 discusses place-based differentials and Chapter 8 focuses on the services sector. We then delve deeper into intersections and intermediaries, charting the global value chain concept and its efforts to develop a multiscalar and multiactor approach in Chapter 9. The best international businesses are aware of the impacts that they make on people and places. These impacts include creating values-in-use that provide solutions to some consumer or societal need. It includes being aware of the immediate and of the future. There is a real danger that corporate decision-makers become too distracted by immediate challenges and in so doing lose sight of the company's overall mission. Too often organizational missions are translated into some type of bland marketing statement and there is often a disconnect between such missions and everyday practice. Chapter 10 draws our analyses together, reflecting on the framework and how it may help us understand responsibility in the contemporary geoeconomy. We conclude that, ultimately, responsible business practice is practice that is informed and very aware, but it is very much practice that is action-centred rather than being positioned around statements that bear limited relation to a company's decision-making processes, everyday routines and processes.

Key terms

Eclectic paradigm – also known as the OLI Model or OLI Framework; an approach developed in the international business literature to explore when and why firms should engage in FDI.

Internalization theory – a theory developed in the international business literature that emphasizes the important contribution to the internationalization of firms of internal markets and processes.

Responsible business practice – business practice that is informed and very aware, but very much practice that is action-centred rather than being positioned around statements that bear limited relation to a company's decision-making processes, everyday routines and processes.

Springboarding – an international business theory that is known as the springboard perspective, or as springboard theory, which argues that emerging economy multinational enterprises engage in international expansion as a springboard based on the acquisition of resources.

Uppsala model – a model developed to explain the internationalization of businesses as a sequential process based on different stages.

Recommended reading

Anand, J., McDermott, G., Mudambi, R. and Narula, R. (2021) 'Innovation in and from emerging economies: new insights and lessons for international business research', *Journal of International Business Studies*, 52: 545–59.

Buckley, P.J. (2002) 'Is the international business research agenda running out of steam?', *Journal of International Business Studies*, 33(2): 365–73.

Buckley, P.J. and Lessard, D.R. (2005) 'Regaining the edge for international business research', *Journal of International Business Studies*, 36(6): 595–9.

Buckley, P.J., Doh, J.P. and Benischke, M.H. (2017) 'Towards a renaissance in international business research? Big questions, grand challenges, and the future of IB scholarship', *Journal of International Business Studies*, 48(9): 1045–64.

Buckley, P.J., Enderwick, P., Hsieh, L. and Shenkar, O. (2024) 'International business theory and the criminal multinational enterprise', *Journal of World Business*, 59(5): 101553. doi.org/10.1016/j.jwb.2024.101553.

References

Anand, J., McDermott, G., Mudambi, R. and Narula, R. (2021) 'Innovation in and from emerging economies: new insights and lessons for international business research', *Journal of International Business Studies*, 52: 545–59. doi.org/10.1057/s41267-021-00426-1.

Billing, C. and Bryson, J.R. (2019) 'Heritage and satellite manufacturing: firm-level competitiveness and the management of risk in global production networks', *Economic Geography*, 95(5): 423–41.

Boccoli, G., Gastaldi, L. and Corso, M. (2023) 'The evolution of employee engagement: towards a social and contextual construct for balancing individual performance and wellbeing dynamically', *International Journal of Management Reviews*, 25: 75–98. doi.org/10.1111/ijmr.12304.

Brouthers, L., Brouthers, K. and Werner, S. (1999) 'Is Dunning's eclectic framework descriptive or normative?', *Journal of International Business Studies* 30: 831–44.

Bryson, J.R. and Ronayne, M. (2014) 'Manufacturing carpets and technical textiles: routines, resources, capabilities, adaptation, innovation and the evolution of the British textile industry', *Cambridge Journal of Regions, Economy and Society*, 7: 471–88.

Bryson, J.R. and Rusten, G. (2008) 'Transnational corporations and spatial divisions of 'service' expertise as a competitive strategy: the example of 3M and Boeing', *Service Industries Journal*, 28(3): 307–23.

Bryson, J.R. and Rusten, G. (2011) *Design Economies and the Changing World Economy*, London: Routledge.

Bryson, J.R., Daniels, P.W. and Warf, B. (2004) *Service Worlds: People, Organisations, Technologies*, London: Routledge.

Bryson, J.R., Billing, C., Graves, W. and Yeung, G. (2022) 'Reframing manufacturing research: place, production, risk and theory', in J.R. Bryson, C. Billing, W. Graves and G. Yeung (eds) *A Research Agenda for Manufacturing Industries in the Global Economy*, Cheltenham: Edward Elgar, pp 1–32.

Buckley. P. (1988) 'The limits of explanation: testing the internalization theory of the multinational enterprise', *Journal of International Business Studies*, 19(2): 181–93.

Buckley, P.J. (2002) 'Is the international business research agenda running out of steam?', *Journal of International Business Studies*, 33(2): 365–73.

Buckley, P. and Casson, M. (1976) *The Future of the Multinational Enterprise*, London: Macmillan Press Ltd.

Buckley, P.J. and Lessard, D.R. (2005) 'Regaining the edge for international business research', *Journal of International Business Studies*, 36(6): 595–9.

Buckley, P.J., Doh, J.P. and Benischke, M.H. (2017) 'Towards a renaissance in international business research? Big questions, grand challenges, and the future of IB scholarship', *Journal of International Business Studies*, 48(9): 1045–64.

Buckley, P.J., Enderwick, P., Hsieh, L. and Shenkar, O. (2024) 'International business theory and the criminal multinational enterprise', *Journal of World Business*, 59(5): 101553. doi.org/10.1016/j.jwb.2024.101553.

Cairns, G. and Śliwa, M. (2017) *A Very Short, Fairly Interesting and Reasonably Cheap Book about International Business*, London: Sage.

Cano-Kollmann, M., Cantwell, J., Hannigan, T., Mudambi, R. and Song, J. (2016) 'Knowledge connectivity: An agenda for innovation research in international business', *Journal of International Business Studies*, 47: 255–62. doi.org/10.1057/jibs.2016.8.

Cantwell, J. (2009) 'Location and the multinational enterprise', *Journal of International Business Studies*, 40(1): 35–41.

Cantwell, J. (2016) 'Innovation and international business', *Industry and Innovation*, 24(1): 41–60. doi.org/10.1080/13662716.2016.1257422.

Casey, C.A. (2025) *Imports and the Section 321 (De Minimis) Exception: Origins, Evolution, and Use*, Congressional Research Service [online]. Available from: https://crsrepo rts.congress.gov/product/pdf/R/R48380 [Accessed 6 February 2025].

Casson, M. (2018) 'The theory of international business: the role of economic models', *Management International Review*, 58(3): 363–87.

Casson, M. and Li, Y. (2022) 'Complexity in international business: the implications for theory', *Journal of International Business Studies*, 53: 2037–49.

Child, J. (1975) 'Managerial and organizational factors associated with company performance: Part II – a contingency analysis', *Journal of Management Studies*, 12: 12–27.

Child, J., Chung, L. and Davies, H. (2003) 'The performance of cross-border units in China: a test of natural selection, strategic choice and contingency theories', *Journal of International Business Studies*, 34: 242–54.

Coase, R.H. (1937) 'The nature of the firm', *Economica*, 4: 386–405.

Cook, G., Johns, J., McDonald, F., Beaverstock, J. and Pandit, N. (2018) *The Routledge Companion to the Geography of International Business*, London: Routledge. doi.org/ 10.4324/9781315667379.

Couper, C. and Piekkari, R. (2025) 'Rethinking international business scholarship as cross-language knowledge production: a dialogical approach to qualitative research', *Journal of International Business Studies*. https://doi.org/10.1057/s41 267-025-00776-0.

Crisogen, D.T. (2016) 'Types of socialization and their importance in understanding the phenomena of socialization', *European Journal of Social Science Education and Research*, 3(1): 1–10.

Danziger, P.N. (2023) '"Guochao" trend may disrupt Western luxury brands' dominance in China', *Forbes* [online]. Available from: www.forbes.com/sites/pamd anziger/2023/01/25/guochao-trend-may-disruupt--western-luxury-brands-domina nce-in-china/ [Accessed 6 February 2025].

Dicken, P. and Malmberg, A. (2001) 'Firms in territories: a relational perspective', *Economic Geography*, 77(4): 345–63.

Dunning, J.H. (1988) 'The eclectic paradigm of international production: a restatement and some possible extensions', *Journal of International Business Studies*, 19(1): 1–31.

Dunning, J.H. and Rugman, A.M. (1985) 'The influence of Hymer's dissertation on the theory of foreign direct investment', *American Economic Review*, 75(2): 228–32.

Gardner, E.C. and Bryson, J.R. (2020) 'The dark side of the industrialisation of accountancy: innovation, commoditization, colonization and competitiveness', *Industry and Innovation*, 28(1): 42–57.

Hall, P. and Soskice, D. (eds) (2001) *Varieties of Capitalism: The Institutional Foundations of Comparative Advantage*, Oxford: Oxford University Press.

Harris, W. (2024) 'Superdry boss says Shein allowed to "dodge tax"', BBC News [online]. Available from: www.bbc.co.uk/news/articles/ckgny3vm6d1o [Accessed 24 September 2024].

Hennart, J.-F. (2012) 'Emerging market multinationals and the theory of the multinational enterprise', *Global Strategy Journal*, 2: 168–87.

Hu, H., Bryson, J.R. and Beaverstock, J.V. (2025) 'Triple-loop springboarding and simulacrum enterprises: financialization and new forms of emerging economy educational international businesses', *International Business Review*, 34(3): 102420. https://doi.org/10.1016/j.ibusrev.2025.102420.

Johanson, J. and Vahlne, J.-E. (1977) 'The internationalization process of the firm—a model of knowledge development and increasing foreign market commitments', *Journal of International Business Studies*, 8(1): 23–32.

Johanson, J. and Vahlne, J.E. (2009) 'The Uppsala internationalization process model revisited: from liability of foreignness to lability of outsidership', *Journal of International Business Studies*, 40(9): 1411–31.

Luo, Y. and Tung, R. (2007) 'International expansion of emerging market enterprises: a springboard perspective', *Journal of International Business Studies*, 38(4): 481–98.

Luo, Y. and Tung, R. (2018) 'A general theory of springboard MNEs', *Journal of International Business Studies*, 49(2): 129–52.

Luo, Y. and Witt, M.A. (2022) 'Springboard MNEs under de-globalization', *Journal of International Business Studies*, 53(4): 767–80.

McAdam, R., Miller, K. and McSorley, C. (2019) 'Towards a contingency theory perspective of quality management in enabling strategic alignment', *International Journal of Production Economics*, 207: 195–209

Meyer, K.E., Mudambi, R. and Narula, R. (2011) 'Multinational enterprises and local contexts: the opportunities and challenges of multiple embeddedness', *Journal of Management Studies*, 48(2): 235–52.

Morawski, J. (2014) 'Socialization', in T. Teo (ed.) *Encyclopedia of Critical Psychology*, New York: Springer. doi.org/10.1007/978-1-4614-5583-7_295.

Mulhall, R.A. and Bryson, J.R. (2014) 'Energy price risk and the sustainability of demand side supply chains', *Applied Energy*, 123: 327–34.

Nooteboom, B. (2000) *Learning and Innovation in Organisations and Economies*, Oxford: Oxford University Press.

Pattinson, T. (2023) 'The rise and fall of guochao: China's nationalistic branding phenomenon', *Focus*. Available from: https://focus.cbbc.org/the-rise-and-fall-of-guochao-chinas-nationalistic-branding-phenomenon/ [Accessed 6 February 2025].

Rusten, G., Bryson, J. R. and Aarflot, U. (2007) 'Places through products and products through places: Industrial design and spatial symbols as sources of competitiveness', *Norsk Geografisk Tidsskrift – Norwegian Journal of Geography*, 61(3): 133–144.

Simmie, J. and Martin, R. (2010) 'The economic resilience of territories: towards an evolutionary approach', *Cambridge Journal of Regions, Economy and Society*, 3(1): 27–43. doi.org/10.1093/cjres/rsp029.

Śliwa, M. and Johansson, M. (2014) 'How non-native English-speaking staff are evaluated in linguistically diverse organizations: a sociolinguistic perspective', *Journal of International Business Studies*, 45(9): 1133–51.

Strange, R., Filatotchev, I., Buck, T. and Wright, M. (2009) 'Corporate governance and international business', *Management International Review*, 49: 395–40.

Vale, G.D., Collin-Lachaud, I. and Lecocq, X. (2021) 'Micro-level practices of bricolage during business model innovation process: the case of digital transformation towards omni-channel retailing', *Scandinavian Journal of Management*, 37(2): 101154.

Vanchan, V., Mulhall, R. and Bryson, J.R. (2018) 'Repatriation or reshoring of manufacturing to the U.S. and UK: dynamics and global production networks or from here to there and back again', *Growth and Change*, 49: 97–121.

Virtanen, Y., Jiang, Y., You, W. and Cai, H.H. (2023) 'International intermediaries: a systematic literature review and research agenda', *European Management Journal*, 41(6): 932–49. doi.org/10.1016/j.emj.2022.11.005.

Weeks, J. and Galunic, C. (2003) 'A theory of the cultural evolution of the firm: the intra-organizational ecology of memes', *Organization Studies*, 24(8): 1309–52.

Whitley, R. (2000) *Divergent Capitalisms: The Social Structuring and Change of Business*, Oxford: Oxford University Press.

World Bank (2023) *The Business of the State*, Washington: World Bank. doi.org/10.1596/978-1-4648-1998-8.

7

Localization, Responsibility and
the Practice of Embeddedness

Introduction

The global economy is not an even playing field. Despite the proclamations of some scholars and managers in the 1990s about the 'death of distance' and the 'end of geography', place continues to play a significant role in international business and is arguably becoming more important. In fact, place differentials drive international business as organizations seek to exploit these differences for their gain. If all places were the same, there would be no need for businesses to move beyond their home markets, other than to seek market growth. As previous chapters have highlighted, the complex configurations of business across different territories – for both production and sales – highlights for us the uneven landscape of the ever-evolving geoeconomy.

This chapter focuses on how and why places are different, the scales at which we can understand these differentials and the implications for managers and entrepreneurs. International business is driven by companies and individuals collecting, analysing and making locational decisions, and is always in flux, subject to change. This can make being responsible more challenging. We then consider the tensions between integration versus localization and responsiveness, exploring how firms negotiate this tension between their global strategies and the degree to which they need to adapt their strategies to local contexts. This chapter outlines international business and social science approaches to understanding the ways in which international business connect to the localities in which they are present. We introduce the concept of 'dynamic embeddedness' in conceptual terms and explore how this can be used in practice. The chapter enters our framework with the cross-cutting themes of practices and conventions and change/evolution and discusses the building blocks of place and territory.

Place-based differentials and their role in international business

The uneven landscape of the global economy is created by differences between locations. These place-based differentials play a significant role in international business – generating the complex mosaic of resources and opportunities that international businesses seek to exploit. They are variations in economic (eg income levels, cost of living), social (eg education levels, access to healthcare), environmental (eg resources, vulnerability to natural disasters), political (eg regulations, business systems) and other conditions that are specific to geographical location.

The discipline of international business has traditionally viewed these place-based differentials as *context* – as the backdrop to international business – with much research focused on the development of universal models that we argue should be more sensitive to context and differences in place. Dunning's eclectic paradigm (2000) seeks to explain the conditions under which firms will internationalize (see Chapter 6). It argues that in order to internationalize, firms need to possess ownership, internalization and location advantages. Dunning (2000) argues that firms will be motivated by one of these forms; however, given the complexity of multinational enterprise (MNE) organizational structures, it is possible to observe overlapping location-seeking activities within the same firms, for locations to offer more than one set of motivation and for firms and places to interact. Firms and places influence each other (Dicken and Malmberg, 2001).

Dunning's eclectic paradigm and dynamic place-based differentials

With the eclectic paradigm, the identification of ownership, location and internalization advantages takes place at a single point in time, when the firm enters a new market. The OLI framework requires us to assess these factors at that moment. But how does this framework operate within a fast-changing global economy? Box 7.1 explores the case of a company with a long history in an international market.

Box 7.1: Location factor change dynamics: IKEA in Poland

IKEA has a long history of activities in Poland and today has a substantial supply chain located there, including production in 20 factories, 90 external suppliers, distribution, sales in 11 stores and wind farms. Some of the most popular IKEA series such as LACK, HEMNES, KALLAX and HÖVÅG are made in Poland (67%, 74%, 70%, 74% share of global production, respectively). Poland is the second most important country for IKEA for production, after China. Annually 20 per cent of global purchases of IKEA come from Poland (IKEA, 2020)

Dunning's OLI aims to understand the conditions required for internationalization to occur. However, the history of IKEA in Poland is complex, challenging the capacity of the framework. In the 1960s, IKEA cooperated with a national Polish company called Fameg to supply chairs. Not much more is documented about this period, but we do know that Poland is a country rich in resources (wood) and artisanal and technical production skills. The location factors were related to these raw materials and production expertise. However, geopolitical changes (the Cold War) prevented

IKEA's presence in the market until the Iron Curtain fell in 1989. IKEA returned to Poland in 1993, initially setting up a sales outlet. What does the OLI tell us about this market (re)entry? During this time, international firms including IKEA analysed the emerging Central European countries, searching for location advantages to exploit. Poland was considered ripe for growth in exports, financial services and retail sales and a flood of investment occurred in the 1990s.

IKEA had ownership factors related to their expertise in furniture design, branding, logistics expertise, low-cost strategy, economies of scale and internal capabilities (codes of conduct, organizational norms and practices). The firm also had internationalization knowledge (having entered 20 markets). The location advantages of Poland included the gaps in retail provision, access to raw materials (including, but not limited to, wood), technical expertise and consumer demand. Poland has one of the lowest rates of single-occupancy housing in Europe. More than half of Poles live in homes with just one bedroom, meaning parents often sleep in the living room. IKEA offers flexible and adaptable furniture that allows consumers to maximize the use of space. Internalization advantages include the capability to produce near the consumer, using their own production facilities to retain independence from suppliers. This allows IKEA to keep control over delivery and quality – important factors when the business model is predicated on standardization and reliability of delivery.

But the static nature of the eclectic paradigm reduces our ability to view IKEA's activities in Poland, causing us to overlook the complexity of their operations and the multitude of subsequent investments the firm has made since 1993. IKEA operates multiple companies in Poland, from Ingka Group (IKEA retail; shopping centres; business services for Ingka group across Europe; IT service desk covering 27 countries; distribution services across Europe; six wind farms); Inter IKEA group (purchasing services working with nearly 90 suppliers; IKEA Industry, the world's largest producer of wooden furniture), IKANO Group (IKANO bank offering banking and financing solutions to customers; mattress manufacture) and finally, Interogo Group (managing real estate).

Internationalization is a process that involves new market entry, but the story does not end there. Firms can fail, exit the market seeking better returns on investment, stagnate or expand and sometimes these processes vary across different business functions. In May 2012, IKEA expanded its operations in Poland, spending €140m on an ultra-thin, high-density fibre-board facility near Orla. They did this to acquire the technological knowledge that had been developed in Poland, gaining strategic control. This is the latest technology in fibre-board production. IKEA have developed and expanded their R&D activities in Orla, working towards new standards in the technology which could enhance its global competitive advantage.

Location factors within a national economy can evolve. IKEA's embeddedness within the Poland market, through its own production facilities and links with Polish suppliers, ensures knowledge flows and enables IKEA to further exploit the ownership, location and internalization factors. The OLI framework is not capable of adequately capturing change dynamics post-internationalization – and nor does it purport to do so. But as we try to understand international business and firm activities across uneven economic landscapes, we need to consider time as a factor in the evolution of locational factors. Places evolve as do companies. Poland's population is shrinking and ageing due to outward migration and low fertility rates. The consumer base is therefore changing, meaning IKEA are developing strategies, including focusing on pre-assembled furniture. Length of time in a market also seems to matter. IKEA state that: To IKEA, the company's success is founded on 'historical bonds and mutual trust built over the years. The entrepreneurial spirit of Poles combined with Scandinavian simplicity and innovation give us amazing development opportunities' (IKEA, 2020). The firm credits the *interaction* over time between ownership and location factors, resulting in Poland now being a central command point for IKEA operations in Europe and beyond. This raises the question of how committed a firm is to a particular place and how embedded it is. It varies over time and is different for each firm. For governments, who often offer incentives to attract foreign direct investment (FDI), a key issue can be how to retain those investments; that is to say, how to enhance the 'stickiness' of place and the spillovers of FDI. Winning FDI should be the start of an ongoing dialogue with the firm, demanding subsequent interactions intended to enhance stickiness and spillovers. This also raises questions regarding responsible business. Is disinvestment responsible or irresponsible business practice? IKEA has developed some degree of commitment to Poland, but the company continually flexes or adjusts these place-based investments in response to place-based and other alterations that impact on the company's strategy.

Advancing location factors?

The greatest academic attention has been paid to Dunning's ownership factor (see critique in Chapter 6), to the neglect of the location factor. As such, international business has made comparatively limited progress in understanding the location factor. Guisinger (2001) encourages the development of an improved definition of the international business environment, arguing that we need to distinguish between the domestic and foreign components of the environment. Following the work of North (1990), he also states that the environment be divided into organizations, which he calls 'interactors' and institutions called 'geovalent components'. Interactors are organizations that interact directly with the firm (suppliers, customers and competitors). The geovalent component comprises all the other environmental forces that impact on the firm but are not themselves organizations. They have the potential to directly and significantly affect the performance of firms and are to some extent quantifiable.

Table 7.1 is not exhaustive. You may want to think about what other attributes you can add to this list. Some elements and attributes will apply to all international investments in overseas markets, others will be of varying significance based on the geographical context and firm activities. Guisinger (2001: 267) chooses not to include international institutions as a geovalent component 'because their effect on MNCs is exercised indirectly through their influence on national policies, such as exchange rates, tariffs and tax systems'. This is a narrow, economic view of the impact of international institutions and there are some geographical contexts in which supra-regional policy-making is significant, such as the EU.

We can question the degree to which Table 7.1 helps us to identify place-based differentials for responsible business. Some elements and attributes may assume greater importance, while others are missing. If you are a responsible clothing company seeking

Table 7.1: Illustrative geovalent elements

Element	Examples of attributes defining each element
Geography	Proximity to major markets Physical size Infrastructure (local/national/international) Digital infrastructure Diversity within one market
Legal systems	Common Civil Religious law Local/place-based adaptations to the legal system
Regulatory system	Employment Environmental Corporate social responsibility Enterprise/Trade zones or other place-based alteration to national regulatory systems
Income profile	GDP or GNP per capita Economic growth Income inequality Consumer segmentation with a significant cohort of consumers able to purchase more luxury goods/services Trade balance
Political risk	Government stability Corruption Bureaucratic stability
Taxation	Effective tax rate for multinational firms Individual tax rate
Exchange rates	Exchange rate variability Exchange rate overvaluation/undervaluation
Government restrictions	Tariffs Quotas Investment controls

Source: Adapted from Guisinger (2001: Table 1)

to manufacture garments in a country, you will need to identify and understand the relevant characteristics of a place. This could include labour laws (national and local). If you are a responsible manufacturer, you will seek places with strong labour laws that prohibit child labour and ensure safe working environments. Going beyond investigating whether these exist, you would seek evidence that the laws are enforced. This requires a contextual approach to the application of responsible business. This would include exploring employment conditions and approaches to sustainability in practice of all companies directly and indirectly involved in a firm's value chain. For example, a company would need to be aware of labour conditions across all firms involved in its logistics and this includes those involved in transporting waste and those employed by taxi companies used by the company. Similarly, if you are a responsible agricultural producer, you will seek attributes that are related to environmental legislation regarding crop production (pesticides, water use, etc). Table 7.1 does not reflect the two key areas of interest for responsible business: 1) labour conditions and 2) the environment (including legislation, incentives, resources, etc). This can be explained by substantive responsible business being an ongoing or applied activity that is much more than simply developing a set of policies or strategies.

What Guisinger (2001: 269) does articulate is the interaction between what he calls 'structural complexity' and 'environmental complexity'. When a domestic firm wishes to enter the international marketplace, it needs to make adaptations to its processes to deal with the scope and scale of its presence in a larger market (structural complexity). The company must *also* adjust its processes to deal with the requirements of the international business environment (environmental complexity). Extending Guisinger's argument, we can see that internationalization to several markets requires multiple adjustments to different contexts of environmental complexity, which may be linked through structural complexity. This also suggests that a company may have a complexity threshold beyond which it should not go or will face substantial challenges if it does so. For this reason, some companies will restrict complexity.

Geographical scale: which places?

International business has a preoccupation with the nation-state or territorial scale. This is partly for good reason – much of the quantitative data used in research is collected at the national scale. 'Growth' is typically monitored and publicized at the national scale (GDP/GNP). However, if a company restricts the unit of analysis to the national scale, they overlook some other dynamics taking place at different scales. There are several other scales that are relevant to international businesses, and firms connect with and are embedded in these multiple scales simultaneously and in different ways:

- Supra-regions are typically trading blocs such as NAFTA and the EU, which have varying degrees of economic and political integration. Firms may be attracted to places based on their inclusion in, or proximity to, these trading blocs. For some sectors, such as automotive or even video games, the global economy is divided up into regions, either by trade tariffs or technological differences that encourage intra-region production and consumption. Brexit highlighted the consequences of exiting a supra-region.
- Regions are subnational areas that have definable characteristics but not always fixed boundaries. In some geographical contexts – the UK, Spain, others – there have been political pressures towards devolution. This can lead to specific areas having greater political and economic powers that can enable regions to offer incentives designed to attract foreign direct investment (including free trade zones).
- Cities, or city-regions, are central command points in the global economy. The vast majority of global capital flows between the world's major stock markets located in key cities. If we consider investments made by large international firms, this often occurs between headquarters in global cities and other cities in overseas territories. As such, we can understand cities as important nodes in the global economy through which capital generation, knowledge creation and sharing and decision-making processes flow.

When we shift the focus beyond the nation-state as a container, we can read places in a more nuanced way. We can observe multiple layers of administration, specialisms, resources and other place-based differentials based on the intersections of multiple geographical scales in each place. For international firms, location decision-making has to be sensitive to different places having different connections to the state within which they are embedded and to the global geoeconomy (Allen, 1992).

Uppsala: internationalization and learning

The Uppsala model (Johanson and Vahlne, 1977) seeks to explain the processes by which firms internationalize (using a behavioural approach, in which knowledge and learning are viewed as having a profound impact on how firms approach foreign markets. It assumes that a major obstacle to international operations is a lack of knowledge about foreign markets, but that knowledge can be acquired. Johanson and Vahlne (1977) argue that such knowledge is experiential, gained through the experience of being in new markets. The Uppsala model's establishment chain views foreign investment decisions as being made incrementally due to market uncertainty. The model therefore claims that through 'learning by doing', firms will lower the perceived market risk and develop a sequential internationalization process. From a practitioner perspective, the model is interesting as it assumes that knowledge is highly dependent on individuals, place-based and therefore difficult to transfer to either other individuals or other contexts (see Table 7.2).

The Uppsala model views learning about new markets as highly embedded in those markets by managers working in a subsidiary or other units in the new market. However, the spatial dimensions of the model are relatively underdeveloped, leading scholars to consider the ways in which firms structure their organizations.

Integration versus responsiveness

Subsidiaries of international firms are simultaneously an integral part of the firm and actors in a specific local context (Andersson et al, 2002; Meyer et al, 2011). They combine the resources of the firm with local resources in the host economy to create products or services they can supply to local markets or export. How firms manage their global and local operations has attracted academic attention, with varying degrees of reflection on managerial implications. Understanding the complementarities and tensions between geographical scales within an international firm and the contexts within which it is embedded is significant for a variety of reasons that relate to relationships with suppliers, supplier origin, local knowledge, composition of workforce and capacity to respond to local and global shocks.

In a contemporary global economy dominated by many 'global' brands, it is easy to imagine that firms are highly standardized (same branding, processes, suppliers, etc, in each location). In reality, firms can find themselves – intentionally or not – adapting to the contexts in which they operate. Even Coca-Cola, one of the world's most recognizable brands, has different production methods (some in-house, some outsourced) and varies its recipes in different markets. This is driven by consumption

Table 7.2: Organization learning in internationalization: academic literature and managerial implications

Core assumption	Academic work	Managerial implications
Knowledge transfer	Literature questions the degree to which market knowledge is limited to individuals. Through their business relationships, organizations can gain access to the knowledge of other firms, without having to go through the same experiences as these firms. Interorganizational learning in a business network can facilitate knowledge exchange and market-specific, tacit knowledge can be acquired through interaction with other organizations. Uppsala model predictions are dependent on an implicit assumption about stability in terms of firm personnel. The turnover of personnel can reduce stability and continuity of the internationalization process – although there is a degree of collective memory in firms in which the lessons of experience are maintained and accumulated.	Consideration should be made of how knowledge can be transferred within and beyond the managers' own organization. What internal sources of knowledge can be drawn upon? Do other parts of the organization have relevant knowledge? The larger the firm, the greater the task of reviewing existing internal knowledge. What external sources of knowledge can be gained about a potential market? What networks can be drawn upon via suppliers and customers, trade associations or even competitor firms? Where is knowledge held in an organization? How is it recorded? Are there codified (written) resources related to internationalization? Think through where knowledge is held, and by whom. This then needs to be considered alongside human resource strategies that aim to retain essential employees (the knowledge holders). If employees do leave an organization, how do firms minimize knowledge loss?
Acquiring knowledge	One 'short-cut' to knowledge can be through acquiring other organizations or by hiring people with the necessary knowledge. Huber (1991) uses the term 'grafting' as an alternative way to acquire market knowledge which therefore shapes the internationalization process differently. It avoids the slow process of learning through one's own experience. Forsgren (2002: 263) suggests that 'internationalization behaviour often seems to be characterized by a combination of learning through experience and learning through the incorporation of units, which already have the knowledge'.	What activities do managers use to gain knowledge from sources external to their organization? How do they use recruitment in their strategy? Managers can identify individuals in competitor firms – perhaps they have led firms of organizations to enter markets/regions other firms are interested in. Managers should think about how they can combine existing internal knowledge with that gained externally.
Mimetic behaviour	Organizations tend to mimic the actions taken by large numbers of organizations. By imitating other organizations, firms can reduce their perceived uncertainty, allowing a less incremental and less cautious internationalization process.	Managers should consider the activities of competitor firms. While there may be some first mover advantages to entering new markets first, later entry may enable them to learn from the successes (and mistakes) of similar firms. They may be able to learn from firms in related sectors.
Strategic behaviour	Learning can happen at different levels of an organization and within different contexts. Knowledge accumulated higher up in the organization (as well as the embedded contextual learning in new markets) also influences strategic behaviour. Market-specific knowledge and general knowledge exist within organizations, with the latter acting as a driving force in taking the firm in new directions. Forsgren (2002) argues that the more hierarchical/centralized a firm is, the closer the relationship between learning and action.	Managers should ask how the structure of their organization can facilitate or hinder how knowledge is shared. With regard to general knowledge, where is this held in the firm? How does this then interact with market-specific knowledge? How can knowledge be more effectively shared? Different firm structures require tailored approaches based on existing communication flows. For example, if a firm is structured by product (different divisions for products), there may be market-specific knowledge held within each division that is not shared. Where firms are organized by geography, it can be assumed that knowledge sharing about markets is more easily facilitated. However, product-specific knowledge may be less easily shared.

(taste preferences) and production (market size and production capabilities) demands in different localities. This example also illustrates an important point around the concepts we use in the context of understanding place-based differentials. 'Localization' is a general term that describes a product that is modified to suit the tastes or requirements of a particular market. This can be food, such as variations on a McDonald's meal, or products, such as video games that have language and/or content localized for specific markets. We also see the term 'localization strategy', which refers to a company strategy that focuses on a number of foreign countries (more on this below). In general terms, when we talk about the integration (or not) of firms in multiscalar contexts, we are conceptualizing more than just the adaptation of a final product or service. We are incorporating aspects that include production, logistics, firm operations and workforce, etc. Companies are complex organizations, and we will now explore how firms, and their managers, develop strategies to manage across international operations.

Prahalad and Doz (1987) developed the 'integration-responsiveness' framework, arguing that international firms develop competitive positions across two dimensions – integration and responsiveness. Integration refers to the coordination of activities across geographical territories in an attempt to build efficient operational networks and to take advantage of similarities across locations (Johnson, 1995). Aggregation benefits such as economies of scale, global innovation and global sourcing often call for global integration. Responsiveness refers to the ability of firms to respond to the specific needs within a variety of host countries (place-based differentials). Each firm takes a strategic decision to either emphasize one dimension over another or to compete on both dimensions. Bartlett and Ghosal (1989) argue that international firms may be able to pursue both objectives simultaneously and view integration-responsiveness as resulting in four strategies: 1) home replication, 2) localization, 3) global standardization and 4) transnational strategy. These are detailed in Table 7.3.

The integration-responsiveness framework can provide some insight into the tension between the local and global within firms and the strategies that firms develop to structure their operations. Typically, the organizational structure of international businesses develops organically over time, so the emphasis on aggregation and adaptation can be in part determined by organizational history. For example, a firm that grows through multiple mergers and acquisitions is more likely to adopt a localized or transnational strategy – certainly in the short term – while it decides whether to keep acquired brands or to standardize brands. An example is Vedior, a Dutch temporary-staffing company that grew during the 1990s and 2000s through acquisition of nationally based staffing agencies. Vedior was a lean organization with a small headquarters performing financial tasks, leaving agencies with high autonomy and allowing them to retain their branding. The rationale for this was that temporary staffing is highly place-based. Labour is not particularly mobile so the vast majority of staffing placements happen within national boundaries (and typically within commuting distances). Vedior appreciated that the local brands possessed local connections with industry and high brand recognition. Through these acquisitions, the firm rapidly became one of the largest staffing agencies globally. Few outside the industry were aware of the connections between the brands. Their Dutch rival Randstad applied a different approach. They adopted a global standardization strategy.

Table 7.3 Integration-responsiveness strategies: advantages, disadvantages and managerial implications

Strategy	Advantages	Disadvantages	Managerial considerations
Home Replication (Low aggregation; low adaptation) Replicates home country-based competencies such as production scales, distribution efficiencies and brand positioning	• Leverages home country-based advantages • Relatively easy to implement	• Lack of local responsiveness • May result in foreign customer alienation • Can under-utilize local staff capabilities • Lack of autonomy can stifle innovation	• Managerial focus is on transferring product-specific knowledge to new markets based on home-country experiences and having direct oversight of subsidiaries • Responsible business strategies are exported to new markets
Localization (Low aggregation; high adaptation) Considers each country as a stand-alone 'local' market worthy of significant adaptation	• Maximizes local responsiveness • Increases capability to exploit place-based differentials • Greater autonomy for local workforce can speed decision-making and innovation	• High costs due to duplication of efforts in multiple countries • Too much local autonomy can dilute strength of strategy • May involve multiple brands which can reduce corporate identity (but may not) • Lower oversight may mean problem solving is delayed	• Managerial focus is on creating the broad frameworks for local business to take place • It may be easier to adapt to local conditions but harder for managers to respond when regional/global problems occur • It is likely to be harder to devise and implement company-wide strategies, ie around sustainability. Can agreement be found? If agreed, strategies are likely to be highly localized and different methodologies can inhibit firm-level monitoring and data collection
Global standardization (High aggregation; low adaptation) Sometimes referred to as 'global strategy'. Involves the development and distribution of standardized products worldwide to reap maximum economies of scale	• Leverages low-cost advantages • Relatively easy to roll out new products/services at speed • Allows for global supply agreements • Typically involves a single, global brand	• Lack of local responsiveness • Too much centralized control • Harder (but not impossible) to identify centres of excellence outside home country • Can be undermined by consumer demand for personalized and bespoke products and services	• Managerial focus is on ensuring standardization across firm network and concentrates on minimizing divergence from the standard • There is much higher transfer of knowledge *to* subsidiaries to the neglect of knowledge *from* subsidiaries • Devising and implementing global strategies is straightforward and greatest effort focuses on compliance
Transnational (High aggregation; high adaptation) Focuses on global learning and diffusion of innovations	• Cost-efficient while being locally responsive • Engages in global learning and diffusion of innovations	• Organizationally complex • Difficult to implement	• Managers, and their teams, can face contradictory and competing demands • Multiple reporting lines can cause confusion, repetition and inconsistency in the development and implementation of strategies

Source: Adapted from Peng and Meyer (2011: Table 5.1)

Their global brand made it easier for them to service their international clients through global supply agreements. In 2008, Randstad acquired Vedior.

Sometimes labour is more mobile, particularly corporate executives. In international businesses, individuals may work in overseas locations and sometimes for long periods. Bryson and Rusten (2008) compare the global executive placement strategies of two firms – 3M and Boeing. They find that while existing service literature highlights the importance of global cities as command points in the global economy, manufacturing companies have developed their own important places as 'different places perform different functions in the global economy' (Bryson and Rusten, 2008: 321). The corporate strategy of 3M identifies and develops local expertise which is supplemented by limited movement of employees between facilities. Boeing exemplifies how a company can develop a supply-chain ecosystem that shares expertise and labour. The firm relies on a global exchange of expertise, particularly in design, within its boundaries and across its supply network. Each international firm has its own 'global' places that reflect the history of the firm and its specific business interests.

Dynamism is inherent in company strategy and the evolution of organizational forms. Nothing is static and there is rarely uniformity in how strategies are developed, implemented or imposed across an international firm's network. Much attention in international business has been paid to the relationship between firm headquarters and subsidiaries, predominately from the point of view of understanding the impact on performance (typically profit maximization). There is scope for extending our understandings, particularly in relation to responsible business practices. No two subsidiaries face exactly the same circumstances, due to place-based differentials, but some do adapt better than others and the difference is reflected in their performance (Lin and Hsieh, 2010). We suggest that the ability of subsidiaries to adapt will also impact on their capabilities to act responsibly.

Based on interviews with managers, Taggart (1997) identifies four types of subsidiary role based on the integration-responsiveness framework. These are outlined in Figure 7.1.

Lin and Hsieh (2010) extend Taggart's taxonomy to consider the operational capabilities (configuration and coordination) and procedural justice (which they term 'implementation variables') of individual subsidiaries.

Configuration – defines the functional activities that the subsidiary carries out. This can vary from dispersed (replicating an entire value chain within each country) to concentrated (disaggregated individual activities of the value chain across countries). Higher integration tends to require more concentrated configuration, while higher responsiveness necessitates a more dispersed configuration. Some concentration is expected to exploit place-based differentials and secure scale economies.

Coordination – the extent to which the subsidiary coordinates its functional activities with those of other subsidiaries in the firm's global network.

Procedural justice – the extent to which a firm's strategy-making process is judged to be fair by the top managers of subsidiaries. The fairness judgements made by subsidiary managers impact on managerial in-role behaviours, compliance and voluntary cooperation that pave the way to exercise strategic decisions. Procedures perceived to be unfair are likely to result in a lack of cooperation and compliance and can cause subsidiary managers to undermine the organization in pursuit of their own gains. Subsidiaries have higher degrees of interdependence and require higher levels of procedural justice (Lin and Hsieh, 2010: 54).

Figure 7.1: Four subsidiary roles

Receptive	Active
Subsidiaries carry out few value-chain functions	Subsidiaries receive strong mandates from headquarters
Highly integrated into parent-firm network	Perform many value-chain activities and these activities are highly integrated with similar or different activities in different parts of the firm network
Less responsive to host-country environment	
Higher configuration	*Higher configuration*
High coordination, interdependence exists in some concentrated functional activities	*Higher coordination, high interdependence exists in some concentrated functional activities*
High procedural justice	*High procedural justice*
Quiescent	**Autonomous**
Considered to be a temporary position while the subsidiary shifts to one of the other three types	Perform most of the value chain functions in relative independence from headquarters and other subsidiaries
Produce and sell some products in the local country and do not replicate all activities	Focus on local requirements
Little connection to sister subsidiaries	*Lower configuration*
Strong links with headquarters (dependencies in technology and finance)	*Lowest coordination, low interdependence with firm network*
Lower configuration	*Low procedural justice*
Low coordination with other subsidiaries but high dependence on headquarters	
Moderate procedural justice	

Left axis: Integration
Bottom axis: Responsiveness

Source: Adapted from Lin and Hsieh (2010: Figure 2)

Lin and Hsieh (2010) argue that firms assign alternative strategic roles to different subsidiaries, thereby creating different implementation requirements. The firm then must differentiate the implementation variables to fit subsidiary roles. The gap between the role of the subsidiary and the implementation variables is a 'differentiated fit'. Lin and Hsieh identify two managerial implications. First, the firm does not always differentiate implementation variables properly across its subsidiaries. Ideally, managers would be provided with a guideline to monitor which implementation variables need to be improved and in what direction. This is particularly important as the role of the subsidiary shifts over time. When this happens, mission creep occurs. Second, by understanding their subsidiary role, they can adjust each implementation variable to approach as closely as possible the ideal profile. This requires an accurate awareness of the shifts that occur over time in subsidiary roles.

The work of Taggart (1997) and Lin and Hsieh (2010) provides us with a typology through which we can understand the different functions subsidiaries perform both within the global firm network and within the national context. However, there are some limitations. As with all taxonomies, the identification of four types (one temporary, three permanent) may reduce our awareness of complexity and differentiation. In very complex global value chains, firm networks can include intra- and inter-firm networks, in which subsidiaries are embedded in multiple supply arrangements that may make identification of a subsidiary type challenging. What is useful about this contribution is the consideration of managerial practices, in particular the power of managers to act based on their perception of procedural justice. This reminds us that the development and implementation of strategy is not always straightforward. It can be contested and can require compromise and adaptation to local contexts. These modifications can be linked to the concept of embeddedness.

Embeddedness

We can extend our understandings of firm internationalization beyond the core international business frameworks of Dunning's eclectic paradigm and the Uppsala model. This includes engaging with work in social sciences around 'embeddedness'. Granovetter's (1985) classic essay argues that economic action is not the aggregate of the actions of isolated individuals or firms but is further 'embedded' in social relationships. In this respect, all actions, whether social or economic, are affected by the social relations of actors and the overall structures of their 'network' of relations. When applied to businesses, industrial networks can be viewed as being composed of companies and individuals engaged in business activities. These networks are dynamic and constantly changing. Firms are seen as being embedded in wider business networks which extend far beyond the boundaries of the individual company. Research into business networks and embeddedness has tended to focus on the connectivity of the networks linking different business units, with the unit of analysis being individual firms and their dyadic connections to other business actors.

Broader perspectives of embeddedness view actors as embedded in markets, stressing the role of 'concrete' personal relations and structures (ie networks) in generating trust and 'discouraging malfeasance' in society (Granovetter, 1985). For Grabher (1993), embeddedness refers to the fact that economic action and outcomes, like all social action and outcomes, are affected by actors' dyadic relations and by the structure of overall networks of relations. The embeddedness approach also allows the significance of 'trust' to be considered and assessment of the balance between cooperation and collaboration between firms.

Grabher and Stark (1997) argue that the proper analytical unit is not the isolated firm but the *networks* that link firms and which connect persons across and within them. Their attention shifted from the attributes and motivations of individual personalities to the properties of the localities and networks in which economic activity is reproduced – the place-based differentials. Shifting the level of analysis from individual firms to networks does not imply that individual firms are conceived as homogenous actors. Networks comprise of broad and heterogeneous spectrum of actors, all of whom exert different levels of control and power. They do not characterize networks in terms of concord and harmonious collaboration among equals (Grabher and Stark, 1997). In short, these socioeconomic perspectives view the firm as embedded in socially constructed networks of reciprocity and interdependence.

As Granovetter's (1985) work has been applied across different disciplines, a range of types of embeddedness have been identified. Some of these are relevant to our understanding of place-based differentials and the ways in which international firms act in foreign markets. A common distinction is made between structural and relational embeddedness:

- *Relational embeddedness* is based on a direct and dyadic tie between two firms (Kim, 2014) and the need for firms to develop mutual dependence and commitment. The ties between the firms can be strong or weak (Granovetter, 1985). Strong ties see firms interacting frequently, circulating knowledge and resources. Weak ties are characterized by a loosely coupled relationship or relative infrequency of interaction.
- *Structural embeddedness* is created in triadic or more complex structures composed of multiple dyadic relationships. This can refer to multipartner alliances, where a focal firm is embedded with suppliers in multiple tiers (Kim, 2014). When examining structural embeddedness we would observe the presence or absence of network connections, the density of linkages and nature of those connections (tight connections with intense communication, sharing information versus sparse networks where there are no direct connections).

This view of embeddedness through the lens of supply-chain arrangements has been broadened to consider the efforts by organizations to become more deeply rooted in the environments in which their activities take place (Rocha et al, 2022). Andersson et al (2002) point to the extensive research conducted on the importance of embeddedness in the relationships of multinational firms with customers, suppliers and local partners, with Jack et al (2015) finding that embeddedness has a positive effect on companies' sales growth, market share and profits. We can extend this to include a firm's customers – how do companies make their customers feel valued and special? Customers can become so embedded – for example through end-user innovation – that they are part of a firm's innovation ecosystem. As embeddedness considers context, research on international firms and their embeddedness can take a range of forms, such as 'local embeddedness, 'social embeddedness' or 'multiple embeddedness'.

When examining multinational firms, we typically see local and social embeddedness employed to understand the overseas contexts in which firms operate. Part of relational embeddedness, local embeddedness refers to the ability of a firm to develop social ties and build social networks into its internationalization and operational strategies. Engaging with work on political economy, this perspective examines the ways in which firms create social capital through tackling issues such as poverty, education, nutrition, human rights and diseases, predominately in the Global South. In the Global

North, issues could include tackling underemployment, living wages and employment security. In emerging markets, the ability of international firms to integrate into host countries and to forge good relationships with local stakeholders both inform their local embeddedness (Mazé et al, 2024). Mazé et al (2024) conducted an in-depth study of Chinese mining multinationals in Peru, finding that their structural embeddedness focused on high-level political lobbying, to the neglect of localized engagement strategies (local embeddedness). They observed that growing grassroots resistance by local stakeholders in Peru was beginning to undermine the bargaining power of the multinational firms. We can therefore observe that there are different ways in which firms can embed themselves; that is to say, different contexts and with various actors – and sometimes they have to make choices between which stakeholders to be most embedded with (as choosing one can limit embeddedness with another).

Given that international businesses are operating in several places, they can often benefit from 'multiple embeddedness' in which they are engaging with institutions and resources from both home and host countries. Firms have to formulate strategies to make use of these differences. Meyer et al (2011) observe firms managing a portfolio of subsidiary activities in numerous and diverse local contexts while constructing strategies to embed operations more *efficiently* into these multiple environments. This highlights what is desired by firms, but less about the realities of making this happen and where potential difficulties, contradictions and even conflict can occur as firms become more embedded in those various local contexts. Two dimensions are important here: first, that of *time* as firm activities and their embeddedness are not static and second, *responsibility*. If we replace the word 'efficiently' with 'responsibly', does this give us a different perspective on international firm embeddedness?

Dynamic embeddedness

As we have discussed above, firms engaging in internationalization learn from this process over time. The ways in which they learn, the information they collect and knowledge they gain will be determined by their network embeddedness. Embeddedness can help firms overcome resource and knowledge limitations and enable activities that would not be possible if the firm were isolated (Rocha et al, 2022). During internationalization, embeddedness in a firm's domestic as well as new market can impact on their success and the shape and scope of their operations in the short and long term.

The geography of a firm's embeddedness matters, too. A firm may begin as a highly localized embedded set of relationships that evolve over time. Some linkages may be displaced as the firm begins to incorporate non-local suppliers and customers (Salder and Bryson, 2019). In their study of local manufacturing enterprises in Staffordshire (a historical manufacturing region in the UK, suffering post-industrial decline), Salder and Bryson (2019) identified what they term 'adaptive embeddedness', taking a dynamic approach to embeddedness. They engage with recent debates about the ability of embeddedness to be replicated elsewhere – some argue that social relations, territorial capital and modes of asset mobilization are too deeply embedded and spatially distinctive (Hamdouch et al, 2017). Salder and Bryson (2019) acknowledge that it can be difficult to replicate the complex concentration of processes and factors that exist locally, but they also see firms as able to adapt to exogenous and endogenous processes. In their study of small and medium-sized firms (SMEs) in small and medium-sized communities, they identify three forms of embeddedness that we can reflect on in the context of international firms:

1. The formation of a firm in a small and medium-sized town or community has several motivations and drivers. The most important of these relates to personal sunk costs, reflecting a form of *emotional embeddedness* in a place compared to that of business considerations. For international firms, we can assume less emotional embeddedness in overseas locations, although there may also be lifestyle and personal connections to places based on the backgrounds of the company leadership (eg a firm may connect with a particular diaspora).
2. Firms are in a constant process of embedding as the relationship between the firm and the place alters. Localized sunk costs constrain this process, limiting adaption (see Table 7.3). This can eventually contribute to failure. Thus, we can observe that embeddedness is not an end point, but rather a constant process of *embedding* and sometimes *disembedding*. The reflection for international businesses is that their efforts to internationalize to, and embed in, overseas territories is a process that requires ongoing attention.
3. Surviving firms engage in a process of *adaptive embeddedness* through which they reconfigure their relationship with place by connecting with outside locations. Altering the nature of local embeddedness through non-local networks is also an ongoing process. International firms may experience adaptive embeddedness differently. When they internationalize, they may rely heavily on non-local (pre-existing) networks, seeking to develop local connections over time.

In an example of the temporary dimensions of embeddedness, Christopherson (2007) analysed Walmart's failed internationalization in Germany. She observed that Walmart's success due to its market power and technological superiority results in market-entry failure (also in Korea and Indonesia), which implies that explanations often reside in the characteristics of the market rather than the context within which corporations develop strategies. Remember that firms and places interact with each other in dynamic ways. Christopherson notes that Walmart's high degree of corporate control over all dimensions of the distribution and retailing process and vertical organization of supply chains was challenged in Germany. Walmart was too rigid, making adaptation to a multiplicity of international market situations problematic. In Germany, the company was operating in a different regulatory and institutional regime, and its own governance structure (a publicly traded company owned by shareholders with short-term goals) limited the capacity to wait for profitability. Walmart gave itself too little time to adapt and withdrew from the market, seeking other opportunities that would produce profits more rapidly (like the acquisition of Asda in the UK). In her broader reflections on this case, Christopherson (2007: 465) notes that developing 'a more dynamic understanding of international economic activity, which recognizes processes of disinvestment as well as investment, is a valuable step toward a more concrete and specific description of globalization'. This is particularly relevant to responsible business as reflection is needed on if, when and how to disinvest from overseas locations. Box 7.2 explores some of the challenges of firm relocation.

Box 7.2: Can a firm be too small to relocate? 3T advanced manufacturing in the UK

The advanced manufacturing firm 3T is located in Newbury, UK. This firm is an SME, employing 40 staff, and is part of an international business headquartered in Italy. They are a responsible business – the 3T factory uses advanced digital manufacturing technologies and processes to achieve sustainable net-zero production. The company has been steadily growing in size over the past three years and is outgrowing its current factory. Growth is positive, but the challenges of business relocation are often neglected in academic research. This case illustrates how firms are not always easily able to 'pick up' operations and establish them elsewhere. Requiring larger facilities, 3T are seeking regional governmental support for their growth and development of their sustainable manufacturing business model.

Theory tells us that they should be seeking the optimal geographical location – the best spot in the UK that provides them with skilled labour, carbon-neutral facilities, energy resources and regional institutional support. The business reality is rather different. To move location would mean disruption that could kill the business. There are two options, each with high costs attached. First, they could wind down their existing facility and then set up a new factory. This would take at least two years and would mean that they were not able to conduct business during this time. No revenue during this period would cause the business to fail. Second, 3T could wind down their existing facility while simultaneously starting a new facility but this would mean costs would be doubled (not within their capabilities and only solved with external investment/support). In either scenario, there is one 'sticky' problem – the relative immobility of labour. If 3T were to move town more than 50 km or so away, many of their employees may leave. The firm would then have to find new employees in the new location, which may not be straightforward (and always has a cost in time and resources). With any relocation the transfer of people is a significant difficulty. It can severely limit the ability of firms to exploit place-based differentials.

In our discussions with 3T, they observed that it is sometimes easier to move country than to relocate within a country. Could they leave the UK? Disembed themselves, shaking off some of the shackles limiting their growth? Could 3T more easily attract investment and support overseas (most countries encourage and incentivize foreign direct investment)? Perhaps they could secure additional resources from their parent company to make an international relocation over a domestic one. Extra complexity results from 3T as a firm within a larger international firm, operating more local. Many of the company's customers are international businesses, so 3T could service them from almost anywhere. At present, the tasks of driving business revenue growth and championing sustainable manufacturing using advanced technologies keep 3T in the UK and their factory relocation will likely be to a very geographically proximate place. This case serves as an example of how firms can be too small to move, reducing the capacity to exploit place-based differentials in the global economy compared to larger firms.

It is possible for firms to become too embedded in a place. However, Andersen (2013) contests the predominant view that (very) high levels of embeddedness by definition equals over-embeddedness. For her, (very) high levels of embeddedness can lead to different outcomes depending on the context. Andersen's primary point of comparison is between domestic and international markets. She finds that in domestic markets, network participants benefit from accumulated knowledge acquired through strong network embeddedness that is beneficial. In contrast, in foreign markets, due to high uncertainty in the form of unknown competition, diverse demand and the liability of foreignness (the extra costs associated with a foreign firm operating in a market), the benefits of accumulated knowledge decrease. The causes of over-embeddedness are a combination of suboptimal allocation of scarce resources and accumulation of localized abilities, which jointly produce a negative effect on performance in foreign markets. When the costs of embeddedness are maintained but the benefits decrease, a firm may experience over-embeddedness. The reason for embeddedness becoming over-embeddedness lies in the nature of network-generated benefits, which causes the cost–benefit trade-off to shift when participants enter foreign markets.

Hagedoorn and Frankort (2008) discuss the 'gloomy' side of firms' embeddedness in networks of inter-firm partnership. They suggest that we need a nested understanding of the effects of three levels of over-embeddedness – environmental, inter-organization and dyadic over-embeddedness – on inter-firm partnership formation and dynamics over time. For them, the major cause of embeddedness is the interaction between dyadic over-embeddedness (when the relationship between two firms becomes redundant through long-term repeated ties) and inter-organizational over-embeddedness (where groups become crowded or congested). What then, does this mean for international firms seeking to exploit place-based differentials? These firms will expect to achieve a degree of embeddedness in foreign markets as this is required to accumulate market-specific knowledge, to engage with relevant stakeholders and to access specific resources. This overview of embeddedness teaches us that there are: 1) multiple interrelated forms of embeddedness; 2) embeddedness is always in the process of becoming and is never final and fixed – it is dynamic and changes over time, due not least to changes in both the firm and the place in which it is operating; and 3) firms need to pay continuous attention to their networks. If over-embeddedness occurs, firms need to spark network evolution, looking beyond their embedded partnerships.

Responsible business and embeddedness

For several decades, certainly up until the global financial crisis in 2008, commentators emphasized the power of international businesses and their capacity to exploit place-based differences in the global economy. They could seemingly invest – and disinvest – rapidly. This contributed to the perception of highly mobile firms, closing factories and reopening them in lower cost locations. While parts of this narrative about place-based exploitation are correct, it does not reflect the ways in which firms become tied to places and the ways in which they become embedded. The previous discussion about over-embeddedness indicates that being too deeply embedded can reduce firm performance in foreign markets. Do embedded firms lose competitive advantages as they become 'stickier' (more tied to place)? If we understand firms simply as profit-generating entities, then perhaps the sole focus on performance is appropriate. However, there are many different types of firms and responsible business means considering more than just performance (and what is 'performance' anyway?). Responsible businesses must consider the ways in which they *exploit* place-based differentials – aiming to reduce exploitation and maximize mutually sustainable relationships with all stakeholders in the markets in which they operate.

There are numerous examples of international firms failing to consider local communities (eg international oil companies operating in Nigeria, Home Depot in China or Uber in Germany). For responsible businesses, the task is to consider who they want to be embedded with, what form their networks should take and what the ideal balance is between the local and non-local. The aim should be to balance local expertise with global knowledge.

Global managers should look beyond their supply chains (although, of course, ensuring ethical supply chains and good working conditions is of primary importance) to consider with whom they wish to collaborate to achieve their corporate social responsibility goals and the nature of their presence in a market. What do international business practitioners wish their legacy to be? How do global managers create deep network relationships and avoid over-embeddedness? Is over-embeddedness possible if those network relationships are not focused on firm performance? What if we take a more nuanced view of what a firm is and how it should behave in overseas markets, particularly in contexts where there are colonial legacies and/or geopolitical power inequalities? Global managers should also think about the responsibilities of being present in an international market. Firms create jobs, build relationships, hopefully conduct philanthropic activities, etc. The implications can be profound if the firm exits the market. Not all responsible decisions are easy. Following the escalation of the Russia–Ukraine War in 2022, international firms were expected to exit the Russian market. Many have not. Some of those who have stayed have cited that they are supplying 'essential' products that the Russian population needs. One such example is Unilever, but this firm has faced criticism for continuing to sell other non-essential items. Benetton, the Italian garment conglomerate, has explicitly defended its position to do business as usual in Russia. They claim that they wish to defend the sanctity of its longstanding relationships with local partners and a network of stores employing over 600 families. One point to reflect upon is the ways in which a firm's governance structure impacts on its ability to act responsibly in response to an immediate alteration in a place's characteristics. A key issue is a firm's ability to flex rapidly and to disinvest. Nevertheless, some types of governance structure are extremely rigid and make rapid disinvestment impossible.

Conclusion

International business aims to find and exploit differences in place. These place-based differentials drive firm internationalization – without them there would be no need to leave the home market other than to access more consumers. The global economy is not homogenizing, the majority of differences we categorize in this chapter are increasing, particularly around resource scarcity and under growing geopolitical pressures. This chapter examines the ways in which firms structure their operations to respond to place-based differentials as well as maintaining a global strategy. This is not straightforward and firms can struggle with the tensions between the local and the global, particularly in times of crisis.

The forms of engagement in foreign markets that international businesses take relate to their embeddedness. This chapter has outlined different types of embeddedness and highlighted that academic literature tends to tell us that firms need different strategies in their home markets compared to overseas territories. For responsible businesses, the mechanisms for market entry and establishment need to focus on sustainable and mutually supportive network relationships with stakeholders at multiple scales. This takes time, learning and a dynamic approach. The next chapter, Chapter 8, will focus on services. Services can be embedded in different ways and these differences are explored in Chapter 8. As well as physical embeddedness, firms can be embedded in online networks (see Chapter 3), such as digital platforms that are almost completely virtual. Firms, such as software firms, face particular challenges around internationalization – demanding place-based differentials such as IT infrastructure including servers and labour regulation (see also the discussion on technology born global firms in Chapter 3). We can therefore consider the ways in which firms are embedded in both physical and non-physical systems, but also noting that even a virtual platform 'touches down' in the physical through the people who design and operate it, the physical infrastructure needed to run the platform and the people using it. Thus, place matters, even as our geoeconomy becomes more digital.

Key terms

Embeddedness – the quality of being firmly and deeply ingrained or fixed in a place.

Place-based differentials – the multidimensional characteristics of a particular place that create uneven investment and operational landscapes for international firms.

Recommended reading

Dicken, P. and Malmberg, A. (2001) 'Firms in territories: a relational perspective', *Economic Geography*, 77(4): 345–63.

Meyer, K.E., Mudambi, R. and Narula, R. (2011) 'Multinational enterprises and local contexts: the opportunities and challenges of multiple embeddedness', *Journal of Management Studies*, 48(2): 235–52.

Rocha, R., Marques, C.S.E. and Galvão, A.R. (2022) 'Embeddedness in internationalization: knowledge map and research agenda proposal', *Journal of General Management*, 48(1): 46–62. doi.org/10.1177/07316844211047161.

Wigren-Kristoferson, C., Brundin, E., Hellerstedt, K., Stevenson, A. and Aggestam, M. (2022) 'Rethinking embeddedness: a review and research agenda', *Entrepreneurship and Regional Development*, 34(1–2): 32–56. doi.org/10.1080/08985626.2021.2021298.

References

Allen, J. (1992) 'Services and the UK space economy: regionalization and economic dislocation', *Transactions of the Institute of British Geographers*, 17(3): 292–305.

Andersen, K.V. (2013) 'The problem of embeddedness revisited: collaboration and market types', *Research Policy*, 42: 139–48. dx.doi.org/10.1016/j.respol.2012.05.005.

Andersson, U., Forsgren, M. and Holm, U. (2002) 'The strategic impact of external networks: subsidiary performance and competence development in the multinational corporation', *Strategic Management Journal*, 23: 979–96.

Bartlett, C. A. and Ghoshal, S. (1989) *Managing Across Borders: The Transnational Solution*, Harvard: Harvard Business School Press.

Bryson, J.R. and Rusten, G. (2008) 'Transnational corporations and spatial divisions of "service" expertise as a competitive strategy: the example of 3M and Boeing', *Service Industries Journal*, 28(3): 307–23. doi.org/10.1080/02642060701856340.

Christopherson, S. (2007) 'Barriers to "US style" lean retailing: the case of Wal-Mart's failure in Germany', *Journal of Economic Geography*, 7(4): 451–69.

Dicken, P. and Malmberg, A. (2001) 'Firms in territories: a relational perspective', *Economic Geography*, 77(4): 345–63.

Dunning, J. (2000) 'The eclectic paradigm as an envelope for economic and business theories of MNC activity', *International Business Research*, 9(2): 163–90.

Forsgren, M. (2002) 'The concept of learning in the Uppsala internationalisation process model: a critical review', *International Business Review*, 11(3): 257–77.

Grabher, G. (ed.) (1993) *The Embedded Firm: On the Socio-economics of Industrial Networks*, London: Routledge.

Grabher, G. and Stark, D. (1997) *Restructuring Networks in Postcolonialism: Linkages and Locality*, Oxford: Oxford University Press.

Granovetter, M. (1985) 'Economic action and social structure: the problem of embeddedness', *American Journal of Sociology*, 91: 481–510.

Guisinger, S. (2001) 'From OLI to OLMA: incorporating higher levels of environmental and structural complexity into the eclectic paradigm', *International Journal of the Economics of Business*, 8(2): 257–72. doi.org/10.1080/13571510110051487.

Hagedoorn, J. and Frankort, H.T.W. (2008) 'The gloomy side of embeddedness: the effects of overembeddedness on inter-firm partnership formation', in J.A.C. Baum and T.J. Rowley (eds.) *Network Strategy* (*Advances in Strategic Management, Vol. 25*), Leeds: Emerald Group Publishing Limited, pp 503–30. doi.org/10.1016/S0742-3322(08)25014-X.

Hamdouch, A., Demaziere, C. and Banovac, K. (2017) 'The socio-economic profiles of small and medium-sized towns: insights from European case studies', *Tijdschrift voor economische en sociale geografie*, 108(4): 456–71. doi.org/10.1111/tesg.2017.108.issue-4.

Huber, G.P. (1991) 'Organisational learning: the contributing processes and the literatures', *Organization Science* 2(1): 88–115.

IKEA (2020) *Made in Poland* [online]. Available from: www.ikea.com/pl/pl/files/pdf/9d/c3/9dc30f67/digital_en_project_made_in_poland.pdf [Accessed 10 July 2024].

Jack, R., As-Saber, S. and Edwards, R. (2015) 'Service embeddedness and its role in a firm's internationalisation process', *International Journal of Operations & Production Management*, 35(3): 346–369.

Johanson, J. and Vahlne, J.-E. (1977) 'The internationalisation process of the firm – a model of knowledge development and increasing foreign market commitments', *Journal of International Business Studies*, 8: 23–32.

Johnson, J.H. (1995) 'An empirical analysis of the integration-responsiveness framework: construction equipment industry firms in global competition', *Journal of International Business Studies*, 26(3): 621–35.

Kim, D.-Y. (2014) 'Understanding supplier structural embeddedness: a social network perspective', *Journal of Operations Management*, 32 (5): 219–31.

Lin, S.-L. and Hsieh, A.-T. (2010) 'International strategy implementation: roles of subsidiaries, operational capabilities, and procedural justice', *Journal of Business Research*, 63(1): 52–9. doi.org/10.1016/j.jbusres.2008.11.008.

Mazé, D., Alcaraz, J. and Buitrago, R.R.E. (2024) 'Emerging market multinationals' embeddedness in Global South countries: an empirical study of Chinese MNEs in Peru', *Critical Perspectives on International Business*, 20(4): 517–38.

Meyer, K.E., Mudambi, R. and Narula, R. (2011) 'Multinational enterprises and local contexts: the opportunities and challenges of multiple embeddedness', *Journal of Management Studies*, 48(1): 235–52. doi: 10.1111/j.1467-6486.2010.00968.

North, D.C. (1990) *Institutions, Institutional Change and Economic Performance*, Cambridge: Cambridge University Press.

Peng, M. and Meyer, K. (2011) *International Business*, London: Cengage Learning.

Prahalad, C.K. and Doz, Y.L. (1987) *The Multinational Mission: Balancing Local Demands and Global Vision*, New York: Free Press.

Rocha, R., Marques, C.S.E. and Galvão, A.R. (2022) 'Embeddedness in internationalization: knowledge map and research agenda proposal', *Journal of General Management*, 48(1): 46–62. doi.org/10.1177/07316844211047161.

Salder, J. and Bryson, J.R. (2019) 'Placing entrepreneurship and firming small town economies: manufacturing firms, adaptive embeddedness, survival and linked enterprise structures', *Entrepreneurship and Regional Development*, 31(9–10): 806–25. doi.org/10.1080/08985626.2019.1600238.

Taggart, J.H. (1997) 'An evaluation of the integration-responsiveness framework: MNC manufacturing subsidiaries in the UK', *Management International Review*, 37(4): 295–318.

8

Services versus Manufacturing and Responsible Business

Introduction

The complexity of the geoeconomy in terms of place-based differentials was explored in Chapter 7. This revealed the multitude of different ways in which the activities of international businesses have to adapt to market variations at local, national, regional and global scales. One of the primary challenges of international businesses is to respond to changes at these geographical scales, a task that becomes more difficult as firms grow their activities across international boundaries. In addition, geoeconomy variegation also occurs based on the types of sectors in which international firms operate. The motivations, values, organizational forms, strategies and geographies of firms can depend to some degree on their primary sector of operation (remembering that some large firms, particularly conglomerates, can have activities across a number of sectors). One of the key distinctions made in international business is between manufacturing and service sectors. Many of the core international business theories were developed based on empirical observation of manufacturing firms – driven by an intense interest in the internationalization of firms in sectors such as automotive and aerospace – and at a time when the sectoral balance of economies was predominately in manufacturing and agriculture. The rise of services since the 1960s has demanded that international business theories catch up and led to a questioning of the applicability of the core theories to understanding service sectors, which now dominate in many advanced economies. This chapter will discuss the cross-cutting themes of practices and convention and motivations. It will examine the building blocks of people, things, place, decision-making, innovations and intersections.

This chapter focuses on the dynamic sector of international services. It draws distinctions between services and manufacturing activities. Understanding the different motivations for international services versus manufactured goods is important for navigating the unique challenges and opportunities presented by international service delivery. The chapter then does two things. First, it makes further distinctions between different types of services (eg business and consumer), presenting a framework for understanding the diversity in this sector. Second, it examines the internationalization strategies deployed by service firms, contrasting these with our existing awareness of manufacturing firms, highlighting the particular challenges faced by services. The chapter also discusses servitization, whereby manufacturing firms increasingly offer services as part of their value propositions. Third, linking back to Chapter 3, it examines the role of technology in driving service internationalization and how technology can support responsible international businesses.

Understanding international services in the global economy

International services are a growing sector. This growth reflects a convergence of factors, including globalization, technological advancements and shifting consumer preferences. Increased interconnectedness has opened new markets for service providers. Digital technologies have facilitated the delivery of services across borders, overcoming some geographical barriers and reducing costs.

In terms of consumer demand, the rise of the 'experience economy' fuels tourism, entertainment and leisure services, contributing to the expansion of the services sector. However, while there is a clear story of growth, navigating this world of the intangible comes with its own challenges. Place-based differentials can influence and change perceptions of international service quality and language barriers can create communication difficulties. Measuring the success of an 'invisible product' (ie service) can be problematic, and regulations can vary widely across geographical territories. For businesses, it opens new markets and opportunities for growth. For individuals, it offers access to specialized expertise and for entrepreneurs and managers it presents a chance to contribute to the global economy in potentially far-reaching ways.

There is a strong interdependence between services and goods in internationalization, and the financial system plays an important role in facilitating both. A robust international financial system, logistics and supply-chain management, marketing and communication services are all important for the successful internationalization of goods. However, in some cases, physical goods can be essential for delivering services. For instance, education services might require books or software, while tourism relies on infrastructure such as hotels and transportation. By recognizing these interconnected aspects, businesses can develop effective strategies for internationalization, regardless of whether they offer services, goods, or a hybrid model of both. Later, this chapter will outline the ways in which manufacturing and services are becoming more interdependent as new forms of business services emerge that support internationalization and an ongoing shift in manufacturing firms in terms of their employees performing service functions. For example, in the automotive sector, in the past, the vast majority of a manufacturer's employees would have been devoted to the physical production and sale of the car. Now, the most advanced electric cars require a substantial team of software engineers, not just in production stages but to support the remote updating of vehicle software and to develop new technologies (such as driverless car software).

Insurance services play a vital role in international business by mitigating risks and protecting assets. Insurance covers physical assets such as factories, equipment and inventory, that is property insurance. Liability insurance protects against legal claims arising from business operations, while other types of insurance cover risks associated with transportation of goods by sea, and political risks, such as currency devaluation or political instability. Credit insurance protects against the risk of non-payment by customers. Insurance providers face various challenges when operating in an international environment. For example, insurance companies face regulatory differences as insurance regulations vary significantly across countries, making it challenging to navigate compliance requirements. Exchange-rate fluctuations can impact insurance premiums and payouts. However, insurance can help businesses manage risks and protect their assets in unfamiliar markets. Adequate insurance coverage can be essential for entering new markets and securing business deals. Insurance can help businesses comply with local regulations and avoid legal issues. By carefully considering these factors, businesses can choose the appropriate insurance coverage to protect their assets and mitigate risks in international markets.

'Fintech' refers to financial technologies. These can offer convenience to consumers and other business users as financial services are often available 24/7 and can be accessed from anywhere with an internet connection (eg mobile banking apps, including Venmo, Cash App and apps offered by traditional banks, such as Barclays or HSBC). Fintech companies often have lower overhead costs than traditional financial institutions, which can lead to more competitive rates and fees for consumers. However, there can be security risks associated with using fintech services, and regulation of the financial industry is still developing, which can create uncertainty for both consumers and companies (Bryson et al, 2020). Fintech services play a critical role in enabling businesses to access new markets and compete with foreign service providers.

Defining international services

In international business, services refer to a diverse range of intangible economic activities exchanged across borders that primarily involve intellectual effort, knowledge or experience instead of the physical transfer of goods (Bryson et al, 2020). Services have certain characteristics such as intangibility, heterogeneity, perishability and simultaneous production and consumption of services, which are fundamentally different from manufactured goods (Lovelock and Gummesson, 2004); services are also knowledge-intensive and relationship-based.

The differences between services and manufactured goods impact how firms approach internationalization. For instance, service firms might need to establish a physical presence abroad sooner than manufacturers, who can initially export goods. Regulations around services can vary greatly by country, requiring more attention from international service providers. While both services and manufactured goods can be a part of global value chains, the nature of service delivery might require different collaboration models. Characteristics of services create unique challenges and opportunities for companies engaged in international trade of services. Understanding these differences is essential for developing effective strategies to successfully compete in the global market. By investing in both knowledge and relationships, service companies can deliver high-quality services that meet and exceed client expectations, ultimately leading to customer loyalty and business growth.

Services and manufactured goods are fundamentally different, and these distinctions have significant implications for internationalization strategies. However, the manufacturing landscape is undergoing a significant shift, with many companies adopting service-oriented models. This 'servitization' trend offers opportunities, it presents unique complexities for these manufacturers-turned-service-providers, particularly regarding internationalization, but the fundamental differences between services and goods still persist. For example, manufacturers traditionally focus on product development and tangible deliverables. The motivation for a transition to a service mentality requires prioritizing customer experience, ongoing value creation and building long-term relationships.

Business services versus consumer services

In international business contexts, services can be broadly categorized into three main groups: 1) business-to-business services or business services (eg financial and insurance services; business-related services); 2) business-to-consumer services or consumer services (eg health services); and 3) consumer-to-consumer services (eg accommodation). Business-related services can be divided into knowledge-intensive business services and capital-intensive services. Understanding this distinction is important for firms motivated to develop internationalization of services. Both target market and focus differ across all three types of services. For instance, the target market for business-to-business services is primarily other businesses. The focus of business service providers in this case is to provide international services that support and enhance the operations of other firms. Examples include professional and financial services (eg JPMorgan Chase & Co., Goldman Sachs investment banking) and other types of services. Another example refers to business-to-consumer services. The target market for these services are individual consumers. Thus, companies provide services that directly cater to the needs of individual consumers. Examples of services include tourism and hospitality (eg Tui Group tourism company), education (eg University of Birmingham) and healthcare (eg Bupa UK healthcare provider). Finally, the target market for consumer-to-consumer services is individuals, but the focus is on facilitating transactions between individual consumers. Examples include online marketplaces (eg eBay, Etsy), ride-sharing apps (eg Uber, Lyft) and peer-to-peer accommodation (eg Airbnb). These platforms act as an intermediary between consumers while consumers interact with each other.

Business services providers are important facilitators of the internationalization efforts of firms across all industries, including consumer services. Internationalization, the process of entering foreign markets, has become a strategic priority for firms motivated by growth and competitiveness. These motivations can evolve over time as the firm grows and matures. For example, accessing new markets can significantly expand a business service firm's revenue potential and those markets may offer opportunities for growth that are not available in the domestic market. Also, operating in multiple markets can reduce risks associated with economic fluctuations or political instability in a single region.

However, successfully navigating the complexities of a new market environment requires a diverse set of resources and skills. For example, business service firms entering new markets require an in-depth understanding of local consumer preferences, regulations and competitive landscape. Another motive for services firms to expand could be linked to accessing skilled staff to navigate in the foreign market. Otherwise, market research firms can provide critical data and analysis, while international business consultants can offer strategic guidance on market entry strategies, competitor analysis and cultural considerations. Business services comprise a broad range of other professional activities that support various aspects of a firm's operations, such as legal and regulatory compliance, financial services, logistics and supply chain management services. By providing a spectrum of specialized expertise, these business-to-business companies aid the navigation of new markets to achieve a successful global expansion.

Categorizing international services in the global services market

The global services market is a complex and dynamic landscape, incorporating diverse sectors with varying sizes, growth trajectories and key players (Tallman et al, 2018). International services markets are a growing sector, ranging from professional services and financial services to education and tourism services. Analysing their dynamics reveals the changing nature of economies. All sectors are expected to grow due to increasing demand in Asian countries for such services. Table 8.1 depicts international service markets and the biggest players in the global economy.

The service is characterized by intangible value that is a two-step process and it can be created by applying knowledge, skills and expertise, and realized through service execution and positive or less positive impact on the customer (Bryson et al, 2020). However, this approach can be considered limiting as some services may not be entirely intangible. In experiential tourism, the service (ie the experience) is intangible, but tangible elements such as logistics/transportation, accommodation and activities contribute to its delivery.

Services can result or manifest in tangible outcomes. For example, a financial consultant's advice might generate a tangible increase in a client's wealth, and a lawyer's expertise may result in a tangible legal document. International services can also involve emotions and relationships (Leonidou et al, 2019). Patient care in healthcare relies on empathy and compassion, while hospitality relies on building rapport and trust. International services can be co-created with the customer (Behl et al, 2023). For instance, in education, the knowledge exchange is a collaborative process between a student and a tutor: the learning process is not one-directional, and in design services, customer input shapes the final product since the designers work collaboratively with their clients and incorporate client feedback into refinements until the client is satisfied with the final design. Another example refers to digital products, which often involve a blend of goods (eg software) and services (eg updates, technical support).

Table 8.1: International service types and representative global companies

International service classification	International service type	Size / importance	Growth	Key players
Producer services	Financial services/digital financial services (Moshirian, 2006)	Remain an important sector for global trade and investment as these services form a large portion of the global economy	Driven by increasing wealth management needs in Asia	JPMorgan Chase & Co, Bank of America, Citigroup, Wells Fargo, HSBC, Godman Sachs
	Consumer services (Bryson et al, 2020)	The market is vast and covers a diverse range of industries, including retail, hospitality, tourism, entertainments and telecommunications	Driven by factors such as rising incomes, urbanization and technological advancements	McDonalds, Coca-Cola, Disney, Uber, Airbnb, etc
Knowledge-intensive services	Professional services (Thakor and Kumar, 2000)	Represent the largest service sector globally, driven by growing demand for specialized expertise	Growth forecast due to increasing demand for consulting, accounting and legal services in emerging markets	Accenture, Deloitte, McKinsey & Company
	Information technology services (Graesch et al, 2021)	A major driver of technological innovation and economic growth, comprises large portion of global services due to digitalization	Growing demand for cloud computing, cybersecurity and digital transformation services	IBM, Accenture, Wipro, Tata Consulting Services, Infosys Limited, NTT DATA Corporation, Capgemini
	Tourism and Hospitality (Fatima and Elbanna, 2020)	Medium-sized sector was significantly impacted by the pandemic but is now recovering	Growing demand for sustainable and experiential tourism	Marriot International, Hilton Worldwide Holdings Inc., Tui Group, InterContinental Hotels Group, AccorHotels, Airbnb
	Education and Training (Macdonald et al, 2007)	Medium-sized sector, used for skills and knowledge development of the workforce	Projected to grow due to popularity increase in online learning, vocational training, and upskilling initiatives	Pearson, McGraw-Hill Education, Kaplan, Udemy, Coursera, LinkedIn Learning, edX, FutureLearn
	Healthcare services (Mosadeghrad, 2014)	Large and constantly growing, incorporates medical care and pharmaceutical products	Expected to grow due to ageing populations, increasing healthcare spending, and technological advancements	Johnson & Johnson, Pfizer, Novartis AG, Roche Holding AG, Abbott Laboratories, Mayo Clinic
Capital-intensive services	Logistics (Nelson et al, 2010)	Relatively smaller sector includes freight transportation (maritime, air, lands) and passenger transportation (aviation, rail, road)	Expected to grow due to economic advances in India and China	Boeing, Airbus, Lufthansa, American Airlines, FedEx, UPS, DHL, DSV Shipping companies A.P. Moller-Maersk Group, Mediterranean Shipping Company (MSC), COSCO Shipping

To illustrate international management consulting business-to-business services, Box 8.1 presents a case study on McKinsey & Company and Siemens.

Box 8.1: McKinsey & Company and the digital transformation of Siemens

This case study exemplifies several key principles of international business services, such as intangibility and collaborative problem-solving. International business services are often intangible, which makes it challenging to assess quality and value before purchase. Collaborative problem-solving requires effective communication, ongoing effort and attention as well as commitment to build strong relationships to achieve goals in international business.

The core competency of McKinsey & Company lies in their deep knowledge of business processes, digital technologies and change management. The company's international business services are knowledge-based, which makes them highly specialized and difficult to replicate.

McKinsey & Company demonstrated a commitment to understand client challenges and tailoring solutions to their specific needs. Collaborative problem-solving was successful because of close collaboration between McKinsey & Company's consultants, Siemens leadership and employees at all levels.

Intangible value creation is evident as McKinsey & Company's consulting services provided intangible value to Siemens in the form of expertise, strategic guidance and implementation support. McKinsey & Company's work with Siemens manufacturer represents a broader trend in service economies and their digital future.

Siemens, a long-standing German industrial giant, needed to adapt to the rapidly changing landscape of industry 4.0, characterized by digitalization, automation and data-driven decision-making. Their traditional manufacturing processes and hierarchical structures were hindering their agility and innovation.

McKinsey & Company (Global), a well-known international consulting firm, partnered with Siemens to develop a comprehensive digital transformation strategy. This strategy focused on several key areas: 1) digital core area with the focus on modernizing Siemens' IT infrastructure to improve data management, analytics capabilities and cloud adoption; 2) smart factories area-focused on implementing Internet of Things (IoT) technologies to connect machines, gather real-time data on production processes and enable predictive maintenance; 3) data-driven decision-making area with the focus on leveraging artificial intelligence and machine learning to analyse data across the entire value chain, optimize operations and gain actionable insights for improved decision-making; and 4) agile culture and workforce development area focusing on a shift towards a more collaborative, data-driven culture that empowers employees to innovate and adapt to change. This included investing in workforce training programs to equip employees with the skills needed to thrive in a digital environment.

Managerial implications are several. First, Siemens gained impact through increased efficiency, enhanced innovation, improved customer experience and new revenue streams. Streamlined operations, predictive maintenance and data-driven decision-making led to significant improvements in productivity and cost savings. Second, by embracing digital technologies and fostering a culture of innovation, Siemens was able to develop new products and services that better addressed business customer needs in this digital age. Third, digitalization enabled Siemens to explore new business models such as offering data-driven analytics services offered to their current and prospective business customers.

Service internationalization entry modes versus manufacturing

When entering international markets, service companies and manufacturing companies face different challenges and require distinct strategies (Laufs and Schwens, 2014). This is reflected in the differing approaches to internationalization for these sectors, particularly regarding the contribution services make to support internationalization. Table 8.2 presents key differences between international services and manufacturing companies and contribution of services to support internationalization.

Considering the above key differences, services companies have a wide range of entry modes available (see Table 8.3), which require making two decisions regarding the level of control and location. It is important for companies to carefully evaluate their options and choose the entry mode that best suits their specific needs. The choice of the entry mode for both services and manufacturing companies depends not only on the level of control desired by the companies (as Table 8.3 suggests) but on many other factors, such as a company size, its resources and capabilities, target market characteristics, service/product complexity, cultural nuances, familiarity with regulatory environment and level of risk tolerance of company managers (Laufs and Schwens, 2014). Service companies may have greater advantage with online platforms due to the intangible nature of their offerings. Such companies can leverage technology and partnerships to minimize investment and adapt their services to international markets. Manufacturing companies often require a more physical presence in the target market. However, these companies may place more emphasis on strategic partnerships to reduce upfront investment and leverage local knowledge in a foreign country (Hennart, 2022).

Globalization in the international service business

Globalization has empowered services trade, reshaping the landscape of global business. Globalization has opened new markets for service providers, allowing them to reach a wider customer base beyond their domestic borders. This situation translates to increased revenue potential and diversification for businesses (Tallman and Fladmoe-Lindquist, 2002). International trade agreements have facilitated the movement of services across borders by lowering tariffs and other restrictions (see Chapter 2). This makes it easier for businesses to enter new markets and compete on a global scale. Technological advancements have made it easier for businesses to deliver services such as software development, online marketing and consulting in different geographical territories. All of this is underpinned by technologies enabling the rapid acceleration of the speed and volume of financial trading (see Chapter 3). This has boosted the growth of digital services, providing new business models and

Table 8.2: Differences between international service and manufacturing companies

	Key differences		Contribution of services
	Manufacturing	International services	Contribution of services to support internationalization
Tangibility of offerings	Tangible goods subject to physical transportation, import/export regulations, and potential logistical complexities	Intangible experiences delivered through expertise, knowledge, or access to resources Physical presence might be required for international service delivery, they can be delivered remotely through technology	Researching target markets, including consumer preferences and competitive landscape Offering logistics and distribution services, including facilitation of the movement of manufactured goods across international borders, ensuring timely delivery and efficient supply chains Facilitating shift towards servitization, including bundling services with manufactured products to create more value to customers
Level of control	Setting up production facilities abroad gives manufacturers greater control over quality, production processes, and inventory management, but requires significant investments	Can be delivered remotely through online platforms, partnering with local service providers, or establishing service operations in the target market; potential trade-offs exist regarding control over service quality and customer interaction	Offering market access and knowledge on foreign markets, helping managers to better understand regulations, and business practices Communication and marketing services enable companies to effectively communicate with international customers
Resource requirements	Requires significant upfront investment in exporting, establishing production facilities, managing supply chains, and ensuring compliance with local regulations	Resource requirements for service internationalization can vary	Consuling services contribute to a better understanding of market dynamics, customer choices and regulations Marketing and communication services assist companies in tailoring their localization and cultural adaptation strategies to resonate with local cultures
Customer interaction and relationships	Customer interaction is often limited to the sales and after-sales stages	Service delivery often involves ongoing interaction, trust and relationship building with the customer	Providing excellent customer services and after-sales support is essential for building long-term customer relationships in international markets
Regulation and trade barriers	Stricter regulations and trade barriers related to product safety, quality standards and environmental concerns	Regulations and barriers between countries can be captured within trade agreements or remain in place, despite agreements, often presenting non-tariff barriers, such as licencing requirements	Management consulting firms, legal services, and accounting firms offer specialized expertise to help manufacturers navigate complex regulatory environments and comply with local laws
Cultural sensitivity and adaptability	Product features may need adaptation to comply with local regulations or cater to specific customer preferences	Services are highly susceptible to cultural influences	Consulting firms provide market research insights to help companies adapt their offerings, communication, and delivery methods to connect more effectively with international customers

Table 8.3: Market entry modes for international services and manufacturing companies

Entry mode	Manufacturing companies	Service companies
Exporting	Minimum level of control and presence required	Minimum level of control and presence required
Exporting via an overseas intermediary / overseas independent service provider	Finding an intermediary to help reduce uncertainties and risks in a foreign market	Partnering with local independent service providers to deliver services to the foreign target market
E-commerce and technology platforms	Not applicable due to a physical product that needs to be manufactured and sold using technology platforms in a foreign market	Delivering services remotely through online platforms and digital technologies
Licencing	Granting a licence to a local company to produce and sell the company's products	Granting a local company the right to deliver the service under the company's brand name and standards; requires strict quality control mechanism
Joint ventures	Some degree of investment is required to enable establishing a shared manufacturing operation when partnering with a local company	Some degree of investment is required to enable quick market entry and leverage local knowledge, expertise and resources
Wholly owned subsidiaries	Involves setting up fully controlled manufacturing facilities in the target market	Offers maximum control over service quality and brand experience

opportunities for international business. The digitalization of money, particularly the rise of cryptocurrencies and digital central bank currencies, has significantly impacted the speed and volume of financial trading, high-frequency trading (HFT) being a prime example. HFT involves using sophisticated algorithms and powerful computers to execute a large number of trades in milliseconds. These algorithms analyse vast amounts of market data to identify fleeting price discrepancies and capitalize on them before the market corrects itself. Digital currencies such as bitcoin and Ethereum offer faster transaction settlement times compared to traditional methods relying on central bank clearing systems. This speed is important for HFT strategies. Digital currencies eliminate physical limitations associated with traditional currencies. Trade can occur 24/7 without the need for bank holidays or operational downtime, further increasing the trading pace. However, a caveat is that complex algorithms used in HFT can make it difficult for regulators and traditional investors to understand the factors driving market movement. This raises ethical questions about fairness and market stability and requires further insight into regulation of such complex and highly competitive systems in the financial landscape (Roncella and Ferrero, 2022).

When accessing new markets, businesses face increased competition from foreign service providers (Tallman and Fladmoe-Lindquist, 2002), business systems, place-based differences (see Chapter 7) and cultural complexities (see Chapter 2). Intense competition can lead to higher quality services and greater value offered to customers. However, competition for businesses means price pressures, lower profit margins and the need for constant innovation and differentiation (Tallman and Fladmoe-Lindquist, 2002) in the context of the international services industry. In addition, businesses face cultural differences in terms of language barriers and clear communication, business practices and consumer preferences, which can be challenging for international services businesses entering new markets. This requires cultural compatibility, cultural adaptation and sensitivity to minimize conflicts and misunderstandings when offering services across borders in terms of language, communication with consumers and business practices for successful service delivery abroad.

It is important to note that when internationalizing, businesses offering services face a steeper language barrier compared to those dealing with physical goods. Language and proper communication in services internationalization becomes more critical because clients rely on clear explanations to understand the value proposition and service delivery process. Physical features and demonstrations can often bridge the language gap for products. Services often require building trust and rapport with clients. Effective communication in the client's native language while understanding jokes in a foreign language is important for establishing trust and ensuring a positive customer experience. International service providers have ongoing interaction with clients throughout the service delivery process. Language barriers can create frustration and hinder effective communication at every touchpoint. For example, Airbnb ensures listings are translated accurately to avoid misleading information and to set clear expectations for guests.

Clear communication in the local language helps Airbnb build trust and establish itself as a reliable platform in international markets. By prioritizing clear communication, cultural sensitivity and adaptation in the target language, international service providers can minimize language barriers, enhance customer experience and build more successful relationships with their customers. The managerial implications are twofold. First, sufficient time and effort needs to be taken to gain knowledge of new markets (cultural, regulatory and contextual factors), with particular attention being paid to communication. This may have implications for how teams are built for new market entry and may require an increase in local employees to facilitate internal knowledge transfer and external customer communications. Second, the need for local knowledges is a reminder that the rollout of services across different geographical territories is not necessarily as quick or seamless as some narratives suggest. If done properly, the development of locally embedded services may take more time than building a standard factory unit in a new market.

Exploring the servitization of manufacturing and implications for manufacturing internationalization

The global manufacturing landscape is undergoing significant transformation, driven by several key trends. These trends include rising automation, the increasing importance of technology and data, and the growing demand for customer-centric solutions (Bryson et al, 2020). In response to these shifts, manufacturers are adopting various approaches, including servitization-based business models. This is a strategic approach that goes beyond simply selling products and offers integrated products and services (Bryson et al, 2020) to unlock new revenue streams and strengthens customer relationships (Behl et al, 2023).

Servitization refers to the process of integrating services with the core manufacturing offering (Behl et al, 2023) to increase the value of physical products (Doni et al, 2019). Servitization process can take various forms, including product-service systems (eg bundling services such as installation, maintenance, repair or upgrades with the sale of a physical product and recycling), customer-centric service (eg consulting, training, financing and logistics support) or outcome-based offerings (eg pay-per-use models, performance-based contracts). Other forms include remote monitoring and service (eg utilizing digital technologies to remotely monitor and manage the performance of products and proactively address potential issues) and data-driven insights (eg using data collected from connected products to offer new services such as predictive maintenance and customized solutions) (Chatterjee et al, 2023). GE Healthcare medical technology company is an example of the servitization process. This company offers a range of services along with its imaging equipment, including remote monitoring, data analysis and training programs. This approach helps hospitals to minimize their equipment usage, improve patient outcomes and builds strong customer partnerships. Another example is Hilti, a well-known construction tool manufacturer, which offers AMaaS (Asset Management as a Service) to its clients: the company goes beyond simply selling the equipment itself, such as drills, hammers and saws. Instead, the company manages the entire lifecycle of construction tools for construction companies. Construction companies pay a subscription fee rather than buying the tools outright. Hilti takes responsibility for maintenance, repairs and replacements, ensuring the tools are always in top working condition. They provide on-site training to ensure workers use the tools correctly and safely. Hilti is a good example of how a company can transition from a product-centric model to a servitization-based model, adding value by taking care of maintenance, repairs and even providing training, ensuring their clients have the tools and knowledge to succeed on the jobsite.

The primary motivations behind servitization are several. First, servitization contributes to the enhanced customer satisfaction with customers through providing value beyond the product itself and fostering long-term relationships (Bustinza et al, 2015). Second, by establishing long-term relationships with international customers through services, manufacturers can collect valuable data on their current product and service usage to improve their new product or service development, increase customer lifetime value (Bustinza et al, 2015; Doni et al, 2019) and sustainability gains. For instance, the Hilti company builds long-term, ongoing partnerships that lead to stronger customer relationships. By taking good care of maintenance, repairs and replacements, Hilti becomes a trusted partner to construction companies. Third, this increases customer retention, leading to a longer-term revenue stream from each client. Fourth, servitization improves resource utilization by creating opportunities for manufacturers to leverage their existing assets and expertise in new ways (Behl et al, 2023). Finally, servitization offers risk mitigation as companies that offer unique services alongside products can be more flexible in managing risks associated with dangers when entering new markets, such as unfamiliar regulations and cultural complexities (Agnihotri et al, 2023).

Servitization can be an effective business model for entering new markets, especially when competing against established players as it offers competitive advantages for new entrants. That is, servitization enables the manufacturer to differentiate itself in a competitive market by offering a unique value proposition accompanied with services that is difficult to copy (Bustinza et al, 2015). Services can be a powerful business-model for building stronger relationships with customers in new markets and fostering trust and loyalty in the long term (Agnihotri et al, 2023). Advancements in digital technology facilitate remote service delivery, enabling manufacturers to offer services in geographically dispersed markets without establishing a physical presence (Feng et al, 2021).

Although servitization offers many benefits, it has some challenges to be considered. Some studies suggest that servitization increases bankruptcy risks and might lead to a company's failure (Dori et al, 2019). The reason behind bankruptcy risks refers to several factors. Implementing servitization often requires considerable investments in technology and infrastructure to support remote monitoring, data analytics and other service-related activities (Paschou et al, 2020). It requires managing service costs and profitability, ensuring that services are delivered efficiently and profitably, for the servitization strategy to achieve success (Paschou et al, 2020). In addition, managing global service delivery can be complex as establishing efficient and scalable service delivery models across diverse geographical locations is challenging. Finally, developing service capabilities and shifting a company's motivation from a product-centric mindset to a service-oriented mindset may be challenging for manufacturers. Box 8.2 provides an illustration of servitization-related challenges.

Box 8.2: Samsung and its challenges in servitization

Servitization can influence how manufacturing companies approach internationalization. For example, when entering new markets, manufacturers need to adapt servitization strategies to different markets. The demand for specific services and the effectiveness of servitization strategies can vary significantly across different countries (eg developed versus emerging economies), various cultures and accompanying regulatory environments (Agnihotri et al, 2023; Akaka et al, 2013).

Samsung, a South Korean multinational conglomerate, has been a major player in the electronics industry for decades. While the company has successfully expanded into various sectors, its attempts at servitization have faced challenges. South Korean culture, which is traditionally focused on hardware manufacturing, may have presented cultural barriers to adopting a service-oriented business model. Customers have expectations of Samsung as a hardware provider, rather than a service provider, making it difficult to establish a strong presence in the services market. The competitive landscape for services, especially in areas such as software and data analytics, is intense, with established players and start-ups competing for market share. Allocating resources to build and maintain a robust services division can be challenging, especially when the focus has traditionally been on hardware manufacturing.

Despite these challenges, Samsung has made efforts to diversify its revenue streams and explore service-based offerings. However, the company has faced difficulties in establishing a strong presence in the services market, particularly compared to Apple and Google.

This highlights three managerial implications. First, managers need to hire experienced professionals in the services industry to lead the company's efforts to utilize servitization strategies in international markets. Second, managers need to focus on customer needs and develop a deep understanding to tailor service offerings accordingly. Business leaders need to focus on value proposition to ensure that it resonates with the target market's specific customer requirements. Finally, managers need to utilize the company's strengths in technology and innovation to develop innovative service solutions.

Managerial implications are several. Before launching a servitization strategy in a new market, the company needs to conduct in-depth research to better understand consumer needs, preferences and existing service models. This will enable companies to tailor their offerings to their target audiences in different cultural contexts. Such manufacturers need to develop new capabilities in various areas such as service design, delivery and customer-relationship management. They have to be ready for intense competition in the new markets and to establish presence and compete effectively against established players with a carefully developed strategy and its adaptation activities (Mihailova, 2023) in the new markets. Next, implementing servitization on a small scale in selected markets first would allow for clearly identifying all costs associated with servitization, including technology development, training and global service delivery along with testing the feasibility of the service model, identifying potential challenges and refining the offering before a full-scale launch. Finally, managers need to develop clear metrics to measure the return on investment from servitization by tracking customer acquisition costs, service revenue and profit margins to ensure servitization is financially sustainable in the long term.

Responsible services in international business

In the context of international services, technological advancements (see Chapter 3) and the rise of digital technologies comprise such advancements as robotics, cloud computing platforms, automation and artificial intelligence (AI) (Bryson et al, 2020; Chatterjee et al, 2023). These advancements are streamlining service delivery, automating repetitive tasks and facilitating the emergence of new service models. AI-powered chatbots can provide 24/7 customer support, while data analytics can personalize service offerings and predict customer purchasing behaviour. Easy access to cloud-based infrastructure allows service companies to scale operations rapidly, collaborate globally and deliver services remotely, contributing to internationalization without significant physical presence. Networked devices and sensors are enabling real-time data collection and analysis, facilitating predictive maintenance, remote monitoring and customized service packages within international sectors such as healthcare and logistics.

The increasing popularity of online platforms such as marketplaces and freelance platforms among businesses is offering ample opportunities for international service delivery (Zakaria and Yusof, 2020) and provides managerial implications. Online platforms foster the internationalization of services such as digital marketing, logistics and customer service. Online platforms allow teams to collaborate effectively across geographic boundaries, enabling the delivery of services such as consulting, design and education across borders (Zakaria and Yusof, 2020). The type of online platform used by businesses depends on the specific service model: 1) marketplaces – these platforms connect service providers with customers directly (Amazon for various products); 2) on-demand platforms – these connect customers with service providers in real time (eg Uber for a ride, TaskRabbit for odd jobs); 3) subscription-based platforms – these offer access to services for a recurring fee (eg Netflix for streaming films, Spotify for music and podcasts); 4) cloud-based platforms – these are platforms allowing for remote access of software and services (eg Dropbox for file storage, Salesforce for CRM). By using platforms such as Upwork or Fiverr, businesses can connect with skilled professionals worldwide for specific tasks or projects, accessing expertise beyond their immediate geographic reach. This opens doors to diverse perspectives and cost-effective solutions. Another example is related to project-management tools. Platforms such as Trello or Asana integrate project management tools, facilitating communication and collaboration between geographically dispersed teams. Real-time file sharing, document editing and communication features enable seamless teamwork across borders.

Additionally, there are intra-firm platforms – internal tools designed to streamline communication, collaboration and knowledge sharing across geographically dispersed teams, which are often overlooked in the context of international service delivery. Such intra-firm platforms empower employees to share best practices, centralize internal resources and facilitate collaboration. For example, the University of Birmingham (UB) uses UoB Core Services as an intra-firm platform to support the delivery of UoB activities in the UK and Dubai. Another example is Deloitte's Greenhouse project-management tool that enables teams to collaborate on projects remotely, tracking progress and sharing resources across international offices.

The surge of online platforms presents exciting prospects for delivering services internationally, through data driven decisions, extended market reach, scalability and efficiency, potential cost reduction associated with physical presence in a new market, as online platforms eliminate such physical need. However, managers need to be aware of the challenges involved, such as data privacy and security and responsible use of technology. Legal and regulatory frameworks need to be complied with to avoid service delivery disruptions, penalties or more severe consequences. Firms must comply with the regulations applicable to their operations in a specific country. This includes different regulations across different countries (eg EU's General Data Protection Regulation [GDPR]). Next, the companies need to respect intellectual property laws in all countries they operate in. This includes avoiding copyright infringement. To address ethical issues, responsible technology service firms can take various steps. For instance, they can develop a code of ethics that sets clear expectations for employee conduct and guides decision-making. For responsible businesses, these ethical codes will relate to their company values.

Managerial implications for responsible international services delivery

It is possible to imagine a world where a British architect uses virtual reality to design sustainable cities in Brazil or where a Kenyan entrepreneur connects local farmers with global markets through a cutting-edge mobile application such as 'GlobalFarmersConnect' that promotes ethical and sustainable food sourcing. The GlobalFarmersConnect mobile application was created by Niger Aaron while studying at a university in the UK (Blake, 2023). Novel services face challenges around trust and transparency along with cultural and logistics barriers. Such services need to ensure fair-trade practices for farmers and affordability for buyers. These services use certain strategies to overcome these challenges: using technology for traceability and transparency, partnering with local farmer cooperatives and distributors, offering competitive pricing and flexible payment options, promoting benefits of sustainable food sourcing to consumers. These are just a small part of services that now fuel the global economy.

In international service delivery, business leaders need to ensure both sustainability and ethical practices. This is no longer a choice but a necessity (Doni et al, 2019). International service delivery can have a significant environmental footprint, including carbon emissions from transportation, resource consumption (particularly energy and water use by data servers) and electronic waste generation. International service delivery can also have a significant negative social impact (Wirtz et al, 2018). For instance, data privacy and data security, unethical labour practices, cultural sensitivity or trust and lack of transparency with customers can negatively impact the social structure in international service destination countries. These are presented as managerial implications below and thought-provoking questions follow these implications.

When delivering services internationally, business managers need to take into consideration data privacy by implementing robust data-security measures, complying with relevant data privacy regulations, protecting customer data (Luo, 2022) across borders with varying regulations and ensuring transparency in data-handling practices. Managers need to tackle the complex issue of balancing their need for data and analysis with the rights of their customers regarding data privacy and data use.

Ethical international service delivery companies need to partner with other international service providers who follow fair labour practices and ethical sourcing standards throughout the global value chain (see Chapter 9). Managers need to ensure fair wages, safe working conditions, and meet ethical labour standards throughout the service delivery chain leading to more ethical international business operations. For example, Veolia, a French multinational company, which specializes in ecological transformation services and offers waste management and recycling, water treatment, sanitation, energy management and optimization services is a leading example of an international service company that leverages partnerships with local businesses to contribute to positive environmental initiatives. Veolia partners with local companies in China to develop and implement a customized solution for treating wastewater generated by several local factories. This partnership helps the local industry company with environmental regulations, reduces water pollution and fosters knowledge transfer between Veolia and the local water-treatment company. Carbon-footprint reduction can be achieved by implementing strategies such as minimizing business travel and utilizing energy-efficient technologies by international service companies. For instance, Veolia partners with local companies in Brazil to establish a dedicated sorting and processing facility for construction waste, where recyclable materials are prepared for reuse of these materials in new construction projects. This partnership diverts construction waste from landfills, promotes circular economy practices in the industry and reduces the environmental footprint of construction activities. The company is not without controversy, suffering from exposure to some questionable practices, including unpaid internships in Ireland and negative environmental impacts following service-plant accidents in the US, one of which resulted in fatalities and over 1.5 million gallons of a mix of storm and sewage water being spilled into a nearby river after a sewage-holding wall collapsed.

Managers also need to consider trust and transparency with customers (Abreu et al, 2021), which are built across different countries when following ethical and sustainable service delivery procedures. International service providers need to clearly communicate the environmental and social impact of services and actively engage stakeholders in sustainability and ethical practices. Managers need to question what their company's role is in ensuring responsible and sustainable international service delivery practices globally. Service providers may partner with organizations that share similar values and commitment to sustainability and ethical practices. For instance, fostering collaboration among service providers, NGOs and governments can accelerate the adoption of sustainable and ethical practices (Abreu et al, 2021) across the international service delivery companies. According to Ameer and Othman (2012: 73), 'companies which place emphasis on sustainability practices have higher financial performance measured by return on assets, profit before taxation, and cash flow from operations compared to those without such commitments in some activity services sectors'. Companies are encouraged to regularly report on sustainability and ethical performance, addressing concerns and demonstrating continuous improvement and efforts. International service providers are advised to regularly review and revise sustainability and ethical practices to adapt to evolving standards and emerging challenges across different countries.

Conclusion

Services form an important part of the geoeconomy in their own right and in supporting other sectors. This chapter discussed international services, their unique characteristics and key factors influencing their success in the global economy. It is clear that the services sector possesses some unique characteristics, particularly when compared to manufacturing. While the core IB theories derive from the study of manufacturing, their application to services still has some relevance and burgeoning academic work across the social sciences is developing our understandings of their specific dynamics further. Of particular interest is the ways in which the industrial sector of a firm impact on its internationalization strategy. This chapter charts the ways in which service firms may internationalize differently, the challenges they face and the managerial implications. There is increasing overlap between services and manufacturing. The chapter outlines the rise of servitization and discusses what the implications for international business may be. The chapter stresses the need to overcome naive perceptions that service internationalization is necessarily easy or seamless. The place-based differentials characterized in Chapter 7 explain why service firms are likely to need to devote time, energy and resources into understanding local markets. With greater embeddedness often comes higher expectations of responsibility and sustainability, thus driving an agenda for change across the sector.

Chapter 9 extends our focus on the interrelationships and interdependencies between the building blocks of the geoeconomy, drawing together our discussions of place-based differentials and sectoral differences and cross-sectoral connections in internationalization. It will discuss global value chains, a framework devised to understand the ways in which international firms are integrated into broader network relationships at multiple geographical scales. Services are integral to this integration, providing mechanisms for communication, financing, intra-, inter- and extra-firm platforms for manufacturing and service delivery and a plethora of basic and advanced business support services. The next chapter extends our understanding of the role of services in the geoeconomy and pays particular attention to how value chains can be configured to create value and what the implications are for practice.

Key terms

International services – a diverse range of intangible economic activities exchanged across borders that primarily involve intellectual effort, knowledge or experience instead of the physical transfer of goods.

Responsible international services delivery – refers to ethical international service delivery and sensibly managing cultural complexities when building trust and transparency with customers across countries.

Servitization – the process of offering additional service components to core manufactured products.

Recommended reading

Agnihotri, A., Bhattacharya, S., Yannopoulou, N. and Thrassou, A. (2023) 'Foreign market entry modes for servitization under diverse macroenvironmental conditions: taxonomy and propositions', *International Marketing Review*, 40(4): 561–84.

Bryson, J.R., Sundbo, J., Fuglsang, L. and Daniels, P. (2020) 'Servitization and manufacturing companies', in J.R. Bryson, J. Sundbo, L. Fuglsang and P. Daniels (eds) *Service Management Theory and Practice*, Cham: Palgrave Macmillan, pp 223–38.

Luo, Y. (2022) 'A general framework of digitization risks in international business', *Journal of International Business Studies,* 53(2): 344–61.

References

Abreu, M.C.S.D., Ferreira, F.N.H., Proenca, J.F. and Ceglia, D. (2021) 'Collaboration in achieving sustainable solutions in the textile industry', *Journal of Business & Industrial Marketing*, 36(9): 1614–26.

Agnihotri, A., Bhattacharya, S., Yannopoulou, N. and Thrassou, A. (2023) 'Foreign market entry modes for servitization under diverse macroenvironmental conditions: taxonomy and propositions', *International Marketing Review*, 40(4): 561–84.

Akaka, M.A., Vargo, S. L. and Lusch, R.F. (2013) 'The complexity of context: a service ecosystems approach for international marketing', *Journal of International Marketing*, 21(4): 1–20.

Ameer, R. and Othman, R. (2012) 'Sustainability practices and corporate financial performance: a study based on the top global corporations', *Journal of Business Ethics*, 108: 61–79.

Behl, A., Kamboj, S., Sarmah, B., Pereira, V., Sharma, K., Rammal, H.G. and Arrigo, E. (2023) 'Customer involvement and servitization in hybrid offerings: moderating role of digitalization and co-creation', *International Marketing Review*, 40(4): 739–73.

Blake, K. (2023) *Nottingham Post* [online]. Available from: www.nottinghampost.com/news/new-game-changer-app-created-8654782) [Accessed 30 January 2025].

Bryson, J.R., Sundbo, J., Fuglsang, L. and Daniels, P. (2020) *Service Management Theory and Practice*, Switzerland: Palgrave Macmillan.

Bustinza, O.F., Bigdeli, A. Z., Baines, T. and Elliot, C. (2015) 'Servitization and competitive advantage: the importance of organizational structure and value chain position', *Research-Technology Management*, 58(5): 53–60.

Chatterjee, S., Chaudhuri, R. and Vrontis, D. (2023) 'Business hybrid offerings by manufacturing SMEs: impact of servitization on internationalization of manufacturing SMEs', *International Marketing Review*, 40(4): 585–611.

Doni, F., Corvino, A. and Martini, S.B. (2019) 'Servitization and sustainability actions: evidence from European manufacturing companies', *Journal of Environmental Management*, 234: 367–78.

Fatima, T. and Elbanna, S. (2020) 'Balanced scorecard in the hospitality and tourism industry: past, present and future', *International Journal of Hospitality Management*, 91: 102656.

Feng, C., Jiang, L., Ma, R. and Bai, C. (2021) 'Servitization strategy, manufacturing organizations and firm performance: a theoretical framework', *Journal of Business & Industrial Marketing*, 36(10): 1909–28.

Graesch, J.P., Hensel-Börner, S. and Henseler, J. (2021) 'Information technology and marketing: an important partnership for decades', *Industrial Management & Data Systems*, 121(1): 123–57.

Hennart, J.F. (2022) 'How much is new in Brouthers et al.'s new foreign entry modes, and do they challenge the transaction cost theory of entry mode choice?', *Journal of International Business Studies*, 53(9): 2116–132.

Laufs, K. and Schwens, C. (2014) 'Foreign market entry mode choice of small and medium-sized enterprises: a systematic review and future research agenda', *International Business Review*, 23(6): 1109–126.

Leonidou, L.C., Aykol, B., Fotiadis, T.A., Zeriti, A. and Christodoulides, P. (2019) 'The role of exporters' emotional intelligence in building foreign customer relationships', *Journal of International Marketing*, 27(4): 58–80.

Lovelock, C., and Gummesson, E. (2004) 'Whither services marketing? In search of a new paradigm and fresh perspectives', *Journal of Service Research*, 7(1): 20–41.

Luo, Y. (2022) 'A general framework of digitization risks in international business', *Journal of International Business Studies*, 53(2): 344–61.

Macdonald, S., Assimakopoulos, D. and Anderson, P. (2007) 'Education and training for innovation in SMEs: a tale of exploitation', *International Small Business Journal*, 25(1): 77–95.

Mihailova, I. (2023) 'Business model adaptation for realized international scaling of born-digitals', *Journal of World Business*, 58(2): 101418.

Mosadeghrad, A.M. (2014) 'Factors influencing healthcare service quality', *International Journal of Health Policy and Management*, 3(2): 77.

Moshirian, F. (2006) 'Aspects of international financial services', *Journal of Banking & Finance*, 30(4): 1057–64.

Nelson, J.D., Wright, S., Masson, B., Ambrosino, G. and Naniopoulos, A. (2010) 'Recent developments in flexible transport services', *Research in Transportation Economics*, 29(1): 243–8.

Paschou, T., Rapaccini, M., Adrodegari, F. and Saccani, N. (2020) 'Digital servitization in manufacturing: a systematic literature review and research agenda', *Industrial Marketing Management*, 89: 278–92.

Roncella, A. and Ferrero, I. (2022) 'The ethics of financial market making and its implications for high-frequency trading', *Journal of Business Ethics*, 181(1): 139–51.

Tallman, S. and Fladmoe-Lindquist, K. (2002) 'Internationalization, globalization, and capability-based strategy', *California Management Review*, 45(1): 116–35.

Tallman, S., Luo, Y. and Buckley, P.J. (2018) 'Business models in global competition', *Global Strategy Journal*, 8(4): 517–35.

Thakor, M.V. and Kumar, A. (2000) 'What is a professional service? A conceptual review and bi-national investigation', *Journal of Services Marketing*, 14(1): 63–82.

Wirtz, J., Patterson, P.G., Kunz, W.H., Gruber, T., Lu, V.N., Paluch, S. and Martins, A. (2018) 'Brave new world: service robots in the frontline', *Journal of Service Management*, 29(5): 907–31.

Zakaria, N. and Yusof, S.A.M. (2020) 'Crossing cultural boundaries using the internet: toward building a model of swift trust formation in global virtual teams', *Journal of International Management*, 26(1): 100654.

9

Responsible Business and Global Value Chains

Introduction

All societies are involved in the movement of people and things, but capitalism continues to intensify the impact, geographic reach and scale of this process. This chapter has the cross-cutting theme of change/evolution as its starting point, with a focus on the building blocks of intermediaries, intersections, place and governance structures. Making sense of how the global economy is evolving is a difficult task. This requires theoretical and methodological tools and different scales of analysis that range from understanding the experience of individuals in different contexts to tracking flows of all types. These tools include the theories that have been explored in the first eight chapters of this book; for example, understanding the role played by different institutional structures, technological innovation and approaches to value creation and monetarization. There is another set of theories or approaches that aim to develop a more integrated approach to understanding internationalization that are known as chain or network theories. These take a very different form to theories of international business; for example, the Eclectic Paradigm or Springboard approach, that are trying to build a general theory of multinational enterprises. These are firm-focused approaches, whilst the chain or network theories are concerned with understanding flows of people, raw materials, components and completed goods between firms and places. These chains are often defined as global value chains (GVCs) and they form around intermediate goods and services which are increasingly traded across national borders and take the form of geographically fragmented production processes (Ponte et al, 2019). An UNCTAD analysis published in 2013 noted that GVCs coordinated by transnational corporations (TNCs) accounted 'for some 80 per cent of global trade' (2013: x). This includes trade in intermediate goods and services.

In this chapter, we compare different approaches to exploring the evolving global economy. The emphasis is on developing a constructive critique that focuses on identifying the practice implications of these theories but framed within an appreciation of responsible business. There are two cross-cutting themes. The first is to explore chain or network approaches with a focus on trying to develop a more integrated but practice-orientated approach to international business. The second is to explore the irresponsibility of GVCs. Too often, GVCs are celebrated for the positive contributions that they make to consumers, producers and governments whilst sidelining the darker sides or negative impacts. These darker sides include GVCs that are configured to reduce costs and increase profits, but too often this includes labour exploitation, unnecessary waste and carbon-intensive forms of production. Reading a business is an exercise that includes exploring GVC configurations and this includes identifying opportunities to enhance efficiency and to reduce negative impacts. Opportunity and scale are critical dimensions of international business. Opportunity is a micro-level process based on the actions of an individual or groups of individuals, but these actions are enveloped by macrolevel or institutional structures. Individual action is framed by these macrolevel structures which are often abstract, remote and anonymous; for example, the legal or tax system or labour regulation. The macro varies by national context whilst micro-level processes reflect place-based cultures and traditions. This is important as opportunity varies by place.

Decision-making and international business

The distinction between local and global represents binary thinking. Binary thinking is challenged by relational thinking that adopts an analytical approach based on 'both/ and' rather than 'or' (Bryson et al, 2021). Relational thinking is opposed to simple binaries; for example, theory versus practice, or international versus local businesses. With relational thinking the emphasis shifts from what characterizes something as being different to understanding interconnections. This emphasis on interconnections highlights the importance of understanding inequalities, power imbalances and exploitation. Power emerges within relationships between people and is inherently a place-based process. It is important to explore the ways in which every international business is embedded in a complex network of relationships and interactions with other companies, countries, places and even individuals.

People are central to all businesses. Here it is important to appreciate that these networks of relationships form around dyadic encounters with a dyad being the smallest possible grouping of people. A dyad is a group of two individuals or things interacting with each other in some way. A dyad includes all types of one-to-one relationships – family, friendships, employment, business transactions – and like all relationships experiences different degrees of asymmetry. This includes asymmetric information, but also other forms of power imbalance; for example, size or scale or existing relationships. Companies are groupings of individuals and represent a consolidation of multiple dyadic encounters. Some of these encounters become formalized in contracts and become a form of strong tie based on regular flows and interactions. Some remain weak ties or acquaintances that open possibilities for informal exchanges (Granovetter, 2017) which may eventually become formalized. The formalization of dyadic encounters results in the configuration of supply chains and also what are known as global commodity chains (GCC), GVCs or global production networks (GPNs). A company consists of many dyadic relationships (see

Chapter 7), but there may be much complexity here. For example, a firm may have multiple suppliers for the same component or raw material. A supply-chain algorithm might make the decision regarding which supplier to use for a specific order based on price, availability and location. Chains or networks form around relationships between companies that are developed to facilitate all types of flows with the outcome being products and services. Products are the outcome of the configuration of some form of business model that is embedded within a complex network of ever-evolving relationships with other companies, and places.

The chain or network literature is very conceptual and focused on firms and there is a tendency for employees to be sidelined in this analysis. Nevertheless, all chains or networks are saturated with people who are directly or indirectly involved in production processes (Herod, 2017). Those involved experience different degrees of exploitation. Labour exploitation occurs when people are abused in workplaces for profit, and this includes underpayment of workers, pay that is not equated with a living wage, various forms of discrimination and modern-day slavery or forced labour (Box 9.1). There is an additional point to consider. Companies do not make decisions as it is people employed by companies who make decisions. The people-centred nature of corporate decision-making processes means that all decisions involve power asymmetries and are complicated by politics, culture and former and existing dyadic encounters. It is important never to assume that businesses make rational decisions; all decisions exhibit bounded rationality in some manner, with the outcome being determined by available information, the time required to make the decision and the cognitive capability of the decision-maker(s). The outcome of people-inflected decision-making processes is that decisions tend never to be optimal, but rather they are acceptable or satisfactory solutions.

Box 9.1: Global value chains: labour exploitation, including modern-day slavery

People play a central role in firms. These include well-paid advantaged employees and under-paid and exploited employees. There is also hidden and visible forms of direct discrimination (including racism, ageism, gender including gender reassignment, sexual orientation, religion) in which an employer treats one potential or actual employee less favourable than others. Women or someone from a minority ethnic community may be paid less than another colleague for undertaking the same job or there might be unequal access to training. Indirect discrimination may occur in job adverts that highlight more masculine characteristics and thus discourage women from applying. An advert, for example, might state that applicants must have ten years of work experience in this sector but this discriminates indirectly based on age. There is then discrimination by perception where an employer makes assumptions about an employee or applicant based on protected characteristics (age, disability, gender reassignment, marriage/civil partnership, race, religion or belief, sex). Discrimination can result in the refusal to employ, dismissal, having shifts cut, denial of promotion, transfers or training, being given impossible tasks and all forms of bullying. Employers must follow local employment legislation, but international businesses should seek to uphold the very best employment practices irrespective of the location. There is a tension here between satisfying local regulations or going way beyond these in locations that have labour regulations that permit or even encourage labour exploitation.

People represent variable costs to an organization, but they are also an organization's most important asset. Artificial intelligence (AI) is unable to substitute for the capabilities provided by people. One of the capabilities that people have over AI is the ability to develop new solutions, but also to identify solutions from accidents and mistakes. Nevertheless, people are much more difficult to manage compared to machines. But there are also great challenges linked to AI and machine learning and in ensuring that AI systems do not acquire discriminatory and biased practices. In workplaces, a core challenge is recruitment, training and promotions. Linked to this is ensuring that employees do not engage in inappropriate behaviour, including harassment or offensive or intimidating behaviours (racial abuse, sexist language) and victimization; for example, excluding someone from company formal and informal social events.

Labour exploitation involves being directly or indirectly complicit with modern-day slavery or the severe exploitation of other people for commercial gain, including sexual abuse and sexual harassment, and all types of discrimination and exclusionary behaviour. In 2016, the ILO estimated that 40 million people were victims of modern slavery, with 25 million being in forced labour; there were 5.9 adult victims of modern slavery for every 1,000 adults in the world and 4.4 child victims for every 1,000 children (ILO, 2017: 5). Too many GVCs are configured around severe labour exploitation combined with environmental pollution and this includes hidden forms of modern-day slavery. Modern-day slavery occurs in all countries. The hidden nature of this form of exploitation makes it very difficult to measure. In the UK, it has been estimated that in 2018, there were approximately 130,000 victims of modern-day slavery (ONS, 2020). There are five main types of exploitation that victims of modern-day slavery may experience: labour exploitation (forced to work for nothing or very low wages), sexual exploitation for financial gain, domestic servitude, criminal exploitation and organ harvesting (ONS, 2020).

All responsible business practitioners must be sensitive to the possibility that their activities are directly and/or indirectly involved with labour exploitation. No practitioner should be complacent about employment practices. They must constantly reflect on labour conditions within their GVCs and seek to identify poor practice and to improve existing practices. A key question to consider is what constitutes responsible employment practice?

For international businesses, decision processes are further complicated, given the difficulties related to cross-cultural management. This includes understanding the ways in which social dynamics are shaped by different cultural environments. In other words, the form, structure and expectations of dyadic encounters are different. In the US, there is a work culture in which success is equated with hard work and long hours. Alternatively, in European nations, there is a greater appreciation of developing a work–life balance. In Japan, a 'karoshi' work ethic exists based on long hours and company loyalty. There are great variations in business practices in India and this includes working long hours and multitasking, but also a more recent appreciation of work–life balance. In China, the work culture includes respect for authority figures – for example managers and supervisors – with employees expected to defer to decisions made by their superiors. Differences in work culture are further complicated by differences in institutional environments. The outcome is that international businesses experience enhanced complexity as they balance tensions between different work cultures and institutional environments. This is an additional dimension of bounded rationality that is experienced by individuals involved in cross-cultural decision-making processes. Too often, international business failure is linked to the failure of managers to adjust firm-level routines to a different work culture and business environment.

It is important to appreciate that all decision-making processes result in some type of prioritization outcome. For international businesses, this includes where to invest or disinvest or to maintain levels of investment. It also includes tensions between decisions that focus on stripping out costs or on process optimization, combined with concerns over responsible business or environmental, social and governance (ESG) concerns.

All businesses are exploitative, and the key issue is the degree and nature of this exploitation. Even the most responsible business will be involved in exploiting place-based differences (see Chapter 7) and in environmental exploitation. There is a paradox here in that some types of exploitation are more acceptable as they have become accepted conventions. Exploitation is also a cross-country issue with cultural and institutional differences, or really varieties of capital, determining what is acceptable in one national context. There is a tension here; products/services may be produced in one country with looser regulations but sold to customers located in another who would find some forms of exploitation unacceptable, and this includes modern-day slavery. And yet, these products/services may have unacceptable exploitations 'hidden' within their GVCs. This would include modern-day slavery, environmental pollution producing localized negative health outcomes and even environmental destruction.

The evolving geoeconomy: new intersections between the local and the global

Local economies or businesses become defined in relation to their opposites – international or global businesses or economies. Local versus international/global is another binary that needs to be treated with considerable suspicion. Local and international businesses form around interconnections and these interconnections are simultaneously in a state of flux as well as being solidified in contracts. Agreements that are solidified by contract experience contract rigidity based on legally binding terms and conditions. The state of flux comes from opportunities to form new relationships, to negotiate new contracts and renegotiate existing ones.

Braudel (1988) distinguishes between the expression 'world economy' and 'world-economy' with the term world economy being applied to the whole world whilst world-economy refers to a fragment of the world that contains an autonomous functioning economy. The concept of a world-economy resonates with Rugman and Verbeke's (2005) theory of regional multinationals. In this perspective, companies located in small open economies must secure access to resources located in the core triad of the US, Japan and the European Community to support their international activities. The outcome is the emergence of regional multinationals that focus on the development of regional rather than global strategies.

There have been world-economies for a very long time, with different configurations occurring as an outcome of a process of constant renewal. These configurations were facilitated by the formation of associations of merchants that formed into networks and joint-stock companies. The Hanseatic League, for example, was a commercial network of merchant guilds and market towns that stretched from England to the Baltic and whose origins can be traced back to the 12th century. The League facilitated trade by establishing trade routes and reducing barriers to trade. Joint-stock companies were established in the 17th century to organize and control trade forming new world–economy configurations. The East India Company was established in 1600 to control trade between England and the Indian Ocean region and became the largest company in the world and even had its own army. The Dutch East India Company was established in 1602 and was granted a monopoly for the Netherlands to engage in trading activities in Asia.

These early joint-stock companies configured trading relationship that take the form of early GVCs. For example, the East India Company entered China in 1637. Chinese porcelain was purchased for the European market, but up to the start of the 18th century, the traditional shapes were modified to suit European fashions, but Chinese decorations and patterns were retained. From the 18th century, Chinese companies began to compete with European producers by designing and manufacturing porcelain for European consumers. This Chinese porcelain example highlights that international business occurs as commercial opportunities are identified based on differences between places. This has been defined as 'the great geographical fact on which commerce depends is that different parts of the world yield different products, or furnish the same products under unequally favourable conditions' (Chisholm, 1925: 1). The outcome of these differences results in '**complicated action and reaction between different parts of the world to which commerce gives rise**' (Chisholm, 1925: 14, bold in the original). These complicated actions take the form of supply chains and led to the emergence of the discipline of operations and supply chain management (O&SCM).

Internationalization's intersection with globalization

An important distinction must be made between internationalization and globalization. There are very different processes. Internationalization refers to a set of processes which extend economic activities from beyond the confines of a nation-state. In other words, economic activity begins to transcend national boundaries. Internationalization includes the increased importance of international trade enabled by developments in international relations including trade agreements and alliances. With internationalization, nation-states continue to play an important role in regulating international economic activity. Globalization represents a qualitative step change in global economic integration. Central to globalization is a set of processes that drive global economic integration with the outcome being the emergence of a globally integrated economy.

This distinction between internationalization and globalization does not represent another binary. But rather, what is occurring are new interconnections between internationalization and globalization. In other words, internationalization continues alongside globalization. There is an important distinction to make. The international business literature's object of study is 'international business' rather than global business.

This distinction is important as there are very few businesses that are truly 'global'. However, there are international businesses that operate within the international economy and those that act globally.

With globalization comes a reduction in barriers to trade and this includes reductions in the regulations that discouraged or prevented migration and free capital mobility. This shift from an international to global economy is ongoing as nation-states experience different degrees of integration into the evolving geoeconomy. The same holds for companies. There are companies that continue to operate based on processes that are more aligned with internationalization. For example, J Hudson & Co was established in Birmingham, UK, in 1870 to produce all types of whistles (police, sports, orchestral and musical whistles). All this firm's whistles are made in the UK and sold within the home market and exported. This approach is aligned with internationalization rather than globalization.

International trade emerges in response to the identification of comparative advantages or place-based differences in factor endowments: land, labour, capital, regulations and entrepreneurship. For J Hudson & Co, the company benefits from the place-based associations that come from designing and manufacturing its products in Birmingham. Alternatively, the application of artificial intelligence to the analysis of Tesla's supply chain has identified 13,428 companies that supply items (NikkeiAsia, 2023). Of these, 42 firms provide non-ferrous smelting, with 40 per cent being based in China. Overall, US companies account for 22 per cent of Tesla's suppliers and Chinese firms account for 17 per cent. The Tesla example highlights the complex fragmentation of a product's supply chain that is a feature of globalization. This provides cost advantages that can be combined with benefits linked to dual supply or ensuring that the same component or input is available from at least two suppliers and locations. A key issue for a company like Tesla is being over-exposed or overdependent on any one company. The NikkeiAsia analysis applied Fronteo's 'chokepoint score' index to Tesla. This index measures a company's degree of dependence on a specific supplier based on a 10-point scale with 10 highlighting the greatest dependence. Tesla has a 6.8 chokepoint score for Ganfeng Lithium, a Chinese provider of Lithium, and a 7.1 score for Novoray, a producer of inorganic components. Globalization, whilst providing a firm with advantages, also comes with risks. These risks include overdependency on a supplier as well as the complexity that comes from managing extremely fragmented supply chains.

With the emergence of globalization, comparative advantage is replaced by companies developing absolute advantage by designing products and services and configuring supply chains. This type of advantage comes from productivity gains that come from a firm's coordinating functionally integrated supply chains based on coordinating a complex spatial division of labour (see Chapter 1).

Geoeconomic fragmentation

The ongoing escalation in the interconnectedness of economic activities across space as places become incorporated into the world economy in complex ways is an accepted fact by international institutions. For example, a report published by the World Bank in 2010 proclaimed that GVCs 'have become the world economy's backbone and central nervous system' (Cattaneo et al, 2010: 7).

This metaphor of GVCs functioning as the world economy's central nervous system is apt. Central nervous systems are subjected to a host of different nervous system disorders. These include nervous systems that become unregulated with individuals experiencing mood swings and irritability along with neurologic diseases that lead to problems with moving, speaking, swallowing, breathing, learning, memory, senses or moods. The world economy's central nervous system experiences a host of known and unknown shocks. These include crises, protectionist policies and regional realignments with the outcome being that:

> Geoeconomic fragmentation is reshaping the landscape of global investment. Trade networks are fragmenting, regulatory environments are diverging and international supply chains are being reconfigured. These shifts create both obstacles and isolated opportunities, with some countries benefiting from investments in global value chain-intensive manufacturing while others struggle to participate in the global economy. (UNCTAD, 2024: iv)

There are two types of fragmentation at play in the evolving world economy. On the one hand, there is the ongoing process of GVC fragmentation that results from the application of an increasingly complex and extended spatial division of labour to production processes. On the other hand, there is geoeconomic fragmentation that is reshaping the geoeconomy into competing and increasingly disconnected economic blocks.

Geoeconomic fragmentation is driven by an ongoing reversal in the process of global economic integration. This can be described as reverse globalization or deglobalization. Nevertheless, all that is happening is an ongoing process of geoeconomy restructuring. This is policy-driven and is a response to distrust combined with national competitiveness that is encouraging some national governments to reinstate trade barriers or develop new barriers that reduce or limit global economic integration. Effectively, three major economic blocks have emerged – the EU, the US and China. Central to geoeconomic fragmentation is an intensification of national sovereignty and security. In other words, policy is driven by the US adopting an 'America first' approach and this also holds for China (China first) and the EU (EU first). There is nothing new here in that every nation-state's approach to international negotiations is founded upon self-interest. Self-interest results in the alignment of converging national self-interests; for example, the evolving political relationship between China and Russia or between Russia, Iran and North Korea. The emergence of these new axis powers distorts global economic integration, with one outcome being a reduction in world economic growth. The signs of enhanced geoeconomic fragmentation include greater trade protectionism. The IMF estimates that geoeconomic fragmentation could reduce global economic output over the long term by as much as 7 per cent or US$7.4 trillion (IMF, 2023). This is equivalent to combining the French and German economies or is three times the size of the annual economic output of sub-Saharan Africa.

Geoeconomic fragmentation reflects a concern for national economic security founded upon governments identifying where their nations are exposed to risks and vulnerabilities that might threaten national economic security. There is an ongoing process that can be traced back to before the COVID-19 pandemic, in which governments engaged in de-risking strategies. De-risking includes government policies that are intended to protect local industries that are deemed to be important for national economic security. This includes tax benefits. The outcome is some degree of reverse globalization that takes the form of adapting supply chains to include the reshoring of production that had been offshored to other countries, combined with friendshoring (Vanchan et al, 2018). A classic example occurred in 2018, when Ypsomed, the Swiss medtech company, reshored the production of its insulin pens after they had been produced in Mexico for over 30 years. Technological innovation led to the introduction of a highly automated production process, and this enabled reshoring to a high-labour cost country (McIvor and Bals, 2021). Shein, the Chinese fast-fashion company, has been altering its business model. This initially involved production being focused in China and included dropshipping. Producing clothing staples like white T-shirts is predictable and an offshore production strategy can be applied, but fast fashion driven by social media and multiple influencers is highly unpredictable. Shein's response had been to begin to localize production in core markets. In 2023, Shein announced that it was investing US$150 million in production in Brazil that was targeted at providing clothing to customers located in Latin America. The plan is to start supplying products made in Brazil to other Latin American markets by 2026 with the ambition to have 85 per cent of Shein's sales in Brazil produced locally. Brazil is one of Shein's five main markets and is the company's most important market in Latin America (Easton, 2023). This reflects the development of a supply lattice strategy with some goods being sourced from offshore, some from neighbouring countries and some close to the point of sale. Some companies adopt a 'world-economy' or regionalized approach and there are many opportunities here. For example, African companies could replace GVCs with much more regionalized African value chains and the same holds true for Asian value chains.

Supply chains

A supply chain is an 'integrated process wherein raw materials are manufactured into final products, then delivered to customers (via distribution, retail, or both)' (Beamon: 1999: 275). Supply chains involve many organizations working together to produce final products and services. The specialist field of operations management focuses on the design, operation, control and updating of supply chains that are required for the production of a product or service. A supply chain contains four types of stakeholder: suppliers, manufacturers, distributors and consumers. Each stakeholder phase may include many companies, locations and facilities. There are simple and complex supply chains. The more complex supply chains involve many stakeholders, locations and facilities and through which information, knowledge, people, raw materials, completed products and money flows.

These complex supply chains take the form of GCCs, GVCs or GPNs. These three terms represent different, but still connected, academic approaches to understanding the world's evolving geoeconomy. The distinctions between these three approaches matter for academics but are much less important for practitioners. These different approaches are explored in the next section.

From World Systems Theory to global commodity chains and global value chains

There have been many alternative attempts to understand the interconnectedness of economic activity. These include the division of labour and spatial division of labour (see Chapter 1). It also includes World Systems Theory (Wallerstein, 1974) as an approach that acknowledged the importance of exploring the ways in which national economies had become integrated into a world system. In this approach, the emphasis is on exploring the evolving division of labour and framing an argument in which the world is divided into core, semi-periphery and periphery countries. Unequal power relations and the dominance of the core countries are central to this analysis.

World Systems Theory drew upon Dependency Theory (Frank, 1967), which highlighted asymmetrical power relationships between rich and poor nation-states. Central to dependency theory is the contention that rich countries exploit poorer countries, and the outcome is countries that are simultaneously impoverished and dependent. Both theories are conceptual frameworks, or metatheories, that are used to facilitate understanding of the evolving geoeconomy. One of the central challenges of social science is with explaining the functioning of some kind of system. This is complex as data points, or observations, cannot be made of the complete system. Usually, data is collected from individuals or organizations. The outcome is that there is a tension in social science between attempts to understand the totality of a system, or system functioning, and empirical research that is often focussed on exploring individual behaviour. Empirical research in the social sciences draws upon the analysis of national statistics collected by governments from individuals or groups, and/or data obtained by interviewing or surveying individuals or groups. World Systems Theory and Dependency Theory were higher-level theories that were unable to explore the particularities of relationships between individual actors or firms. An alternative approach emerged with the work of Gary Gereffi, an economic sociologist, who was interested in exploring the configuration and power dynamics of global commodity chains (GCCs). To Gereffi, GCCs are 'sets of inter-organizational networks clustered around one commodity or product, linking households, enterprises, and states to one another within the world economy. These networks are situationally specific, social constructed and locally integrated, underscoring the social embeddedness of economic organization' (Gereffi, 1994: 2).

Theory builds on theory. The GCC approach builds on transaction cost theory (TCT) that was introduced by Coase in 1937. To Coase a firm (organizational hierarchy) versus the market 'are alternative methods of coordinating production' (Coase, 1937: 388). The argument is that outside firms, relationships between firms/individuals are coordinated by market transactions based on price movements. Markets come with costs related to information searching and managing knowledge asymmetries. Firms are established to internalize these costs and 'a firm will tend to expand until the costs of organizing an extra transaction within the firm become equal to the costs of carrying out the same transaction by means of an exchange on the open market or the costs of organizing in another firm' (Coase, 1937: 395). The TCT approach focuses on understanding the configuration of inter- and intra-organizational structures. In other words, the ways in which firms decide to internalize transactions inside the hierarchy of a firm or alternatively to draw upon the market to externalize, or outsource, tasks. Every firm, every product, involves a multitude of transaction cost decisions. Combined, the outcome of all these individual decisions, made by just over 330 million firms, form the geoeconomy.

The complicated actions and reactions that result in the flows that form supply chains are driven by place-based differentials that take two forms; companies search to access assets or production inputs, and/or search to increase market share. Gereffi makes an important distinction between two types of asset as 'driver' (1994: 97). On the one hand, there are *producer-driven commodity chains* that are configured by transnational companies (TNCs) and other corporate forms. These supply chains are designed to produce products and services, with the TNC making strategic decisions that include backward and forward linkages. A backward linkage involves relationships with suppliers whilst forward linkages are with consumers, and this includes intermediaries; for example, retailers and wholesalers. Typically, these types of supply chains are found in capital-intensive industries; for example, automotive, aviation, computers, smartphones. On the other hand, there are *buyer-driven commodity chains* which are configured by retailers; for example, supermarkets, trading companies and e-commerce platforms like Amazon. Such firms establish transnational supply chains with the emphasis being placed on price, quantity and availability. These buyer-driven supply chains are configured around buyer power, or the ability of these buyers to deploy scale to negotiate favourable procurement terms. This can include requiring suppliers that are highly dependent on one buyer to accept after-sales rebates, discounts and retrospective payments. This can also involve slotting fees that suppliers must pay to secure access to more desirable shelf space.

The GCC approach evolved into the GVC approach, with this repositioning reflecting an appreciation that the evolving geoeconomy was heterogeneous. The GCC approach emphasized the internal governance structure of supply chains and the roles played by very different firms (producer versus buyer-driven). The GVC approach highlights 'the relative value of those activities that are required to bring a product or service from conception, through the different phases of production – involving a combination of physical transformation and the input of various producer services – delivery to final consumers, and final disposal after use' (Gereffi et al, 2001: 4). An important feature of the GVC approach is the appreciation that accessing international markets is much more complex than simply designing, producing and marketing products. An important challenge is the need for firms to gain 'entry into international design, production and marketing networks consisting of many different firms' (Gereffi et al, 2001: 1). In other words, how a firm navigates the processes, relationships and forms of governance that enable it to participate in GVCs.

The GVC literature includes a focus on understanding development inequalities. A core issue is with understanding how emerging economy value chains are included in GVCs. The literature explores different types of upgrading that can be facilitated by government policy (Gereffi et al, 2001). This includes a concern with product upgrading or with encouraging firms and emerging economies to transition towards the production of higher-value products and services. It also includes process upgrading based on productivity enhancement. Intra-chain upgrading concerns firms altering the contribution they make to a GVC, including developing new functions. In contrast, inter-chain upgrading involves firms applying capabilities acquired in being involved in one type of product or service to other commodities. Bit Source, a pioneering software development and digital services company located in Pikeville, Kentucky, is an excellent example of upgrading. This company was established in 2014 by Rusty Justice, an engineer, who was concerned about the downturn in Kentucky's coal industry. Justice realized that mine workers were intelligent, trainable and technologically aware and had capabilities that were akin to computer programmers. A decision was made to try to bring coding to Pikeville by retraining out-of-work miners and the outcome was the establishment of Bit Source.

One aspect of the GVC approach is with understanding the ways in which 'firms and industries are profoundly influenced by the local and national institutional environments in which they are situated' (Sturgeon, 2001: 9). This is to accept that GVCs do not exist in a vacuum, but that they are enveloped in a complex matrix of supporting institutions and industries. This includes the global financial service system, which is a GVC in its own right. In fact, there are a number of interlinked financial service GVCs that include banking services, but also insurance. Insurance is a core service required to support imports and exports as insurance is required both for the goods, components and raw materials that are being moved, but also for logistics infrastructure: ports, airports, vessels, aircraft. Every stage of a GVC involves critical support inputs, including infrastructure, human capital, equipment and services.

Occasionally, an academic paper is published that is pathbreaking and which redefines an ongoing debate. For the GVC debate, this occurred in 2005, with the publication of a paper by Gereffi et al that set out a typology of value chain governance. This approach was based on the identification of three variables that play important roles in determining the governance and dynamics of value chains: the complexity of transactions, the codification of information and the capability of suppliers. Complexity includes lead firms placing new demands on those companies involved with their value chains; for example, adding expectations regarding just-in-time supply. The complexity of information that is transmitted between firms within a value chain can be reduced with the adoption of technical standards and codification. The introduction of value-chain modularity enables companies to reuse elements within a value chain, or modules, which can be incorporated into new products. With the introduction of value chain modularity, suppliers can be introduced or removed from a value chain with the outcome being the configuration of a 'very fluid and flexible network structure' (Gereffi et al, 2005: 85). The selection of firms to be included in a value chain includes an appraisal of their capabilities as these relate to the value chain transaction that is required. These three variables led Gereffi et al (2005) to identify five types of governance relationship in global value chains:

Markets – With market exchange, transactions are configured between participants in a value chain when they are easily codified with simple product specifications. When this occurs, the lead firm can purchase these inputs using simple market-based transactions.

Modular – Codification increases the potential for value chain modularity. With codification, complex information can be exchanged simply, reducing the costs of switching partners and the outcome may be a lead firm who can deploy a modular form of governance for this transaction.

Relational – A product specification might not be suitable for codification and in this circumstance, transactions may be complex and require suppliers with high capabilities. Mutual dependence occurs that includes trust, making it difficult for either party to the transaction to break the contract.

Captive – When the ability to codify is high and product specifications are complex, but supplier capabilities are low, then a captive value chain form of governance is likely to be applied. The lead firm will seek to lock in the supplier and suppliers would also experience significant switching costs.

Hierarchy – With product specifications that cannot be codified and with complex products for which competent suppliers cannot be identified, the lead firm may be forced to configure an in-house solution.

This framework provides a useful typology for considering different types of supplier transaction within a GVC. To Gereffi et al the 'governance framework that we propose takes us part of the way toward a more systematic understanding of global value chains, but much remains to be done' (2005: 99) and this includes the development of policy tools to support GVC upgrading. The GVC for a product may include all governance types. There are complications to this approach – for example, products that must be accredited or certified – with this process tending to lockdown a GVC making it impossible, or costly, to substitute one firm within a value chain with another. It is important to appreciate that this 2005 paper is the starting point for a discussion of value chain governance. This approach, for example, has been criticized for underestimating sector-based differences and the evolution of value chains (Ponte and Sturgeon, 2014). A GVC may evolve from an initial emphasis on relational governance types that then transition to a form of captive relationship as the lead firm is able to enhance codification.

All production has within it varying degrees of exploitation (Bolwig et al, 2010). For GVCs, there are three issues to consider. First, the type of value chain governance that a company or regional economy is orientated towards. Regions, or nation-states, that tend to be involved in more captive type supplier relationships may have limited opportunities to upgrade and to break their dependency on the production of lower-value and highly codified products for TNCs. Alternatively, modular value, or relational forms of governance may enable upgrading. There is the smile metaphor that has been applied to GVCs. In this approach, the argument is that some countries benefit from the 'smile of value creation' in that 'the activities at the ends of the overall value constellation are largely located in advanced economies, while those in the middle of the value chain are moving (or have moved) to emerging economies' (Mudambi, 2008: 706). The implication being that value-added activities along a value chain are distributed to form a smiling curve with the middle part of the smile representing lower-value more codified tasks. Either side are positioned higher value-added processes; for example, research and development (R&D), design and commercialization on one side, and on the other marketing, advertising, specialist logistics and after-sales services.

Responsibility, circularity and global value chains

The production of all types of goods and services, from raw agricultural products (vegetables, fruits, livestock) to the most technically advanced manufactured products, is extremely heterogeneous (Bryson et al, 2022). There are many different approaches to producing raw agricultural products that include varying amounts of inputs and capital investment. Manufacturing companies range from those producing comparatively simple and highly codified products that involve very few inputs, to goods that contain millions of components. Every good or service is the outcome of a distinctive process involving the configuration of a division of labour that then becomes a spatial division of labour and this then may be configured as a GVC. A GVC forms around decisions regarding what is going to be produced and how it is going to be produced. The how also includes decisions regarding where the products or services are going to be produced, sold and increasingly recycled. All these decisions include explicit or implicit decisions that define a product's degree of engagement with responsible business or a firm's commitment, or otherwise, to an agenda based around an ESG agenda that is intended to prioritize environmental issues. The application of an ESG agenda to a complex GVC involving many companies and places is a challenging task for all businesses. Every company decision has ESG implications.

Heterogeneity is the key word to reflect on here as there is no single approach to producing the same goods and services. Four manufactured products with similar functionalities can have very different environmental, social and governance impacts. One might be produced and sold locally with very limited engagement with GVCs. Moreover, a company may be committed to recycling and persuading consumers to return products for recycling once they reach their end of life. This company may only produce and sell locally to ensure that it can regulate labour conditions to avoid labour exploitation and any involvement of highly exploited labour, including modern-day slavery in its value chain. An alternative approach might be a similar product produced using a GVC that has been configured to reduce costs and to ensure that the final product can be sold as cheaply as possible. There might be no concern with minimizing ESG impacts. The heterogeneity of production takes four forms: by type of firm (small, large, transnational, local/foreign, cooperative/social enterprise/for-profit/private/listed), by the configuration of the production process (to maximize profit, to minimize production costs, to reduce ESG impacts), by market segment (cover all segments or target some segments and ignore other segments) and by the ostensive and performative nature of a company's approach to responsible business.

There are four approaches that a firm can apply to acting responsibly (or appearing to):

1. As a form of greenwashing or the act of proclaiming that a company is acting responsibly, but these are claims that are unsupported by actual practice.
2. Through applied practice based on an ostensive and performative approach in which the company tries to do the right thing by reducing the firm's negative ESG impacts and trying to treat employees, consumers and all living on this planet responsibly.
3. By configuring a firm from before it is established as a responsible business. These firms are often established by an individual or groups of individuals who want to form for-profit businesses based around minimal exploitation. All firms exploit and the issue is the degree of exploitation of people, consumers, the environment and society. These firms can be termed *born responsible businesses* as they think and act as responsibly as possible.
4. By reconfiguring a firm as a result of leadership or ownership changes. Rather than being born responsible, firms can be *reborn responsible*. This requires firms to overhaul their motivations, goals and strategies to enable them to think and act as responsibly as possible.

There is a fundamental challenge facing all firms that are involved in configuring value chains at different spatial scales. This book's focus is on responsible international business, but it must be acknowledged that international business does not have to involve the configuration of GVCs, but instead a firm may configure distributed localized production systems that are intended to serve local markets. These are two very different approaches to configuring production approaches. An alternative approach is to have one production site that provides goods and services to all markets via exports. One example of this is VEJA, the French footwear and accessories brand founded in 2005. VEJA produces its sneakers in Northeast and Southern Brazil as these locations are close to the cotton and rubber producers. In addition, the factories and workshops must meet International Labour Organization (ILO) standards to ensure that work is fair and safe, and this includes freedom to form groups, fair pay and employee benefits (Bryson et al, 2024). Here it is important to distinguish between high-value, low-weight products, and which might have place-based associations, that can be exported, and products in which the application of a GVC approach to product/service realization has become the accepted convention. One of the challenges faced by all companies is the complexity of products and the ways in which they are linked directly and indirectly to all types of GVC.

Thus, a product that is sold as being eco-friendly and in which considerable care and attention has been given to minimizing its environmental impacts may still include materials and components that have significant negative environmental and societal impacts.

A firm that seeks to act responsibly must consider all dimensions of its value chain. The more fragmented and geographically dispersed a value chain becomes, the more opportunities exist for negative environmental and societal impacts to be hidden within a GVC. There are some principles that all firms should consider when configuring a GVC:

1. The complexity of the GVC and this includes the company's ability to monitor and regulate all stages in the value chain.
2. Avoiding illicit or illegal practices.
3. Be aware of company ownership and the motivations of those firms involved in a GVC.
4. Logistics and the GVC's exposure to different forms of logistics. This can result in supply-chain blockages. The configuration of appropriate logistics is critical for minimizing a product's carbon footprint.
5. Waste and ensuring that the GVC has a focus on minimizing waste. This reduces costs, but also enhances a product's eco-credentials.
6. Production efficiencies and ideally production processes that are designed to maximize circularity and to minimize inputs. This includes an emphasis on renewable energy, water recycling and the application of closed-loop systems.
7. People play a central role in all firms. Appropriate processes must be in place to ensure that labour exploitation is minimized, and this includes trying to avoid being indirectly or even directly complicit in modern-day slavery and proactively seeking to employ people from disadvantaged backgrounds.
8. Product/service design should include an emphasis on design for circularity, repair, recycling and product inclusiveness.
9. Product/service design should include a concern with designing out product obsolescence.
10. GVC configuration including a concern with avoiding negative forms of highly exploitative captive governance relationships.
11. Training must be central to all companies that seek to act responsibly. There are companies that invest in training, and this includes early career training. Nevertheless, there are companies that have decided not to invest in early career training programmes. These are parasitic companies as they seek to recruit those who have been trained by other companies.
12. Taxation and tax avoidance. A company should seek to pay appropriate levels of tax in the jurisdictions in which it operates.

Circularity and global value chains

Since McDonough and Braungart (2002) published *Cradle to Cradle: Remaking the Way We Make Things*, much thought has been given to how to (re)design production processes to create circular economies (CEs). A central goal behind building these CEs is to decouple economic growth from natural resource depletion and environmental degradation through activities that reduce, reuse and recycle materials in production, distribution and consumption processes (Bryson et al, 2024). Key to this is shifting away from production processes configured around linear flows of materials and energy towards circular or 'closed loop' systems configured around questions of resource use and waste residuals (Du et al, 2025). The majority of GVCs are configured around a linear approach to production in which raw materials and components flow along these chains and come together in finished products that are sold. Too frequently, once these products reach their end of life, they become waste and may be incinerated, disposed of in a landfill or sent to an emerging economy for resale, recycling or disposal.

This shift towards circularity requires a fundamental change in how products are designed, produced and consumed so as to place sustainability, closed-loop thinking and post-consumer practices at the centre of business models (Hvass and Pederson, 2019; Bryson et al, 2024). For manufacturers, a CE approach can include engineering products for greater longevity and for better circularity through designing them to be more easily taken apart by recyclers and/or making them easier to repair (Du et al, 2025). Nevertheless, no production process or product can be completely circular as there will always be some degree of waste and some of this waste may not be recyclable.

A GVC involves different stages; for example, acquisition of raw materials, component inputs and the provision of production-related and after-sales services. There are also stages related to the management of discarded products and materials. All responsible businesses should be concerned with minimizing waste materials and the proportion of their products once they reach their end of life that are either incinerated or sent to landfill. Global Destruction Networks (GDNs) have been configured as 'networks of places where products are disassembled and their constituent parts are extracted for processing and re-use' (Herod et al, 2014: 427). This includes shipbreaking or the process of breaking up obsolete vessels, and companies that specialize in recycling electronic equipment. Companies that seek to develop CE-inflected business models try to ensure that their end-of-life products are disposed of appropriately. Regulatory change is also driving this process with governments introducing *extended producer responsibility* (EPR) policies that are intended to extend producers' operational and/or financial responsibilities for the post-consumer stages of their product's lives. Companies are increasingly configuring Waste Reduction Networks (WRNs), which are networks '*of actors who are involved in extending commodities' lives to delay their entering the waste stream*' (Bryson et al, 2024, italics in the original). A WRN includes additional value-creating stages that are added to a product's lifecycle and these include 'on-going processes of value creation [which] come through the labour involved in repairs, alterations, upcycling and in reselling and/or renting items, which might be conducted by the original manufacturer or may be undertaken by others' (Bryson et al, 2024).

Exploitation is central to all production processes and to the configuration of all GVCs. Thus, negotiating the best deal with a captive supplier is good business but it might not be responsible business. The important point to note is that all decisions involving a GVC reflect trade-offs between risk, cost, quality, location and people. In other words, trade-offs between risk against product design and characteristics, production characteristics, place, people, production costs and profit. There are GVCs that are optimized to reduce costs and maximize profit, but these are often highly exploitative. Alternatively, there are GVCs that have high returns that come from configuring a GVC as responsibly as possible. However, there will always be known and unknown forms of negative ESGs within a GVC. The key is to minimize the unknown. There is always the danger of consumers and lobbying groups discovering these unknowns and revealing them via social media.

Responsible business, global fragmentation and risk

The ongoing process of increasing the fragmentation of GVCs results in new forms of risk. It is important to differentiate between complicated problems compared to complex problems (Nason, 2017). A complicated problem may be challenging to solve, but solutions are possible through the applications of procedures, systems, processes, techniques and technology. The fragmentation of GVCs comes with an escalation in their complexity and for some chains complexity is transformed into a process that has become complex. A complex problem is very different to a complicated problem as complexity comes with many unknowns and this is combined with interrelated processes that include unexpected or unpredictable feedback loops. The shift from internationalization to globalization is one in which GVCs transition from being complicated to being complex. The outcome is unexpected supply chain disruptions.

GVCs are enabled by technological developments that facilitate and catalyse global economic integration. Central to this is a rapidly evolving *cyber–energy–production plexus* that is forming around 'multiple connections between telecommunications, energy and production networks' (Bryson et al, 2022: 21). Industrial control systems (ICS) are central to GVCs that integrate hardware with software through network connectivity. ICSs are central to the critical infrastructure that supports production systems. The cyber–energy–production plexus forms around directly and indirectly linking ICS components to the internet, and this exposes core operational systems to cyberattacks and failure that occurs within some part of the plexus (Bryson, 2025). The integration of many systems within this plexus means that any failure produces a domino effect (Box 9.2). Such effects emerged with COVID-19 and resultant supply chain disruptions. The pandemic was an unusual shock event given its reach and duration. Other shocks tend to have more restricted geographic reaches and durations; for example, a temporary blockage of the Suez Canal or the localized impacts of terrorism.

All GVCs are saturated with risks, and include those that come from ongoing value chain fragmentation. Bryson and Vanchan (2020) argue that GVCs produce 'extra-network' effects that arise from their configuration. A geographically extended GVC comes with enhanced mobility that supports rapid virus transmission but also adds pollutants produced from transporting materials, components and completed goods over long distances. The risks that are embedded in supply chains can result in global supply chain disruptions. This can lead to reshoring or what has been defined as reverse globalization or even deglobalization (Bryson et al, 2022). Deglobalization and reverse globalization is not occurring. Instead, a new form of globalization is emerging that reflects a new balance between the local and global aspects of value chains. This includes lead firms paying more attention to GVC resilience, with one outcome being a growth in dual sourcing or ensuring that the same component is available from at least two different suppliers located in different countries. It also includes companies being able to produce some components close to the point of assembly using additive manufacturing (three-dimensional (3D) printing). A company like Toyota, the Japanese automotive company, strategy involves continuing to invest in China, but this includes extending its assembly and supplier networks in Southeast Asia. For example, in 2023, Toyota Indonesia shipped 285,000 completely built-up (CBU) vehicles to over 100 countries across Asia, South America, Africa, the Middle East, Australia and Oceania (Kurniawan and Kurniawan, 2024). This also includes exporting completely knocked down (CKD) vehicles or vehicles in a disassembled form. This type of strategy is based around spreading investment to reduce risk. A company should not be too overdependent on one market or a GVC that has been overoptimized with the outcome being a reduction in flexibility and resilience.

Box 9.2: The cyber–energy–production plexus and the dark side of global economic integration

As I write this sentence the global economy is crippled by a digital pandemic that has occurred due to an unexpected global disruption to the cyber–energy–production plexus. On 19 July 2024, CrowdStrike, the US cyber security firm, released a software update that included a defect. This update impacted the Windows operating system, and the outcome was a domino effect that rippled across the world economy. Companies located in China tended to avoid this effect, given the reluctance of the Chinese government to permit Chinese firms to use foreign software. Outside China, IT systems failed, and this included online payment systems that affected airports and flights, train services, hospitals, GP surgeries, banks, cafes, restaurants and shops, payment apps, taxis, betting websites, payroll systems, football clubs, stock exchanges, supermarkets, TV channels and water companies. But the key point is that this disruption was nearly global, with shops in Australia closing as their digital checkouts failed, US emergency service lines failed and in the UK, railway companies and the NHS were disrupted. For this global digital pandemic, the key bellwether indicators, or something that indicates a trend, appear to have been disruption to online payment systems and to airlines. Heathrow Airport's departure boards, for example, failed and at Berlin's airport there were problems with the check-in systems and all Spanish airports were impacted. During this incident, Crowdstrike noted that it would be some time before all systems would be back up and running.

Global economic integration comes with many positives, but there is also a dark side. This dark side includes labour exploitation, with some involving modern-day slavery. It also includes the threat of global pandemics. Enhanced global economic integration is associated with increased movement of people. The implication being that a localized virus can rapidly spread to become a global pandemic. We can expect global pandemics to become frequent occurrences. The other part of this dark side concerns a reduction in national economic security. I am writing this chapter with a laptop that was assembled in China and includes many components made in China. The UK has limited laptop-production capacity; for example, a company like Scan manufactures hundreds of 3XS system laptops every month in Bolton, UK. However, these still rely on components made across Asia and, in any case, the UK does not have the capacity to meet national demand for laptops and other types of computers. The other dark side originates from the complexity of the ever-evolving cyber–energy–production plexus (Bryson, 2025). This includes layers upon layers of interacting algorithms, with each algorithm representing complex computer codes that few people can understand. There is then the added complexity of legacy code, or source code that has reached or crossed an end of the support cycle. This type of old code occurs throughout the cyber–energy–production plexus. Legacy code is not inherently bad. However, it is important that efforts are made to understand the code's functionality and how this relates to the complete programme. The danger is that a trivial software update might have perverse impacts on legacy code and the outcome could be outage.

Conclusion

The evolving global economy includes companies that think and act globally alongside firms that think and act internationally or locally. There is no one current or dominant way of generating value from configuring the value chains that support the production of products or services. There are many different approaches to value realization. This chapter has explored the ongoing evolution of the geoeconomy, with a focus on supply chains or GVCs. There are many sides to this analysis. On the one hand, a firm-level analysis can be applied that identifies the trade-offs that a firm must make as they configure a value chain. This configuration may be more locally or globally orientated. The use of the word 'more' highlights that there is a continuum at work rather than a simple binary between local versus global. A company will be involved in the configuration of many different value chains. Sometimes it will be the lead firm and sometimes it will act as a supplier to a GVC configured by another company. Samsung is an excellent example. This company configures GVCs to create its own products but is also a supplier for GVCs configured by Apple. On the other hand, a country perspective highlights the different roles countries play in GVCs. This includes countries that are in a very peripheral or dependent position compared to countries that benefit from having concentrations of higher-value activities.

A key issue that comes from this chapter is the relationship between GVC configuration, trade-offs and risk. All GVCs come with known and unknown risks, and all come with different degrees of exploitation. A responsible business is one that should be seen to be acting responsibly. This comes with many challenges and complications. It is important that a firm is aware of the degree of actual and potential exposure that it has to risks and irresponsible behaviours of firms and people that are part of its GVCs. This is about being aware of these risks and remaining vigilant.

Key terms

Internationalization – the process by which companies adapt their strategies and products as they seek to enter different national markets. This is a quantitative process with the outcome being an extension in a company's geographic reach.

Globalization – the label given to the outcome of a set of processes that result in the development of an increasingly interconnected world. This is a qualitative process involving functional integration.

Global value chains (GVCs) – involve the configuration of a production sequence for the creation of final goods, with each stage adding value (raw materials, processing, production, services, marketing, logistics) and with at least two stages taking place in different countries.

Recommended reading

Bolwig, S., Ponte, S., Du Toit, A., Riisgaard, L. and Halberg, N. (2010) 'Integrating poverty and environmental concerns into value-chain analysis: a conceptual framework', *Development Policy Review*, 28(2): 173–94.

Bryson J.R., Billing, C., Graves, W. and Yeung, G. (2022) 'Reframing manufacturing research: place, production, risk and theory', in J.R. Bryson, C. Billing, W. Graves and G. Yeung (eds), *A Research Agenda for Manufacturing Industries in the Global Economy*, Cheltenham: Edward Elgar, pp 1–32.

Bryson, J.R., Herod, A., Johns, J. and Vanchan, V. (2024) 'Localised waste reduction networks, global destruction networks, and the circular economy', *Cambridge Journal of Regions, Economy and Society*, 17(3): 667–82.

Ponte, S., Gereffi, G. and Raj-Reichert, G. (2019) *Handbook on Global Value Chains*, Cheltenham: Edward Elgar.

References

Beamon, B.M. (1999) 'Measuring supply chain performance', *International Journal of Operations & Production Management*, 19(3): 275–92. doi.org/10.1108/01443579910249714.

Bolwig, S., Ponte, S., Du Toit, A., Riisgaard, L. and Halberg, N. (2010) 'Integrating poverty and environmental concerns into value-chain analysis: a conceptual framework', *Development Policy Review*, 28(2): 173–94.

Braudel, F. (1988) *Civilization and Capitalism: The Perspective of the World*, London: Collins.

Bryson, J.R. (2025) 'Jenga capitalism and the cyber-energy-production plexus: new forms of risk and uncertainty that are reshaping economic geography', in T. Neise, P. Verfürth and M. Franz (eds), *The Changing Economic Geography of Companies and Regions in Times of Risk, Uncertainty and Crisis*, London: Routledge.

Bryson, J.R. and Vanchan, V. (2020) 'COVID-19 and alternative conceptualisations of value and risk in GPN research', *Tijdschrift voor Economische en Sociale Geografie*, 111: 530–42.

Bryson, J.R., Vanchan, V. and Kalafsky, R.V. (2021) 'Reframing urban theory', in J.R. Bryson, V. Vanchan and R.V. Kalafsky (eds), *Ordinary Cities, Extraordinary Geographies: People, Place and Space*, Cheltenham: Edward Elgar.

Bryson, J.R, Billing, C., Graves, W. and Yeung, G. (2022) 'Reframing manufacturing research: place, production, risk and theory', in J.R. Bryson, C. Billing, W. Graves and G. Yeung (eds) *A Research Agenda for Manufacturing Industries in the Global Economy*, Cheltenham: Edward Elgar, pp 1–33.

Bryson, J.R., Herod, A., Johns, J. and Vanchan, V. (2024) 'Localised waste reduction networks, global destruction networks, and the circular economy', *Cambridge Journal of Regions, Economy and Society*, 17(3): 667–82.

Cattaneo, O., Gereffi, G. and Staritz, C. (2010) 'Global value chains in a postcrisis world: resilience, consolidation, and shifting end markets', in O. Cattaneo, G. Gereffi and C. Staritz (eds), *Global Value Chains in a Postcrisis World: A Development Perspective*, Washington: World Bank, pp 3–20 [online]. Available from: https://openknowledge.worldbank.org/handle/10986/2509 [Accessed 19 July 2024].

Chisholm, G.G. (1925) *Handbook of Commercial Geography*, London: Longmans, Green and Co.

Coase, R.H. (1937) 'The nature of the firm', *Economica*, 4: 386–405.

Du, B., Bryson J.R. and Qamar, A. (2025) 'Aspiring towards automotive circularity: a critical review and research agenda', *Journal of Environmental Management*, 380: 125150.

Easton, J. (2023) 'Shein plans to distribute Brazilian-made products around Latin America by 2026', *Retail Systems* [online]. Available from: www.retail-systems.com/rs/Shein_Brazil_Products_Latin_America.php [Accessed 11 September 2024].

Frank, A.G. (1967) *Capitalism and Underdevelopment in Latin America: Historical Studies of Chile and Brazil*, New York: Monthly Review Press.

Gereffi, G. (1994) 'The organisation of buyer-driven global commodity chains: how U.S. retailers shape overseas production networks', in G. Gereffi and M. Korzeniewicz (eds) *Commodity Chains and Global Capitalism*, Westport: Praeger, pp 95–122.

Gereffi, G., Humphrey, J. and Sturgeon, T. (2005) 'The governance of global value chains', *Review of International Political Economy*, 12(1): 78–104.

Gereffi, G., Humphrey, J., Kaplinsky, R. and Sturgeon, T.J. (2001) 'Introduction: globalisation, value chains and development', *IDS Bulletin*, 32: 1–12.

Granovetter, M. (2017) *Society and Economy: Frameworks and Principles*, Cambridge: Harvard University Press.

Herod, A. (2017) *Labor*, Cambridge: Polity.

Herod, A., Pickren, G., Rainnie, A. and McGrath-Champ S. (2014) 'Global destruction networks, labour and waste', *Journal of Economic Geography*, 14(2): 421–41.

Hvass, K.K. and Pedersen, E.R.G. (2019) 'Toward circular economy of fashion: experiences from a brand's product take-back initiative', *Journal of Fashion Marketing and Management*, 23(3): 345–65.

ILO (2017) *Global Estimates of Modern Slavery*, Geneva: ILO.

IMF (2023) 'The high cost of global economic fragmentation' [online]. Available from: www.imf.org/en/Blogs/Articles/2023/08/28/the-high-cost-of-global-economic-fragmentation [Accessed 19 July 2024].

Kurniawan, H. and Kurniawan, H. (2024) 'Toyota Indonesia aims to export 300,000 cars in 2024' [online]. Available from: https://jakartaglobe.id/business/toyota-indonesia-aims-to-export-300000-cars-in-2024 [Accessed 30 July 2024].

McDonough, W. and Braungart, M. (2002) *Cradle to Cradle: Remaking the Way We Make Things*, New York: North Point Press.

McIvor, R. and Bals, L. (2021) 'A multi-theory framework for understanding the reshoring decision', *International Business Review*, 30(6): 101827.

Mudambi, R. (2008) 'Location, control and innovation in knowledge-intensive industries', *Journal of Economic Geography*, 8 (5): 699–725. doi.org/10.1093/jeg/lbn024.

Nason, R. (2017) *It's Not Complicated: The Art and Science of Complexity in Business*, Toronto: University of Toronto Press.

NikkeiAsia (2023) 'Tesla relies on China for 40% of battery supply chain: analysis', NikkeiAsia [online]. Available from: https://asia.nikkei.com/Business/Automobiles/Tesla-relies-on-China-for-40-of-battery-supply-chain-analysis [Accessed 18 July 2024].

ONS (2020) *Modern Slavery in the UK: March 2020* [online]. Available from: https://www.ons.gov.uk/peoplepopulationandcommunity/crimeandjustice/articles/modernslaveryintheuk/march2020#measuring-modern-slavery [Accessed 30 July 2024].

Ponte, S. and Sturgeon, T. (2014) 'Explaining governance in global value chains: a modular theory-building effort', *Review of International Political Economy*, 21(1): 195–223.

Ponte, S., Gereffi, G. and Raj-Reichert, G. (2019) *Handbook on Global Value Chains*, Cheltenham: Edward Elgar.

Rugman, A.M. and Verbeke, A. (2005) 'Towards a theory of regional multinationals: a transaction cost economics approach', *Management International Review*, 45(1): 5–17.

Sturgeon, T.J. (2001) 'How do we define value chains and production networks?', *IDS Bulletin*, 32(3): 9–18. doi.org/10.1111/j.1759-5436.2001.mp32003002.x.

UNCTAD (2013) *World Investment Report: Global Value Chains: Investment and Trade for Development*, Geneva: United Nations.

UNCTAD (2024) *World Investment Report: Investment Facilitation and Digital Government*, Geneva: United Nations.

Vanchan, V., Mulhall, R. and Bryson, J. (2018) 'Repatriation or reshoring of manufacturing to the U.S. and UK: dynamics and global production networks or from here to there and back again', *Growth and Change*, 49: 97–121.

Wallerstein, I. (1974) *The Modern World-System I & II*, San Diego: Academic Press.

10

Responsible International Business

Introduction

Managing an international business is complex as it requires understanding and managing many conflicting priorities, and this process is saturated with all types of risks and shocks (Bryson, 2022, 2025). This involves prioritizing investment decisions that encompass decisions about continuing to invest in a particular market, product segment or technology. Of course, limited finance is available and there is always the possibility of disinvestment as business priorities change. The practice of international business is an exercise involving predictions about the future, managing and enhancing existing processes, developing new processes, problem solving and searching for new opportunities.

In this chapter, we reflect on the process of managing international businesses and some of the challenges involved in this process. There is a major challenge for students studying a module on international business and the same problem is experienced by researchers. The challenge is that a module, or this book, is constructed around a set of themes, issues or topics. Business scholars also tend to focus on one business activity area. Consequently, the object of study is divided up into a series of relatively isolated parts. Practitioners must consider all aspects of a business, and this includes being aware of positive and negative feedback loops as one business decision impacts on other business areas. This chapter is intended to encourage you to reflect on this challenge and to instigate a discussion on the complexity of managing an international business.

Trade-offs

All business practitioners have trade-offs to make, or choices, regarding the current and future directions of the companies that they are involved with (Bryson et al, 2024). These choices differ by employment grade. The junior manager is constrained to make operational choices that concern the implementation of strategy decided by senior managers. Their ability to influence the evolution of a company's strategy and values is limited. The chief executive officer (CEO) has much more influence in shaping, implementing and evaluating strategy. However, CEOs are constrained by the board of directors or owners and by decisions and investments that have been made in the past. No business decisions occur outside the constraints of context. Context includes all types of risks and shocks (Bryson, 2022, 2025). It is important to appreciate that a risk may be anticipated or unanticipated and that anticipated risks might not become shocks. A shock is a risk that has occurred, and a risk is an event that might occur (Bryson, 2025). Context also includes time, place, sector, competition, governance structure and decisions that those working for a firm have made in the past.

Trade-offs include decisions regarding optimization or resource efficiency that are related to productivity. Productivity is important as it is a measure of the relationship between outputs and inputs. This then is a measure of efficiency as productivity increases when more output is produced for the same level of input. Another way of defining productivity is as a process linked to cost control and resource optimization. Nevertheless, over-focusing on productivity reduces company resilience or the ability to respond to shocks, and it might also undermine a firm's long-term competitiveness. There is an important tension between a management focus on optimization and with flexibility or agility (Bryson, 2025). Another tension is with acting responsibly as some approaches to optimization may result in irresponsible corporate behaviour. All this is to highlight that there are many alternative approaches to managing a business and each comes with different outcomes and challenges.

The most important decision that a company makes concerns its overall mission and motivation. Motivation is extremely important but is too often assumed or overlooked. Too often, business motivation is equated with profit. Nevertheless, there are many different approaches to generating profit. On the one side, a business might focus only on profit generation and have no concern for negative environmental or societal impacts. Such a business might be involved with all types of labour exploitation. On the other side, a business might be profit-focused but framed within a real concern with acting responsibly and with due attention to limiting negative environmental and societal impacts (Bryson and Buttle, 2005; Bryson and Lombardi, 2009). The word 'limiting' is used deliberately as it is very different for an international business to avoid some involvement in activities that have negative impacts.

A company may position itself as a responsible business, but implementation of this ambition is extremely difficult. All company procedures, routines and strategies must be configured around some applied definition of responsible practice. This includes employee recruitment, training, appraisal and incentive schemes. Nevertheless, self-proclaimed responsible businesses will still have incidences where they are perceived to have acted in an irresponsible manner. A core question concerns who has the right to make a decision that might have financial consequences, and this is combined with individual employees or intermediaries making mistakes and seeking to hide these from senior managers. An excellent example is outlined in Box 10.1.

Box 10.1: McCann versus Snozone: responsibility and employment practice

In 2015, an employment tribunal between McCann versus Snozone Ltd was held in the UK. In this case, McCann applied and was interviewed for a job as a maintenance engineer by an employment agency appointed by Snozone. McCann received two phone calls from this agency, in which it was stated that Snozone wanted to offer him the job. McCann accepted this offer, but the salary and start date had not been agreed. Subsequently, the agency learnt that Snozone had decided not to employ McCann. McCann took Snozone to an employment tribunal and this upheld his breach of contract claim.

The *McCann* v. *Snozone* case is a reminder of basic contract law; a contract can be entered into verbally or in writing on the basis of some offer, consideration, acceptance and intention. This case also highlights the dangers of making verbal offers. An individual working for a responsible business may inadvertently enter into a binding contract and the key question is the willingness of the company to uphold such a contract.

It is important to consider the responsible business aspects of this case. Did Snozone act in a responsible manner? There are many aspects to consider here. First, Snozone initially withdrew the job offer and then denied that an employment offer had been made. Second, Snozone's decision to withdraw the job offer was made on the understanding that the company considered that McCann would be unable to work with the company's engineering consultant and that McCann did not have the capability to acquire the skills needed to work on the company's new equipment.

Acting responsibly for any business requires a willingness to accept that human error is always possible, and that responsible business practice must not only be done, but also must be seen to be done. This is to paraphrase the legal dictum laid down by Lord Hewart in 1924. Hewart was then Lord Chief Justice of England and he stated that: 'Justice must not only be done, but must also be seen to be done.' For business, this approach applied to acting responsibly is much easier to state than to enact. Thus, responsible business must not only be enacted, but it must also be seen to be enacted. The problem is that an incident might occur that requires a solution that comes with budgetary implications. Those involved might not have the authority to make a decision and might try to hide the error or problem. This type of event would challenge a company's claim to be acting responsibly; everyday practice and the politics involved in such practice might result in events in which the company was not seen to be acting responsibly.

Company decisions are never made out of context, but the context can change rather rapidly. In Chapter 6, the OLI or eclectic paradigm was explored as we mapped international business theory to our building-block framework. The OLI was developed to understand a firm's decision to enter a foreign market. However, the OLI does not consider change in circumstances. All companies seek to make correct decisions based on available information, but over time the decision might no longer reflect present-day circumstances. Florence termed this 'obsolescent logic'; a frequent occurrence affecting firm adjustment (1953: 90). A company's decision to enter a market might ultimately come to represent a form of obsolescent logic. Investing in a market includes sunk costs, or investments that have already been incurred and cannot be recovered but would have to be written off. Sunk costs are conventionally associated with firm-based investments limiting flexibility and movement. A firm may invest in what eventually becomes a suboptimal location; even the most rational locational decision might eventually be undermined by processes leading to 'obsolescent logic' (Florence, 1953). An excellent example of this type of process has occurred in Russia as one of the many negative consequences of this country's war with Ukraine. Russia is an important market, but since the invasion of Ukraine in 2022, over 1,000 companies have voluntarily curtailed operations in Russia. Some companies sold their Russian operations at a loss whilst others abandoned them, and an alternative approach was to scale back operations. McDonald's, for example, initially suspended its operations in Russia on 8 March 2022, and in May 2022 announced that it was going to sell all its restaurants in Russia. Burger King's Russian operations had a very different legal structure based on a joint venture involving three partners. This has made it difficult for this firm to exit Russia and has led to criticisms that it is a company that is sustaining Putin's regime. This example highlights the importance of governance structure and the constraints that this can place on a business as it tries to be seen to be acting responsibly. In our framework, this would be considered as an important intersection between governance and the ability of a firm to react to alterations in a territory. The lesson here is for companies to be aware of the possibility that sudden forced disinvestment might be required. A flexible governance structure is required that enables sunk costs to be written off immediately, as any delay could result in reputational damage.

Transparency and accountability

In Chapter 9, we explored global value chains (GVC), but this approach tends to overlook environmental and other negative impacts. Recently, there has been a major conceptual and methodological development that has the potential to overcome the impasse being experienced by studies that adopt a chain or network metaphor. In 2019, Goldstein and Newell introduced the 'TRAcking Corporations Across Space and Time' (TRACAST) methodological framework (Goldstein and Newell, 2019). The development of the TRACAST approach was inspired by NGOs and activism aimed at enhancing corporate transparency and monitoring. Such groups investigate specific companies, and this is the TRACAST object of study. The TRACAST approach focuses on revealing a company's unsustainable production processes with the aim being to enhance transparency and accountability. This methodological process 'enables us to more deeply understand why and how supply chains take the forms that they do and their corresponding impacts on people and the planet' (Goldstein and Newell, 2019: 106492). This approach can be applied by academics, non–governmental organizations (NGOs) and corporate actors to enhance supply chain transparency and to shift towards more environmentally and socially responsible sourcing. This approach identifies 'hotspots' or places with severe social and environmental impacts related to a specific product's supply chain. The TRACAST approach involves rigorous academic research, but the papers name the companies responsible for the negative impacts identified.

One of the most exciting aspects of the TRACAST approach is the application of methodologies developed in environmental science and physical geography, including GIS data and environmental sensors, to identify the localized environmental impacts of supply chains. This includes linking Costco's beef supply chain in California to the environmental burden of air pollution related to the emission of $PM_{2.5}$ in the San Joaquin Valley (Chamanara et al, 2021). TRACAST also includes an appreciation of 'teleconnections' as an additional approach to understanding the complex linkages that exist between 'geographically separate sites of production and consumption' (Goldstein and Newell, 2019: 106492). In atmospheric science, teleconnections are climate anomalies that are related to one another over long distances. This concept highlights the importance of exploring the positive and negative impacts of all types of interrelationships that form between specific companies and places. Teleconnections are another form of intersection.

Values, purpose and responsible business: the dangers of trying to be too responsible

The challenge faced by all businesses is with recruiting, retaining, incentivizing and managing people. This is why businesses develop vision or ethics statements and mechanisms that are intended to try to ensure that the actions of all those representing the firm are guided by these values. Ensuring that a company's values inform everyday practice requires training, employee engagement, monitoring and enforcement. There will always be times when an employee engages in practices that are counter to their employer's values and often these practices remain hidden from those who need to know. For all businesses, a key question concerns what types of values should be articulated. To explore this issue, in Box 10.2 we consider two companies that compete in the same sector.

Box 10.2: Comparing sectoral business values: Lockheed Martin and Northrop Grumman

Lockheed Martin is the largest defence company in the world with revenues of over US$67 billion in 2023 and with 96 per cent of this being defence related. Northrop Grumman had revenues of over US$39 billion in 2023 and 89 per cent was defence related. These two companies have different approaches to value or to what is often now defined as a firm's purpose.

Lockheed Martin's values are to 'do what's right', 'respect others', 'perform with excellence' (Lockheed Martin, 2025a). This is supported by an approach based on asking questions, obtaining data, talking to others, reframing issues and reporting violations. Lockheed Martin has developed 'Voicing our Values Techniques' that challenge employees to check their motivations, check the facts and to develop a dialogue with others (Lockheed Martin, 2024). This involves employees being encouraged to reflect on 'what about this situation is bothering me?' Central to this approach is a statement about being 'good citizens and we take responsibility for our actions'. The Lockheed Martin approach is based on encouraging employees to set an example, and this should cross the boundaries of departments, business units and business areas.

Northrop Grumman's approach is configured around the phrase, 'Own it, live it, lead it,' and this is underpinned by four 'We' statements: 'We do the right thing, We do what we promise, We commit to shared success and We pioneer' (Northrop Grumman, nd: 3). At a high level, there are some commonalities with Lockheed Martin's approach as both firms proclaim that they will do the right thing. Nevertheless, there is an important difference. Northrop Grumman raises the value bar by declaring that the value statement of 'We do what we promise' applies 'to each of us at Northrop Grumman, regardless of position or level of authority'. In addition to our employees, our Values apply to our Board of Directors, consultants, agents, contractors and other third parties who are authorised to act on our company's behalf.' (Northrop Grumman, nd:3)

This difference is critical, as it exposes Northrop Grumman to the actions of individuals employed by other companies and who cannot be directly monitored or disciplined by the company. There are many difficulties that come from this statement. An agent/subcontractor will be working for many companies and thus will have difficulties in enacting or even remembering different clients' values. Conflicts of interest will also occur between agents and their clients. Lockheed Martin is very aware of the relationship between the company's performance and its partners and has developed a 'partner for excellence' approach that includes exploring ethical issues as part of their supplier training programme (Lockheed Martin, 2025b). Extending Northrop Grumman's values to all within its value chain is a commendable ambition. The key is how this is enforced and how far the company is willing to go to ensure that what has been promised by anyone working directly or indirectly for the company has been delivered.

The learning point for reflection that comes from the evaluation of two different corporate approaches to value in Box 10.2 concerns corporate governance. A board of directors should take care to avoid making decisions that expose a company to uncontrollable and unknowable risks (Bryson, 2025). The Lockheed Martin approach to acting responsibly is concise and pragmatic and provides a considerable degree of assurance that here is a company that tries to act responsibly. The Northrop Grumman approach is much more complex but clearly positions the firm as a responsible business. Nevertheless, the Northrop Grumman board has set itself an approach to value that means that the Board is exposed to promises made by all directly or indirectly involved in its business activities. And here lies incalculable risks, and a major corporate challenge.

Reading international business: an exercise in identifying and understanding intersections

In Chapter 1, we set out a framework for reading international business. This approach highlights that understanding a business to make informed managerial decisions requires an understanding of a vocabulary that also requires a grammar. In the nineteenth century, there was a concern with identifying the grammar of geography (Kenny, 1841) or the rules, procedures and concepts that support the development of a geographical imagination or an approach to understanding the intersections between people, place and space. Business schools are involved in a similar project based on understanding the rules, procedures and concepts that inform business practice. In other words, the vocabulary and grammar of doing business.

It is important for all interested in the practice of international business to have an appreciation of its grammar. All business endeavours, all new innovative business models, are the outcome of someone identifying an actual or potential business opportunity that sits at the intersections between the grammar of geography and that of business. Early accounts of what was called commercial geography, a practice-orientated subdiscipline of geography intended to support 'those entering on commercial life' (Chisholm, 1925: v), identified two general facts regarding the localization of industry. There were 'the psychological action of the sense of opportunity as a stimulus to exertion' and 'that great economies can always be effected where it is profitable to work on a large scale', but there are also 'economies peculiar to small scale production' (Chisholm, 1925: 99). These two general facts remain important for understanding international business. Place-based differentials present opportunities that can be read by some but not all business practitioners. Economies of scale are still important, but this is not to overlook the advantages that come from smaller-scale production.

Every chapter in this book has contributed to understanding some aspect of the vocabulary and grammar of international business. Our approach includes four cross-cutting themes, and every firm will develop its own distinct interpretations and application of these themes. This is to highlight the importance of distinguishing between the application of universal theory, or approaches to business, versus the particular or the ways in which one firm and its management respond to all types of contingencies. Value reflects the motivation of a company's founders, managers and owners. Practices are developed by a firm around these values and then all companies are in a continual process of change. New corporate routines are established, and existing ones altered or removed. There is no absolutely correct way of running an international business. There is no textbook solution. Every firm develops its own approaches and solutions, and these represent a blend of decisions made in the past, sector conventions, regulations and also idiosyncratic behaviour. There is a real danger in assuming that the practice of establishing and running a business is one that is completely focused on rational decision-making. Chance or serendipity plays a significant role in business, but the key point is that someone must recognize that a chance incident represents a commercial opportunity. Thus, chance, capability, a willingness to take risks are all combined with some of the more formal vocabulary of business practice.

The grammar of business includes approaches to developing a distinctive business model or configuring a GVC. Existing approaches can be applied, but innovative approaches emerge that challenge established ways of doing business. It is important to understand the contribution managers make to business. In 1973, Mintzberg (1973) observed managers and identified 10 managerial roles: figurehead, leader, liaison, monitor, disseminator, spokesperson, negotiator, disturbance handler, entrepreneur and resource allocator roles. These roles are divided into three types: interpersonal, informational and decisional. Acting responsibly cuts across all ten roles. It is important to appreciate that decision-making is a non-linear process. It is too simple to assume that information is gathered and an informed decision made. Often, a decision will be made intuitively but with this intuition founded on experience. In addition, the implementation stages of the decision-making process come with feedback loops during which the best managers will make adjustments. Less able managers may continue to try to implement the initial decision and there may be negative consequences for business performance and competitiveness.

Reading a business involves understanding business motivations, values and the ways in which these relate to how value is perceived by a firm. Value creation involves complex interplays between people, things and places. This is to highlight that managing an international business is about understanding all types of intersections. These include intra- and inter-firm intersections; for example, business practitioners must understand a company's internal interpersonal dynamics as well as being able to configure and oversee the ongoing evolution of a GVC. There are many important aspects of business to consider here. Understanding money and money flows is critical. A company's board and executive team is constantly making decisions that involve the allocation of company funds to people, product lines, places and investments. These are complex decisions that must be placed in the context of differences between territories or national jurisdictions. Differences in national regulations, and this includes taxation and trade tariffs, matter for some business decisions. For example, there is an ongoing debate in the US about the negative impacts that come from American companies offshoring production to lower cost locations. There is a perversity here as the US tax code operates to encourage US firms to invest offshore. For US multinational companies, income that is earned outside the US is often not taxed in the US or taxed at a rate that is half the rate that is applied to US earnings. Thus, the more investment made by a US company outside the US, the less US tax will be paid by the company (Clausing, 2024). These US companies are acting responsibly as they respond to the constraints imposed on them by the US tax code, but they can also be considered to be acting irresponsibly as they have shifted investment from the US to other nation-states.

Pathways towards responsible international business

There is no one pathway or approach to managing an international business in a responsible manner. There are multiple pathways and approaches. All businesses, and their owners and managers, which have ambitions to act in a responsible manner are on a journey that involves continual adjustments and adaptations. It is important to appreciate that there are ebbs and flows here. A company's direction of travel towards some type of responsible business practice may include initiatives in which a management team is forced due to circumstances beyond their control to act in what might be perceived to be a less than responsible manner. Volkswagen, for example, has always sought to maintain and even increase its employment in Germany. This has been part of this company's management philosophy that is also hardwired into the company's ownership structure. Yet enhanced international competition in the automotive industry is forcing Volkswagen to consider what was always considered by the company, its employees and owners to be an unimaginable company strategy. This forced strategy is driven by a need to cut costs and the outcome might be to close factories in Germany and to offshore production.

There are many examples of responsible international businesses. But it is worth noting that the pathway that these firms have configured as part of a step-by-step process is often complex. A good example is Ebac, the UK-based manufacturer of dehumidifiers, water coolers and washing machines. This company was established by John Elliott who had a chance meeting in a hotel bar in 1972. This serendipitous encounter led to a contract for Elliott to design and manufacture industrial dehumidifiers. A one-person business was founded that has evolved into a small international business. However, this is an international business with a difference. Like all businesses, Elliott experienced many setbacks and failed projects. Nevertheless, his strategy includes designing and manufacturing world-class products in the UK. The manufacture of all washing machines sold in the UK had moved overseas. In 2016, Ebac introduced its own washing-machine range and returned the manufacture of washing machines to the UK. In 2012, Elliott joined a small group of entrepreneurs who have made the decision to gift his company to a foundation. He established the Ebac Foundation. This organization is charged with running Ebac as a successful enterprise by reinvesting all profits to enhance the strength of the business, to create more jobs and to contribute to the prosperity of the local community. Any surplus after reinvestment goes to assist good causes in the local community.

The case of Ebac raises the question of whether Ebac is a responsible company. The answer to this question is not straightforward. Like all companies, Ebac is the outcome of a set of trade-offs. One trade-off involves maintaining manufacturing in the UK. The Ebac foundation includes a constraint that states that the business cannot be relocated anywhere other than in County Durham, UK. The focus is on ensuring profits are used to support long-term manufacturing investment and related jobs in a predefined area. This is commendable. There is, however, the question of whether too many constraints have been placed on this business and that ultimately these constraints might at some time in the future work against the long-term interests of the Ebac Foundation and those employed by Ebac. This raises the question of the intersection between timing and responsibility. At some time in the future, these constraints might limit business performance with the outcome being that what initially appeared to be a company that was acting responsibly becomes an organization that has become irresponsible as it experiences constraints related to obsolete logic.

Concluding reflections on responsible business practice

Last paragraphs of books are important. It may be that the term 'responsible business' is one of the latest management fads that will rapidly be replaced by another such fad. There is, however, substance to the concept of acting responsibly due to positive and negative impacts that come from immediate actions, and also future impacts. The term responsible business is much broader than corporate social responsibility and is not as precise as the principle of Environmental, Social and Governance (ESG) investing. Geographic and temporal context is always important. A business that is perceived to be acting responsibly in one country in 2025 might be perceived in another country to be an irresponsible company and the same holds for time. The most responsible international business in existence in 2025 might in a decade's time be considered as a classic example of an irresponsible business. The most important point to reflect upon is the complexity that is related to acting responsibly.

Decisions are the outcome of prioritization processes involving trade-offs. All businesses and managers have choices. Sometimes choices are constrained and there might be no choice or no option. Nevertheless, business practitioners must make decisions and often an immediate decision must be made based on limited evidence. The key here is for decision-makers to be aware of the impacts of these decisions and how decisions build on decisions and the outcome is the emergence of some form of applied theory of business. This theory of business must include a focus on profit and cost control, but profit maximization does not have to involve irresponsible business practices.

There are inherent tensions with a business acting responsibly that hinge around the question of responsibly for whom, what, where and when. Thus, a business may focus on being a responsible employer whilst treating the environment or even consumers less responsibly. What this means is that a responsible business may still act irresponsibly. A truly responsible company must enact a strategy that simultaneously involves acting responsibly for all stakeholders – for current and future employees and consumers, for the communities in which it is embedded, for all places in which it transacts business and for all intermediates involved in its value chains. Such a company must take responsibility for limiting waste and this includes post-consumer product initiatives based around repair, recycling and remanufacture (Bryson et al, 2024). This is an extended definition of a responsible business, and every company that identifies with the term will include some of these processes, but there will be very few companies which can truly proclaim that they are completely responsible. The question then is the degree to which a company is responsible and what are the challenges that still need solutions to enhance the firm's claim to be acting in a responsible manner.

Recommended reading

Bryson, J.R. (2022) 'Reading manufacturing firms and new research agendas: scalar-plasticity, value/risk and the emergence of Jenga Capitalism', in J.R. Bryson, C. Billing, W. Graves and G. Yeung (eds), *A Research Agenda for Manufacturing Industries in the Global Economy*, Cheltenham: Edward Elgar, pp 211–43.

Bryson, J.R. (2025) 'Jenga capitalism and new forms of risk and uncertainty that are reshaping economic geography', in T. Neise, P. Verfürth and M. Franz (eds) *The Changing Economic Geography of Companies and Regions in Times of Risk, Uncertainty and Crisis*, London: Routledge, pp 47–65.

Bryson, J., Herod, J. Johns, J. and Vanchan, V. (2024) 'Localised waste reduction networks, global destruction networks and the circular economy', *Cambridge Journal of Regions, Economy and Society*, 17(3): 667–82.

References

Bryson, J.R. (2022) 'Reading manufacturing firms and new research agendas: scalar-plasticity, value/risk and the emergence of Jenga Capitalism', in J.R. Bryson, C. Billing, W. Graves and G. Yeung (eds), *A Research Agenda for Manufacturing Industries in the Global Economy*, Cheltenham: Edward Elgar, pp 211–43.

Bryson, J.R. (2025) 'Jenga capitalism and new forms of risk and uncertainty that are reshaping economic geography', in T. Neise, P. Verfürth and M. Franz (eds) *The Changing Economic Geography of Companies and Regions in Times of Risk, Uncertainty and Crisis*, London: Routledge, pp e-47–65.

Bryson J.R. and Buttle M. (2005) 'Enabling inclusion through alternative discursive formations: the regional development of Community Development Loan Funds (CDLFs) in the United Kingdom', *The Service Industries Journal*, 25(2): 273–86.

Bryson, J.R. and Lombardi, R. (2009) 'Balancing product and process sustainability against business profitability: sustainability as a competitive strategy in the property development process', *Business Strategy and the Environment*, 18: 97–107.

Bryson, J., Herod, J. Johns, J. and Vanchan, V. (2024) 'Localised waste reduction networks, global destruction networks and the circular economy', *Cambridge Journal of Regions, Economy and Society*, 17(3): 667–82.

Chamanara, S., Goldstein, B. and Newell, J.P. (2021) 'Where's the beef? Costco's meat supply chain and environmental justice in California', *Journal of Cleaner Production*, 278: 123744. doi.org/10.1016/j.jclepro.2020.123744.

Chisholm, G.G. (1925) *Handbook of Commercial Geography*, London: Longmans, Green and Co.

Clausing, K.A. (2024) 'Reforming U.S. international taxation to meet the challenges ahead', testimony before the U.S. Senate Committee on the Budget [online]. Available from: www.budget.senate.gov/imo/media/doc/drkimberlyclausingtes timonysenatebudgetcommittee.pdf [Accessed 13 September 2024].

Florence, P. Sargant. 1953. *The Logic of British and American Industry*, London: Routledge and Kegan Paul.

Goldstein, B. and Newell, J.P. (2019) 'How to track corporation across space and time', *Ecological Economics*, 169: 106492. doi.org/10.1016/j.ecolecon.2019.106492.

Kenny, W.S. (1841) *Goldsmith's Grammar of Geography*, London: T. Allman.

Lockheed Martin (2024) *Voicing Our Values 2024* [online]. Available from: www.loc kheedmartin.com/en-us/who-we-are/ethics/awareness/index.html [Accessed 7 February 2025].

Lockheed Martin (2025a) *How the Ethics Process Works* [online]. Available from: www. lockheedmartin.com/content/dam/lockheed-martin/eo/documents/ethics/How-the-Ethics-Process-Works.pdf [Accessed 7 February 2025].

Lockheed Martin (2025b) *Supplier Training Excellent Program* [online]. Available from: https://www.lockheedmartin.com/en-us/suppliers/training.html [Accessed 7 February 2025].

Mintzberg, H. (1973) *The Nature of Managerial Work*, New York: Harper and Row Publishers, Inc.

Northrop Grumman (nd) *Standard of Business Conduct* [online]. Available from: https:// cdn.northropgrumman.com/-/media/corporate-responsibility/ethics-and-busin ess-conduct/NGC-Standards-of-Business-Conduct-English-UK.pdf?rev=d91be 040a5c34d1897ceabd6efaf8724 [Accessed 7 February 2025].

Index